BEING BOTH

BEING BOTH

*Embracing Two Religions in
One Interfaith Family*

Susan Katz Miller

BEACON PRESS
Boston

Beacon Press
Boston, Massachusetts
www.beacon.org

Beacon Press books
are published under the auspices of
the Unitarian Universalist Association of Congregations.

17 16 15 14   8 7 6 5 4 3 2 1

This book is printed on acid-free paper that meets the uncoated paper
ANSI/NISO specifications for permanence as revised in 1992.

Text design and composition by Kim Arney

Library of Congress Cataloging-in-Publication Data
Miller, Susan Katz.
   Being both : embracing two religions in one interfaith family / Susan
Katz Miller.
       pages   cm
   Includes bibliographical references and index.
   ISBN 978-0-8070-6116-9 (paperback) — ISBN 978-0-8070-1320-5 (ebook)
1. Interfaith families—United States—Religious life. 2. Interfaith
marriage—United States. 3. Children of interfaith marriage—United
States. 4. Families—Religious life—United States. 5. Jewish families—
United States—Religious life. I. Title.
   HQ1031.M55 2013
   306.84'3—dc23
                                                        2013023147

For my loving interfaith family:

My parents, William and Martha

My husband, Paul

My children, Aimee and Ben.

And for Reverend Julia Jarvis and Rabbi Harold White,

my pastor and my rabbi.

CONTENTS

 INTRODUCTION

The Kaleidoscope

E ACH YEAR, MY EXTENDED clan gathers for a huge Passover
seder in Florida. My eighty-eight-year-old father presides over
the ritual meal, leading us through the prayers and songs of religious freedom. The family at the table includes believers, seekers,
and secularists, Jews, Catholics, Protestants, Buddhists, and those
who claim interfaith identity. A Jewish nephew who is about to
become a bar mitzvah and a Catholic nephew who just received First
Communion compete with my interfaith son to find the traditional
hidden matzoh. We are a joyous, motley crew, intent on celebrating together.

In twenty-first-century America, we live in a kaleidoscope of
religious identities: complex, swirling patterns of faith, spirituality,
heritage, and practice. Many of us attend more than one place of
worship. We change our religions more than once in a lifetime. We
may believe in God or not but still seek spiritual experience inside
and outside of churches, synagogues, mosques, and temples. And
we are marrying across traditional lines of race, ethnicity, gender,
and religion.

In the midst of this religious flux and flow, interfaith couples are
making a new and controversial choice: raising children with both
family religions. As an interfaith child and an interfaith parent, I

feel exhilarated by this new fluidity, empowered by the transition away from restrictive either/or identity labels and into the inevitable and more expansive both/and future.

Americans are leaving behind traditional single-faith identities. Almost a quarter of us attend religious services of more than one faith or denomination, according to a 2009 study by the Pew Forum on Religion and Public Life. "The religious beliefs and practices of Americans do not fit neatly into conventional categories," that study concludes. At the same time, according to Pew researchers, more than one in four American adults change faith affiliation at least once, and that rises to almost half of us if it includes denomination changes (for instance, from Lutheran to Methodist).

Meanwhile, the proportion of religiously unaffiliated Americans has grown rapidly—to almost 20 percent of the population. And yet, the majority of those 46 million unaffiliated adults believe in God or a universal spirit. This seeming paradox—belief in God without religious affiliation—will not come as a surprise to those in interfaith families, many of whom have rich spiritual lives but do not belong to a church or synagogue. My family would be classified as religiously unaffiliated, even though we light *Shabbat* candles on Fridays, sing Christian hymns in church with extended family, and wrestle with theology as we educate our children in both religions.

I am not advocating for a "spiritual but not religious" rejection of community. The hunger for community, for belonging, is universal. As human beings who evolved in clans and tribes, we crave social networks. Religious community provides intergenerational bonding, the support of wise clergy, preservation of our shared history and texts, and the comfort of ritual—not to mention the arrival of casseroles in times of trouble.

I argue here that it is not necessary to share a single faith in order to share such benefits. In fact, I contend that it is indeed possible to raise children with two religions, and that both couples and children experience the distinct benefits of this choice. This book describes a grassroots movement of interfaith families claiming the right to create their own communities beyond a single creed or dogma, bound instead by respect for both Judaism and Christianity and a desire to explore the similarities, differences, and points of historical and theological connection. In these pages, I seek to answer three questions about this movement: Why are intermarried couples choosing two religions for their children despite pressure to choose only one? What are the benefits and drawbacks of raising children with both family religions? And how do these children feel, as they enter adulthood, about their interfaith education and complex religious identities?

Growing up Jewish, I learned that no choice made by parents can eliminate completely either the challenges or the gifts of being born an interfaith child. Each pathway—choosing one religion, choosing two religions, choosing a third religion, choosing no religion—has advantages and disadvantages. Books, outreach programs, and couples groups sponsored by religious institutions push, with varying degrees of subtlety, for couples to choose a particular pathway. Here, I acknowledge my own bias as I argue for the legitimacy of the pathway that works for me, my husband, and my children: doing both.

Clergy often state that children raised with two faiths will be confused. The scant evidence they cite dates from an era when there were no interfaith communities. Some of those who claimed they were raising children with both religions were actually raising them with very little religion at all, in part because society disapproves of choosing both. Extended family mourned for the intermarried couple; clergy rejected them. In short, many early attempts to raise children in two religions were doomed by lack of support.

A child raised in a community of supportive interfaith families, with clergy from both traditions, has a very different experience from a child raised by parents who are isolated by their interfaith choice. My own two teenagers have been loved, challenged, and guided by a rabbi and a minister working as a team. And they have been welcomed at church and synagogue by family on both sides. This book presents preliminary evidence that children raised in interfaith family communities can become sensitive and articulate interfaith spokespeople, drawing strength from two religions.

WE ARE ALL INTERMARRIED

Whether Jews or Christians or Hindus or Buddhists, no two individuals have identical beliefs and practices; thus, every marriage could be considered an interfaith marriage. Many interchurch couples share some of the same challenges and benefits of intermarriage, whether the marriage is Baptist/Quaker, Lutheran/Unitarian, or whether it's an "inter*shul*" Jewish marriage such as Modern Orthodox/Jewish Renewal. Even if both partners are Roman Catholic, they may not share identical beliefs on the power of prayer or the role of women in the Church. Even if both partners are Reform Jews, one may be an atheist and one a Kabbalistic mystic.

Most of the couples in this book are Jewish and Christian, but I believe their stories will inspire interfaith Buddhist, Hindu, Muslim, and Pagan families. I focus on Judaism and Christianity not only because of my own experience as the middle generation in a happy three-generation Jewish and Christian family but also because Jewish and Christian families constitute the first great wave of religious intermarriage in America, on the forefront of creating programs to educate children in both family religions.

Interfaith marriage is the norm in many communities now, rather than the exception. The Pew Forum's 2008 *U.S. Religious Landscape Survey* found that 37 percent of all Americans married or living with a partner are in interfaith (or mixed denomination) relationships. Some religious institutions feel threatened by the rise of intermarriage, queasy about the religious kaleidoscope. Many Jewish institutions and some Christian denominations, including Roman Catholicism, the Greek Orthodox Church, and Mormonism, have policies discouraging intermarriage.

And yet the intermarriage rate continues to increase. A 2005 report from the U.S. Conference of Catholic Bishops found Catholics marrying out at a rate as high as 50 percent. The intermarriage rate for Jews married since 1996 was calculated to be 47 percent by the 2001 National Jewish Population Survey (NJPS). There are over a million of these Jewish/non-Jewish families in America, a number that is growing by at least forty thousand each year.

The statistics on Jewish intermarriage have been both mourned and challenged; the NJPS study became so controversial that no new ten-year survey was done in 2010. Part of the issue has been the heated ongoing disagreement in Judaism over "Who is a Jew?" Are demographers to use the Orthodox definition (Judaism is matrilineal)? Or the Reform definition (either parent can be Jewish)? Or allow Jews to self-identify, even if they claim a second religion?

What we can say is that the majority of American children with Jewish heritage now have Christian heritage as well. In other words, children are now more likely to be born into interfaith families than into families with two Jewish parents. And Jewish institutions are just beginning to grapple with this fact.

Some Jewish leaders still call intermarriage the "silent Holocaust." Others view it as an opportunity to increase the number of Jewish conversions or at least the number of Jewish children. When two Jews marry out, rather than marrying each other, the number of children with Jewish heritage doubles. "The 'extended' population of Jewish ancestry in the U.S. is continually expanding as a result of mixed unions," observed demographer Barry

Kosmin in a 2009 paper based on the American Religious Identification Survey (ARIS).

Many now call for greater acceptance of Jewish intermarriage in the face of this demographic reality. Rabbi Arthur Blecher goes even further in his book *The New Judaism*, arguing that such marriages are not only genetically healthy for Jews but have been common throughout Jewish history. He contends that the low rate of Jewish intermarriage in the first half of the twentieth century was actually an exception, and that the panic over Jewish intermarriage today is caused in part by the abrupt transition from a period when American Jews were isolated as an immigrant culture, back to a higher rate of intermarriage in recent decades.

Some of us are audacious enough to believe that raising children with both religions is actually good for the Jews (and good for the Christians or for any other faith or denomination represented in the marriage). The children in these pages have grown up to be Christians who are uncommonly knowledgeable about and comfortable with Jews, or Jews who are adept at working with and understanding Christians. Or they continue to claim both religions and serve as bridges between the two. I see all of these possible outcomes as positive.

LIKE IT OR NOT, COUPLES ARE CHOOSING BOTH

For years, religious institutions have attempted to portray choosing both religions as completely outside the norm. And yet, 90 percent of intermarried Jewish families reported having Christmas trees, while over half of them also lit Hanukkah candles, according to an ARIS report as far back as 1990. But only in recent years have researchers begun to acknowledge the existence of dual-faith families as a significant category.

Faced with the failure to conduct any national survey of the Jewish population in 2010, individual Jewish communities around the country conducted their own local studies. Most of these studies measured the percentage of children being raised as "Jewish and something else" or "partially Jewish." In other words, they acknowledged a separate category for children being raised with two religions. And they discovered that in some areas, more interfaith children are being raised with two religions than as exclusively Jewish, according to a compilation of these studies by the North American Jewish Data Bank. Such places included Minneapolis (33 percent "partially Jewish," versus 30 percent "Jewish only"), San Diego, and Philadelphia. And at least a quarter of all children of intermarriage were being raised with two religions in places including Chicago, Saint Paul, and Tucson. Meanwhile, the percentage of adults in "Jewish" households self-identifying as "Jewish and something else" or as "partially Jewish" in the New York area shot up from 2 percent in 2002 to 12 percent in 2011.

In all of these communities, adding together the categories for "raised solely Jewish" and "raised partially Jewish," yields a majority of interfaith children being raised with some connection to Judaism. Rabbi Blecher, based on his own experience with over one thousand intermarried families in the Washington, D.C., area, concluded, "It is rare for a child of intermarriage, even someone living a Christian life, not to identify as a Jew to some extent."

Sociologist Steven Cohen of Hebrew Union College labels the children of Jewish intermarriage who claim more than one religion as part of what he calls the "borderland Jews," a term with a kind of Wild West flair that appeals to my rebellious side. However, this term has the same limitation as "half-Jew" or "partial Jew"—all these labels define us by Jewish fraction while ignoring the rest of our (Christian or other) identities. The panic over Jewish continuity dominates both the research and the discourse on interfaith families.

Despite the significant number of parents choosing both religions for their children, until now, this choice has received little attention in the press or academia. Often, as I mentioned, these families have been accused of hastening the destruction of Judaism. And yet, many of these parents feel they are helping to preserve Judaism, or other minority religions, by educating their children in two faiths, rather than no faith, or only with the "default" religion of Christianity. My children have only one Jewish grandparent. Would it have been better for them, or Judaism, or the world, if I had raised them without any Jewish education?

THE JOY OF BEING BOTH

The vast majority of books on intermarriage have focused on the challenges of interfaith life. While I am well aware of these challenges, in this book I set out to tell a different side of the story: how celebrating two religions can enrich and strengthen families, and how dual-faith education can benefit children. In addition to interviews, I conducted two original surveys: one survey of 256 interfaith parents with children in interfaith education programs throughout the country, and one of fifty teens and young adults raised in these programs. On the basis of the accumulated wisdom of these parents and children, and the teachers and clergy working with them, I make the case here that we are raising interfaith ambassadors, not lost and confused souls. As testament to the fact that interfaith families are feeling a new confidence in celebrating two religions, most of the people quoted in this book were willing to use their real names. (In a few cases, I used first-name pseudonyms instead.)

I begin with my own story of growing up Jewish in an interfaith family, and then describe why my husband and I joined the grassroots movement to form interfaith family communities. I explore the specific benefits of choosing both religions and then address the most common objections to this choice. I profile couples that have chosen this pathway, and the clergy and teachers who support them. I describe interfaith birth rituals, coming-of-age rituals, and education. At the heart of the book, the first generation of teens and young adults to graduate from interfaith education programs relate their own experiences. And finally, I explore the next wave: Muslim, Hindu and Buddhist interfaith couples.

My intention is to share the joy that I have found in "being both." I am motivated by the tremendous spiritual strength and comfort I feel when sitting with my Christian husband and my two interfaith teenagers, surrounded by over a hundred other interfaith families, singing and reflecting together in a community that provides each of us with equal rights and responsibilities. In this setting, it does not matter whose mother or father (or grandmother or grandfather) was which religion. It does not matter who had, or did not have, a bris or a baptism. There are no prohibitions on which of us can read a text, or sip the wine, or touch a ritual object.

My own journey has convinced me that interfaith children, no matter what religious education they receive, no matter what religious labels they choose, embody two cultures and two religions. I argue that American religious institutions must acknowledge, rather than ignore, the reality of dual-faith identity and the children who represent the flesh and blood bridges between religions. Is it unfair to expect interfaith children to play this novel role? Is it a risky experiment to educate children in two religions, a leap into the unknown? I don't think so. Instead, I think being both may contribute to what the mystical Jewish tradition of Kabbalah calls *tikkun olam*—healing the world.

CHAPTER ONE

Claiming My Interfaith Identity

W HEN I WAS A week old, my Episcopalian mother secretly baptized me in the kitchen sink of our walk-up apartment on Beacon Hill in Boston. She had promised to raise Jewish children, and yet there she was, in those first sleep-deprived days of motherhood, dripping water on my forehead. She says she simply wanted to hedge her bets, to give me every possible protection. I also suspect that my baptism comforted her in a last moment of connection to her churchgoing youth, on the cusp of her transformation into being the mother of a Jewish family.

Weeks later, not knowing that my mother had already performed the ritual, my grandmother quietly performed my second baptism in her own kitchen sink. And then my mother's sister graced me with a third private and unofficial baptism. My mother, aunt, and grandmother did not admit, even to one another, what they had done until years later.

As a mother myself, I have nothing but empathy and gratitude for my mother's brave but covert gesture. These are the sacred duties of a mother: to love and to protect her child and to transmit her history and culture. I think about my parents now, frail in their old age, still fiercely loyal to each other, still deeply in love. Together, my parents have made it impossible for me to view interfaith marriage as a dilemma, a problem. Instead, they bequeathed to me their joy and a sense that in joining together two or more cultures, we share in an act of creativity and inspiration, an act of defiant spirituality and love.

One could theorize that my secret baptisms were the gestures that launched me on a journey beyond the labels and boundaries of religious institutions. Perhaps because I was blessed with tap water and illicit prayer, I was destined for an alternative pathway, drawing from both sides of my religious heritage.

But then, consider the more traditional pathways taken by my three younger siblings, all of them also secretly baptized: one is raising Jewish children, one is raising Catholic children, one prefers Buddhism. The lesson of my family may be that no choice by parents, no set of rituals, can guarantee a particular religious outcome for children or grandchildren, given the inevitability of intermarriage and the increasing religious fluidity of our culture and of our world. Children, whether or not they are interfaith children, go out into this world and make their own religious choices.

NO PATHWAY IS PERFECT: RAISED IN ONE RELIGION

After performing her secret baptisms, my mother held strictly to her commitment to raise us as Jewish. She never once took us into a church. When my parents got engaged in 1960, clergy of every stripe were urging couples to choose one religion—as is still the case today—and that is what my parents did. My mother threw herself into the project, becoming the perfect "all but conversion" parent of Jewish children in an interfaith family. She learned to cook matzoh balls and even took Hebrew classes so that she could follow the prayers when she accompanied us to synagogue. My siblings and I learned Hebrew, and became bar and bat mitzvahs.

My parents worked hard to make us Jewish, in part because they knew our status was questionable in the eyes of the Jewish community. According to traditional Jewish law, or halacha, Conservative and Orthodox Jews do not consider the children of Christian mothers Jewish, and my father's Judaism—Reform Judaism—is, well, chopped liver. In the 1960s, individual Reform Jewish synagogues tended to accept the small number of children of intermarried Jewish fathers, including me and my siblings, without having a concrete policy on the subject. But I am sure my parents thought that by sending us to Jewish religious school, celebrating Jewish holidays, taking us to shul (synagogue), and abstaining from church, they could convince the world we were "real" Jews.

In Sunday school, we embroidered yarmulkes and matzoh covers, we prayed for Israel during the 1967 war, we read Anne Frank's diary and wept over the Holocaust. How could we be anything but Jews? And in 1983, the year I graduated from college, the efforts of our family seemed to be rewarded when Reform rabbis voted to accept the children of Jewish fathers as Jews, provided that the children were raised scrupulously as Jews, as we had been.

I believe my parents made the right choice for our family in that time and place. In the 1960s, when intermarriage was still unusual, without the possibility of finding or forming a community that would support them in giving their children access to both religions, they made a necessary and logical decision. I experienced the benefits of being given a single religious identity but also the drawbacks.

In a different era, in a different place, faced with the same decision, I have made a different choice. I am raising my children as interfaith children, educating them in both of their cultures, in both of their religions. As interfaith marriage has become common among Jews, a growing number of families are refusing to choose one religion. These families are giving priority to the full intellectual exploration of both religions by their children. They want their children to feel proud, rather than conflicted, about their dual heritage. And they are forming communities of like-minded inter-faith families to support them in this decision.

Will raising interfaith children with both religions doom Judaism? My children are only quarter-Jews by "blood," and it is even the "wrong" quarter according to Conservative and Orthodox Jews, because it comes through a patrilineal line. The logical choice might have been to choose to raise our children Episcopalian, the religion of three of their grandparents. Nevertheless, I see no reason not to give my children as much education in, and love for, both religions as I can. Maybe they will end up marrying Jews and choosing Judaism for their own families. Maybe they will end up Buddhists, or Unitarians, or Catholics. But they will never say that I withheld knowledge about their Jewish, or Protestant, heritage. Indeed, I cannot imagine suppressing such a compelling story.

PIONEERS IN INTERMARRIAGE

Emanuel Michael Rosenfelder, my German Jewish great-grandfather, was a circuit-riding rabbi serving Jewish communities up and down the Mississippi River in the late nineteenth century. While overseeing a Jewish orphanage in New Orleans, he met my great-grandmother, whose parents had both died in a yellow fever epidemic. Together, they fled the tropical swamplands and moved upriver to Kentucky. My grandmother, Aimee Helen Rosenfelder, was born in Louisville in 1896 and moved to Pennsylvania, to the little town of Honesdale in the foothills of the Poconos, to marry my grandfather, Edward David Katz.

Their son, my father, William Emanuel Katz, became a bar mitzvah in 1937 at Temple Beth Israel, a one-room white clapboard building on the banks of the Lackawaxen River. At seventeen, he left Honesdale to study chemical engineering at MIT. He interrupted his studies to serve as a radioman on the Pacific island of Tinian during World War II, then returned to Boston, earned a graduate degree, and joined a small water-treatment company in Cambridge, where he worked for over fifty years. Tenacity is my father's most notable quality. He never left his first job, and he never gave up on the woman he wanted to marry.

Blonde, blue-eyed, and beautiful, Martha Elizabeth Legg had graduated from Sweet Briar College, a women's school in Virginia. Yet beneath this traditional Protestant exterior, my mother had an adventurous spirit. As a comparative religion major, she had studied Eastern religions as well as the Bible as history, preparing her for a lifetime of comparative religion in an interfaith marriage. After graduating from college, my mother took a job as a social worker in a Boston hospital.

One rainy night in 1953 at Boston's Logan airport, Martha and Bill found themselves vying for the one taxi left at the stand, and then sharing a ride to Beacon Hill. Martha was aware from the start that this man with curly red hair and owlish horn-rimmed glasses was Jewish. He, in turn, took note of her prim tweed suit and sensed from their first meeting that she hailed from a different tribe. For seven years, they dated on and off in the lively singles scene on Beacon Hill. The issue of religious difference slowed their courtship, but at last, in 1959 they became engaged.

Even though my mother had agreed to raise Jewish children, finding a rabbi was not easy. My father first approached Rabbi Roland Gittelsohn of Temple Israel, the Reform synagogue where my father had been a longtime member. He recalls the rabbi saying, "I'm sorry, I can't marry you unless your wife is going to convert." Which she was not going to do.

My mother has not forgotten that day: "I was there, and I was mad as a wet hen. He treated us as if we didn't know what we were doing. And I was twenty-nine, and Bill was thirty-five, and I thought, 'He might have given us credit for having thought this out, you know?'" After a long search, they finally found a rabbi who agreed to officiate, with my mother's Episcopal minister adding a blessing. I was born the following year, and over the next decade, my parents were fruitful and had three more children.

RAISED AS A JEW, WITH CHRISTIAN ROOTS

When I was five, we moved to the Boston suburbs and joined a new synagogue. Nevertheless, we were close to both sides of our extended family tree. At Christmas and Easter, we would visit my Episcopalian grandparents in Binghamton, New York. We opened mounds of presents under the tree, awoke to Easter baskets magically brimming with chocolate, feasted and sang at the holiday meals with my grandparents and cousins. My parents made clear to us that we could participate in these holidays, but that we were Jewish.

By traveling every Christmas, we avoided the question of whether or not to have a Christmas tree in our own house until my grandfather, my last Christian grandparent, died when I was sixteen. With most of her family gone, my mother felt very emotional about Christmas. Decorating a tree became an important link to her family's past, and so we began celebrating a secular Christmas and Easter at home. By that time, three out of four of us were teenagers anyway, with our Jewish identities safely rooted, or so my parents hoped.

As a teenager, I felt solely and completely Jewish. In part, this was a tribute to my parents' united front on our religious identity. On the High Holy Days in the fall, I was eager to spend long hours in the synagogue with my father, while my mother often attended one service with the younger children and then stayed home taking care of them. When I fasted with my father on Yom Kippur, I experienced how the light-headedness caused by an empty stomach, coupled with chanting and praying, could bring about an interesting alteration in consciousness, a sense of transcendence.

At the same time, I understood Judaism as being particularly compatible with modern scientific thought. I believed that the simplicity and rationality of Jewish theology had somehow inspired the multitude of great Jewish scientists. All in all, I felt lucky to be born into a religion that was spiritually, aesthetically, and intellectually satisfying.

STRADDLING THE LINE

Socially, the synagogue was another question entirely. Perhaps it was because my mother never felt comfortable with the "real" Jewish mothers, but our family never seemed to fit in there. While my mother came with us to synagogue, she did not join in the more social activities at the temple: baking challah, or working for the "Sisterhood" selling Jewish ritual items. While I certainly did not see myself as Christian, or even, at that point, as an interfaith child, I knew I was different from my Sunday school classmates. I remember one day when the teacher drew a chalk line down the middle of the floor and asked us to pick a side. One side was for people who identified themselves as "Jewish Americans," the other side for "American Jews." It was clear to me that the teacher hoped we would choose to be American Jews—to place our greater loyalty with our religion and reduce our nationality to a modifier. It was also clear to me that I considered myself a Jewish American.

I felt paralyzed when faced with this choice. What I wanted to do was to straddle the line. In retrospect, part of my paralysis came from my subconscious insecurity about trying to "pass" as a real Jew. Would I be outed as a half-Jew if I stepped to the wrong (though perhaps truthful) side of the room? Part of my paralysis came from the discomfort I felt when faced with labels, boxes, dividing lines, choices. I was already beginning to feel that the box labeled "Jewish" never seemed to contain my whole being. And I was keenly aware of the divisive implications of this type of litmus test. As a child of intermarriage and as a Jew versed in the history of the Holocaust, the act of separating people out based on their beliefs or religion felt very wrong to me.

The realization that Christianity could not be cleanly erased from our home or family narrative came gradually, through an accumulation of short conversations that rose, disconcertingly, to the smooth surface of the Jewish family life my parents had worked so hard to create for their children. One day in the early 1970s, I returned home from junior high and asked my mother, "But who do the Jews think that Jesus was?" My Jewish education had been so thorough that I could not imagine believing that Jesus was the Messiah. But in asking the question, I realize now, I was attempting to integrate the two worldviews present in our household: one overt, the other unspoken. "Jews might believe," my mother ventured carefully, "that Jesus was a prophet, like Moses or Elijah. He just happened to live long after the Torah was written, so he's not in it."

That is precisely the answer I give my own children today. But at the time, I felt the need to test my mother's opinion against an "authentic" Jewish source: the Hebrew teacher hired to tutor me in preparation for my bat mitzvah. When I related my mother's suggestion that Jews might think of Jesus as a latter-day prophet, his face went crimson. "Jesus," he muttered, "was a two-bit rabbi."

This was probably my first experience with the sort of allergic response that many Jews have to the mention of Jesus, even as a historical figure. Considering the atrocities committed against Jews by Christians, this reaction is understandable. In some Jewish families, Jesus is the "J word," a name never spoken aloud. Children in such families grow up with the idea that Jews don't "believe in" Jesus, often with the vague impression that Jesus was a mythical figure. They do not have an opportunity to think about Jesus as a

Jew, or the fact that both Christianity and Judaism changed dramatically in the century that followed his death.

OH, THEN YOU'RE NOT JEWISH

It was only when I began to enter the adult world that I started to encounter overt external resistance to my self-identification as a Jew. Despite the Hebrew, the bat mitzvah, and all of my mother's sacrifices, I began to meet people who told me that I simply wasn't Jewish. As a student at Brown University, I met many Conservative and Orthodox Jews from New York, steeped in the Ashkenazic culture of Eastern Europe and "the City." Having grown up in Protestant New England, I didn't know the difference between a bagel and a bialy (to start with, the bialy has no hole in the center). And again and again, I was told I didn't "look" Jewish—this said with varying degrees of hostility.

For interfaith children, the amalgam of race and culture and religion that is Judaism often causes cognitive dissonance. Despite the way I see myself—as a spunky little Jewish woman—Jews and non-Jews often remark that I don't look Jewish, perhaps because of my small "Irish" nose. The remark is never really welcome. From non-Jews, it feels like an anti-Semitic compliment, as in, "You were lucky not to get Jewish looks." When the remark comes from a Jew, I take it as a challenge, as in, "You don't even look Jewish. You aren't part of the tribe."

But the most persistent argument I faced was that I was not Jewish because Judaism is matrilineal, and my mother was not Jewish. Ironically, in the same years I faced the greatest rejection as a patrilineal Jew in college, Reform Jewish rabbis were working to pass the historic 1983 resolution allowing the children of Jewish fathers to be accepted as Jews. But this policy shift served merely to provoke the Conservative and Orthodox Jews I met on campus.

Suddenly, I was the public embodiment of a bitter struggle between the different Jewish movements over "Who is a Jew?"

I remember a date with a pre-med student—a Conservative Jew from New York. Apparently, he thought having dinner with me was rebellious. "You're not Jewish," he informed me. "My parents would rather have me marry a *Falasha* [an offensive term for an Ethiopian Jew], than marry you." There was no second date. The racism inherent in his declaration only struck me later. At the time, I was busy being stunned by the rejection.

Matrilineal descent has nothing to do with religious belief, and everything to do with identity as a tribe. As a college student studying biology and deconstructing race in courses on the history of science, I found the concept of matrilineal Judaism infuriating. I knew that there were Jews of every ethnicity, some of them Jewish converts, and I was not going to accept Judaism as a race.

In the university post office one day, a man from the Jewish Chabad movement approached me with a *lulav* and an *etrog*, the ritual palm frond and citrus fruit associated with the Jewish holiday Sukkoth. His intent was to bless Jewish students for the holiday. While Jews do not generally proselytize, this particular Orthodox sect is known for their global outreach mission to nonpracticing Jews. He squinted at my frizzy Jewfro, pale skin, and glasses, and asked, "Are you Jewish?"

I spat back, "That seems to be a matter of debate."

"What do you mean?" he asked.

"My father is Jewish but not my mother. I was raised as a Jew, learned Hebrew, became a bat mitzvah."

He started to walk away, mumbling, "You're not Jewish."

Boiling over, I shouted at his back, "That's based on a biological fallacy. Don't you know any genetics? The mother and father contribute equally to the child." I knew that there was no point in arguing. But I couldn't help myself. My period of innocent and enthusiastic Judaism was giving way to frustration at being told I could not be what I thought I was.

In this climate, I had no real way of solidifying my Jewish identity as a college student. Hillel House, Brown's chapter of the national Jewish campus support organization, was intended as a safe haven for practicing Jews, many of whom found my existence as a half-Jew troubling. I steered clear of their celebrations. Even when I returned to my childhood synagogue, I began to feel like an outsider. In the sixties and seventies, my formative years, Reform Judaism enjoyed a spirit of openness, reflecting the openness of American culture. Very few men wore yarmulkes, and almost no one besides the rabbi wore the fringed prayer shawl, or tallit. Whether one labels this period with the derogatory term "assimilationist" or with the positive term "inclusivist," it did make it easier for our interfaith family to feel comfortable there.

But by the 1980s, Reform Judaism, which began in Germany, was being transformed by Eastern European Jews with more traditional roots. They brought with them the yarmulke and tallit, and more Hebrew. At the same time, the waning of American anti-Semitism emboldened Jews to become more public and more traditional in their practices. And the birth of Israel and the Six-Day War sent a strong current of Zionism through American Judaism. (Yet patrilineal half-Jews are not accepted as legal Jews in Israel and do not have the right to religious marriages or burials there.) So the increasing emphasis on loyalty to Israel, as well as the more conservative religious practice, posed a problem for me.

AN INTERFAITH WEDDING: CHOOSING BOTH

Alienated from what had begun to feel like an insular and exclusionary Judaism, I was eager as a young adult to explore other worldviews. As fate would have it, in high school I met Paul Miller, an Episcopalian with a truly global spirit. By the time we got married,

Paul had already lived in two Catholic countries (France and Haiti) and one Muslim country (Morocco). Paul feels most alive when immersed in other cultures, speaking other languages, discovering new ways of being in the world. Our family joke is that, stranded as a teenager in New England, he gravitated to the most exotic woman he could find: a half-Jew. We first began dating when I was fourteen, spent years living apart, sometimes on different continents, and dating other people, but always gravitated back to each other.

After college, I spent three years working my way up from factchecker to full reporter at *Newsweek*, living in New York, Los Angeles, and Washington, D.C. When Paul was offered a job with a Catholic agency in Dakar, Senegal, we decided, after more than ten years of circling like orbiting planets, to get married. Suddenly, I had six weeks to pack a shipment of personal effects and 220-volt appliances, get tropical vaccinations, work my final two weeks in Washington, and plan an interfaith wedding.

In the midst of this flurry of prenuptial activity, my father bravely took on the task of approaching our rabbi about officiating at the wedding. While intermarriage is officially discouraged, each Reform rabbi makes his or her own decision about whether or not to witness such marriages. My father reported back with the rabbi's words: "I can't touch it."

A decade later, the rabbi who helped to reconnect me to Judaism explained to me that many Reform congregations prohibit rabbis from officiating at intermarriages in their employment contracts. But in that moment, the words the rabbi used seemed very personal: they labeled my marriage as something untouchable.

In the end, we had a strangely perfect wedding, witnessed by my husband's cousin, Reverend Rick Spalding, a Protestant minister and pioneering interfaith educator, and Rabbi Benjamin Rudavsky, a civil rights activist. This was my first experience with the creative thrill and jolt of power involved in designing an interfaith service. Choosing the elements to include in our wedding, rather than following a prescribed liturgy, imbued the words and rituals with a glow of meaning. It was the first time I felt both sides of myself represented in a religious service. But it would be years before I experienced this cohesion again. I still saw myself solely as a Jew, though perhaps a Jew on the fringe.

Many of our friends and relatives experienced our wedding as a symbol of hope for peace between world religions, a sign that love can overcome differences, and an education for those from both sides of the aisle. Galvanized by these ideas, we began to think about educating our future children in both religions, even as we left the United States to begin our married life as expatriates in Africa.

LIFE ABROAD: BEYOND CHRISTIANITY AND JUDAISM

Each adventure in my young adulthood seemed destined to push me closer to the moment when I would claim my interfaithness and choose this pathway for my children. Three days after our wedding, I found myself formulating a new identity as a nice Jewish girl, married to a Protestant boy, working for a Catholic organization, living in a Muslim country. The first year in Africa was lonely, as I struggled through full-blown culture shock. One minute I was a single woman with an enviable job. The next minute, I was a married woman living in Senegal, completely dependent on my husband, struggling to become fluent in French.

But in my second year, I began to fall for the giant baobab trees, the mangrove swamps, the lively fish markets along the beach. I conquered French and learned enough Wolof, the most widely spoken Senegalese language, to bargain for a mango in the open-air market. And I grew to appreciate the progressive form of Sufi mysticism practiced in Senegal, a predominantly Muslim country.

Three years in West Africa gave me breathing space to consider religion without feeling pressure from American society to label myself. Sometimes, Senegalese acquaintances would ask my religion and I would proudly proclaim my Judaism. Often, I would be the first Jew these African Muslims or Christians had met, and I was glad to make a good impression on behalf of my people, to serve as a sort of unofficial Jewish ambassador.

Removed from the tensions of American politics and Middle Eastern strife, I began to understand exactly how much Islam and Judaism share. Shortly after we arrived in Dakar, we found ourselves in the home of a Senegalese schoolteacher on the outskirts of the city, as guests for the Muslim holiday Senegalese call Tabaski (known in other parts of the Muslim world as the *Eid al Kabir*). Tabaski celebrates Abraham's sacrifice of a ram in lieu of his son. All day we sat, as friends and relatives came and went. The conversation was in Wolof, a language I didn't yet speak, but slowly, I began to understand that Tabaski is the Muslim day of atonement. Our host, dressed in a long damask robe, finally explained to me in French: "God forgives us for sins against God. But for sins against our fellow man, we must ask our forgiveness from our fellow man. So today, we go from house to house, asking our friends and family for forgiveness."

I was stunned. This was the exact language that Jews use during the High Holy Days of Yom Kippur and Rosh Hashanah. I knew, intellectually, that Islam grew in part from Jewish roots. But after a lifetime of reading about Middle East strife, I was emotionally unprepared for this complete synchronicity. It seemed to me at that moment that, in actually traveling from house to house, asking forgiveness, these Muslims were celebrating the true spirit of the Jewish High Holy Days.

Our experience with Islam in Africa broadened my thinking beyond the "Christian or Jewish" duality that had dominated my childhood. I began to understand the three Abrahamic religions as variations on a monotheistic theme. But although I began to see each religion as an equally valid system, I still saw them as mutually exclusive entities.

On our next overseas assignment, three years in northeastern Brazil, I discovered the possibilities of syncretism—how the simultaneous practice of two religions can yield a powerful synergistic effect. In Brazil, I was immersed in a culture formed through racial and religious mixing. Brazil is roughly the same size as the continental United States, with an equally diverse topography and culture. Both countries were built on the backs of enslaved African laborers, and both countries still struggle with this political and socioeconomic legacy. There is a huge difference, however, in the way the two countries responded to the African influx. In the United States, African culture was forbidden and suppressed, and through most of American history, we have continued to categorize people as either black or white, with "one drop" of African blood often enough to color a person black. In part because of this dualism, biracial children in the United States have had little choice but to self-identify as black.

As an interfaith child, I see parallels between the state of being interracial and the state of being interfaith in the United States. Society tags us with our minority status, no matter how fractional. And claiming the majority culture may feel cowardly—we do not want to abandon the minority. Caught between two identities in a binary system, we may feel marginalized and misunderstood.

In contrast, in Brazil a third of the population claims mixed-race heritage. While skin color is noticed in Brazil and has socioeconomic repercussions, people do not tend to self-identify as black or white. Fluid identity in Brazil extends beyond race to religion. About two-thirds of Brazilians are Catholic, but almost two-thirds of these Catholics (many of them "white" by American standards) also practice New World African or native Brazilian religions, such as Candomblé and Umbanda. While living in Brazil, we danced every year in what may be the greatest syncretic festival on the planet—Brazilian Carnival.

In the midst of this Brazilian religious and racial fluidity, the rigid boundaries of institutional Judaism came into stark relief. The only rabbi in town was a Chabadnik who rejected me as a Jew, excluding me from his community seder, while welcoming another American who had been raised Christian but had a Jewish mother.

By the time we moved back to the States, my connections to institutional Judaism felt tenuous indeed, and my mind was certainly expanded on issues of identity. While religious institutions often demonize the idea of religious syncretism, I began to understand that all religions have syncretic elements, in that they continue to evolve and change and influence each other—even Judaism. And I began to resist the idea that this blurring of boundaries, this religious layering, threatens the well-being of practitioners. It may threaten institutions, but that's another story.

FINDING AN INTERFAITH HOME

We arrived back in the United States in 1997, with an infant son and a toddler daughter in tow, all of us weary of travel. It was time to plant our family in an American community and make some decisions about the religious education of our children.

Living overseas in a city without a synagogue had allowed us to delay these decisions, though we celebrated both sets of holidays at home. When we married, my chivalrous husband, the great-grandson of an Episcopal bishop, offered that he would be willing to raise our children as Jews. Ironically, I was the one who could not imagine trying to shield my children from the Christian reality of three-quarters of their family tree. At the same time, I didn't necessarily want to subject my quarter-Jew children to the experience I'd had of constantly having to defend my Jewish identity.

I wanted my children to be able to understand their Christian heritage, to be educated about and comfortable with Christianity in a way I never had been. I also knew I wanted them to be educated about their Jewish heritage, and to have a positive relationship with Judaism. I did not want them to feel that they were trying to "pass" as Christians. And a more universalist pathway, such as Baha'i or Unitarianism, seemed to ignore the detailed funk and grit of our two family traditions. I wanted to give our children the specificity of our religions and a sense of their place on the family tree.

We settled in Takoma Park, Maryland, a diverse and unusually freethinking suburb of Washington, D.C. It is probably no coincidence that the Interfaith Families Project of Greater Washington (IFFP) was founded there. By the time we arrived, IFFP was four years old and had already grown from four families to fifty-five. IFFP describes itself as "an independent community of interfaith families committed to sharing, learning about, and celebrating our Jewish and Christian heritages." My daughter, then four years old, entered the Sunday school, where she immediately began learning about Judaism and Christianity in equal parts, taught by paired teams of Jewish and Christian teachers.

We thought we were joining this community for the sake of our children. But when I found IFFP, I found the community that I myself had been searching for all my life: A community where interfaith marriage was the norm. A community where no one would challenge my right, or the right of my children, to claim Judaism. A community where people with patrilineal and matrilineal Jewish heritage had equal standing. A community where I could safely explore the role that Christianity has played in the history of Judaism and in my family. A community where my husband and I could feel equally respected, where neither of us would feel like a guest. And finally, a community where I felt my family could be at the center, rather than on the periphery.

In my second year at IFFP, I found myself on the board of the organization. Members referred to me as the "interfaith poster child," since I was the first adult child of intermarriage to take a leadership position in the group. In my fourth year, I became one of the two board co-chairs.

Meanwhile, my parents watched with growing fascination as I immersed myself in the local and national movement to raise children with two religions. They attended IFFP functions, where they proudly held court, wearing name badges that read "Interfaith Pioneer." At last, they were getting some credit for their long and successful intermarriage.

As I became more comfortable discussing Jesus as a historical figure and a Jew, the party line in our family—that my mother had agreed to raise us as Jews because she didn't care that much about religion—was revealed as a bit of a myth. Only as an adult, as I began my first tentative attempts at a remedial education in basic Christianity, did I learn that after college, my mother had applied to Union Theological Seminary, the historic and progressive Protestant seminary in New York City.

I was astounded by this revelation. Through years of encouraging her daughters to get good educations, my mother had somehow never mentioned that she had applied to graduate school? Clearly, not too many years before her marriage, Christianity had meant quite a lot to her. In the end, she did not enter the seminary; in part because, as a woman, she could not become an Episcopal priest. (The Episcopal Church did not ordain women until 1974.) And she did not want to go to seminary "just" to become a Sunday school teacher.

So, if my mother had entertained aspirations of priesthood, why were we raised as Jews? Because my father wanted it, but also because my mother thought it was impractical for us to try to "pass" as Christians. "It didn't seem reasonable to me to raise you as

Christians," she says. But my mother also thought her own spiritual questioning disqualified her as a strong religious role model. As she recalls, "I didn't even know what I believed at that point, and I still don't. So raising you as Christians didn't seem fair." And thus she put aside her Christianity and instead devoted herself to raising Jewish children. Now, when my mother visits our interfaith community, she often comments that she wishes that such a support group had existed when we were children.

Almost fifteen years after joining IFFP, with my teenagers now graduated from their formal interfaith education program, I still feel the euphoria of belonging. The Jewish people will always be my people, and I will stand up for them and against anti-Semitism whenever I am needed. And I still do not describe myself as a Christian, having been raised exclusively as a Jew. Like most of the children being raised in our community, I see Jesus as a teacher, not as a personal savior. Most often, I define myself as a Jew who celebrates my interfaithness.

Nevertheless, I have chosen as my primary religious community a fully interfaith community: a community in which I can be completely myself—my whole self, not "half" anything, someone without an asterisk, without need of explanation or qualification. We decided that this was the greatest gift we could give our children—a community where they can feel that they are at the heart, not in the extremities. Yes, they can learn Hebrew, they can learn the history of the Jewish people and claim that history as their own. But they can also learn the Sermon on the Mount and contemplate all that has made the Jew named Jesus so compelling to the world. And they can learn that their grandmother, my mother, continued our interfaith family tradition by baptizing them in her kitchen sink. They can celebrate her loving gesture, without any need for secrecy or guilt.

CHAPTER TWO

A Grassroots
Social Movement

FOR INTERFAITH FAMILIES, FINDING community has been a historical challenge. Some have found a home in Unitarian Universalist congregations, in Quaker meeting houses, in Baha'i temples, in Ethical Culture, in Secular Humanistic Judaism, or in progressive churches and synagogues. Many other families abandoned hope of finding a community that would accept them, and felt forced to become "do-nothings." Some became embittered by rejection and abandoned the idea that religious community could be beneficial.

The radical vision of designing a community specifically for interfaith families—which values both religions and both spouses equally—began to crop up spontaneously in cities around the country in the 1980s. With the increasing rate of intermarriage, the density of families in urban areas who yearned for such a solution became high enough that interfaith communities began to naturally coalesce.

In this chapter, I trace the evolution of this grassroots movement. For interfaith families, and for clergy who want to help them, this history may provide inspiration to find or form such a group, or to at least borrow ideas from these groups. At the same time, the story of the growth of this movement may help explain to skeptics why so many volunteers have been willing to work to build interfaith communities from the ground up.

DOVETAIL: NATIONAL SUPPORT

Many of the earliest interfaith communities found each other and became loosely connected through the Dovetail Institute for Interfaith Family Resources. Dovetail, founded in 1992, served as a clearinghouse that maintained a virtual bulletin board for people seeking to find other interfaith families, published a newsletter, and organized a series of national conferences where leaders from the various groups met to share ideas and resources.

Over the years, some interfaith family communities rose up and then naturally phased out when the children graduated, or families decided to affiliate with churches or synagogues, or parents simply lacked the energy and time to continue. Groups in the San Francisco Bay area, Memphis, Minneapolis, and New Haven all flourished for a while and then became less active. Such smaller, informal groups can serve a real and important purpose. But eventually, in order to become sustainable, the largest groups have invested in some combination of staffing, communications, programming for adults, and space for growth. It is not easy to keep a group running on volunteer energy alone, without endowments, church buildings, or institutional support. In spite of this, the three largest and most successful programs profiled below (in New York, Chicago, and Washington) have continued to expand and thrive, and spin off new groups.

Dovetail did not necessarily promote the idea of independent interfaith communities. Mary Heléne and Ned Rosenbaum, who formed the heart and soul of the organization until they retired (and retired Dovetail with them), raised their own children with both religions in the 1960s and '70s through separate attendance at both church and synagogue, before the advent of interfaith communities. They describe their pioneering family in the joint memoir, *Celebrating Our Differences*. But through the 1990s and 2000s, Dovetail was the only national organization even open to discussing the idea of interfaith communities.

Most religious institutions gave Dovetail a wide berth, fearing that the organization was somehow encouraging a "mixing" of religions. "The mere fact that the organization acknowledged the possibility of a successful dual-faith approach meant the Jewish establishment saw Dovetail as promoting that option," recalls Mary Heléne Rosenbaum. Nevertheless, Dovetail board members and conference speakers included many forward-thinking rabbis and people in the Jewish outreach movement who appreciated the need for, or at least wanted to understand, this independent organization. Important early support came from Egon Mayer, the hugely respected sociologist who both studied intermarriage as an academic and advocated, as a founder of the Jewish Outreach Institute, for better treatment for non-Jewish spouses within Jewish communities.

The rejection of Dovetail by Jewish institutions is ironic in light of the religious journey of Dovetail founder Joan Hawxhurst. A Protestant married to a Jew, Hawxhurst founded Dovetail after an uncomfortable experience in a synagogue group for interfaith couples, where she felt she was "steered firmly, if surreptitiously, toward the decision to create a Jewish home," and where she felt "excluded and faintly disrespected." A decade later, in what she describes as a "beautiful irony," Hawxhurst and her husband ultimately joined a Jewish congregation and raised their children as Jews, in a Jewish home. She wrote, "Within the supportive Dovetail community, we were able to explore the possibilities, talk about the tough issues, and come to our own mutually acceptable solution."

THE NEW YORK MODEL: START WITH EDUCATION

The novel idea of an intentional community for interfaith families first took root on the Upper West Side of New York in 1987. What eventually became the Interfaith Community (IFC) began with the vision of two women, both parents at the private Trinity School. Lee Gruzen, a Protestant married to a Jewish man, first articulated the idea of raising dual-faith children in *Raising Your Jewish/Christian Child* (1987). "My book started with the premise that the children of mixed marriage have an incredibly rich heritage, and to amputate it by pushing away the 'other,' or being afraid of the 'other,' and not mining it for everything that both sides have to offer would be an incredible missed opportunity," Gruzen told me.

Gruzen's vision inspired Sheila Gordon, a Conservative Jew married to an Episcopalian man, who worked with Gruzen and other like-minded parents to create the first interfaith education program as an afterschool program at Trinity. Today, some twenty-five years later, Gordon still leads the IFC board, coordinating six chapters in four states.

Gordon recalls her motivation to launch the original group: "My husband and I felt there must be a way to respect and engage seriously in our own religious traditions, and that we had just hit a complete brick wall with the institutions," she says. "Some of the rest of us were feeling marginalized, diminished by whatever powers that be, public opinion, all of that. We were looking for a place to go and do it in an authentic way. Some of us were concerned about Jewish continuity in addition. I was constantly getting that question, 'Haven't you broken that chain? Don't you feel responsible to your heritage?' That kind of question was very prominent at that time."

After several years, the original cohort of children had graduated, and the religious education program lapsed into dormancy. And yet, the original families continued to gather for holidays, including popular lay-led Jewish High Holy Day services. The experience of being together remained powerful. And Sheila Gordon knew that with increasing intermarriage rates, the need to support interfaith families had only grown. So she retired from her career in academia and foundation work in 2001 and put her considerable managerial skills into relaunching the interfaith education program and professionalizing the organization. She drew on the successful programs in Chicago and Washington but also hired Jewish and Christian educators to design a new curriculum. And she recruited an advisory board filled with supportive clergy.

In the decade since the relaunch, Gordon has seen religious institutions begin to open up to the reality of intermarriage. In 2001, the original tag line for the group was "A safe and neutral space for Jewish/Christian families." She says, "Ten years later, that really is no longer the way we think about our work. It really was defensive and apologetic. Those words were pretty powerful, and they still are for some people. But it is much more apologetic and marginal than our new tag line, which is 'Two religions, one family, a model for Jewish/Christian families.' That's a big shift."

Gordon specifically designed the new program in a format that could be easily replicated to form branches in other locations. Now, in addition to the original program in Manhattan, there are IFC chapters in Boston; Danbury, Connecticut; New York's Westchester County and Long Island; and the Orange/Rockland/Bergen counties of New Jersey and New York.

THE CHICAGO MODEL: GROWING FROM A COUPLES GROUP

In New York, where the founding families already had children, the driving factor in creating a group was the desire for an interfaith religious education program, with adult support and education and community following later. An alternative model involves gathering young intermarried couples into a circle for discussion, holiday celebrations, and socializing. Eventually, when children are born into the group and reach school age, the need for an interfaith school naturally follows.

This was the case in Chicago, where, in 1988, young couples founded the Jewish Catholic Couples Dialogue Group ("the Dialogue Group") as a resource and discussion forum to wrestle with the common issues of weddings, extended family, and balancing the religious practices of intermarried adults. By 1993, when many of the couples had young children, some of the original members had formed a religious education program, the Interfaith Family School, with a curriculum developed by founding member Patty Kovacs. Later, Eileen O'Farrell Smith spun off a separate organization, the Interfaith Union, dedicated to helping with baby-welcoming ceremonies and to providing interfaith education in the Chicago suburbs.

The Chicago groups were very fortunate to have the involvement of clergy from the outset. Their situation was somewhat unusual, with a historically progressive local Catholic leadership centered downtown at Old Saint Patrick's Church, coupled with a significant demographic of Jews and Catholics intermarrying. The Catholic Church has a very wise requirement for pre-marriage counseling, the Pre-Cana program, and clergy in Chicago help connect interfaith couples to the Dialogue Group. Families in the Interfaith Family School are welcomed both at Mass at Old Saint Pat's, and in some local Jewish congregations.

In other cities, groups have not necessarily found that type of institutional support from churches or synagogues. "Movements always come from the ground up, not the top down," muses Chicago's Father John Cusick. "The only advice I would give couples who want to make something like this happen is, don't go running to authority for permission. You go to your leaders for counsel and encouragement, not for permission."

Almost twenty years after its creation, the Interfaith Family School is thriving, with some 80 families and 120 students enrolled in kindergarten through eighth grade. Group founders Patty and David Kovacs have two children, now in their twenties. "If you're going to do both, it's hard," says David, the Jewish spouse. "It's a commitment. You can't do this and be the bagel-and-lox-kind of Jews," he says. He believes that giving children both Catholicism and Judaism works best when families are committed to attending Mass, synagogue, and the Interfaith Family School. This model may require more effort, but Kovacs is not surprised that the Dialogue Group and Family School continue to thrive. "It's gotten easier for people to get intermarried, and Jewish congregations are getting more welcoming," he notes. "But interfaith families are always going to have this independent stripe to them."

THE BAY AREA MODEL: FAMILY COOPERATIVES

Meanwhile, in the East Bay Area of San Francisco in 1989, rabbi and psychotherapist Yeshaia Charles Familant began meeting with young interfaith couples in his converted garage office once a month on Friday nights, for Shabbat blessings and discussion. Many Jewish institutions now provide support groups for intermarried couples, led by rabbis or lay Jewish counselors. But in California, Rabbi Familant's group evolved into something revolutionary when he brought in a Catholic priest, Father John Hester, as a fellow adviser to the couples. "The rabbi quickly realized that either people were asking questions about Christianity that needed answers, or that it would be better with balance, but it happened that he was very good friends with Father Hester and asked him to join us," recalls Alicia Torre, an original member of the group.

As the couples began to have children, Rabbi Familant and Father Hester continued to provide support. "All of our kids had joint Hebrew baby-namings and baptisms with Rabbi Familant and

Father Hester," recalls Torre, the mother of three sons who are now in their twenties. Torre was raised Episcopalian; her husband, Jonathan Nimer, was raised Jewish. They knew from the start of their marriage that they wanted to celebrate both religions with their children. "We both had very strong cultural values that mattered to us, and neither of us were interested in converting," explains Torre. "Part of our marriage vows were committing to a home in which there would be celebrations in both traditions."

Having made this decision, Torre was highly motivated to help create an interfaith religious education program for her family. While on maternity leaves in 1991 and 1994, she traveled to both New York and Chicago to research the successful programs already under way. "Lee Gruzen's was the only book that was positive about dual upbringing," she recalls. But she felt called to build a community of her own.

What evolved in the Bay Area was a series of small, cooperative family interfaith education programs, consisting of six to eight families meeting in private homes. As in a cooperative nursery school, parents accompanied the students, learning alongside them. Torre's family participated in three of these co-op interfaith Sunday schools over the years.

There was no attempt to institutionalize or grow these programs, and the Sunday schools dissolved when the children aged out or families chose larger communities. As Torre described it, many of the families were leery, at least at first, of religious institutions. The dual-faith education concept, says Torre, attracts "a lot of people who have negative feelings about institutions, or were simply raised outside them, or who have a discomfort with labeling." Some people overcame this hesitancy during their years in an interfaith group and went on to join churches and/or synagogues. "The people who were seekers—who most wanted a community of like-minded people, to be involved with progressive work in the community, or have services with words that speak to their souls—those people came to our group, they worked out their issues with institutions, and then went on to find something more substantial," says Torre. For others, the interfaith community fulfilled their needs and remained their only religious community. Twenty years later, Torre and Nimer still get together with some of the original couples for occasional social gatherings.

Fellow Bay Area parent Amy Bassell Crowe recalls launching one of those family-run interfaith schools as "one of the greatest things I think I've ever been involved in." Bassell Crowe grew up Jewish in New York; she describes her husband, Jeff Crowe, as a "CEO" (Christmas and Easter only) Catholic. Until their oldest daughter reached second grade, they carted her to two Sunday schools: Jewish in the morning, Christian in the evening.

But Bassell Crowe, a psychologist, had her doubts about having her daughter educated in two separate schools, neither of which would address the issues raised by the other religion: "We realized she felt like a ping-pong ball." Clergy urged the family to pick one religion. But Bassell Crowe pushed back: "I asked for data that showed that we needed to choose one faith, and there wasn't any." Determined to teach their children both, Bassell Crowe traveled to New Haven to get advice and resources from Debi Tener, who was running a Sunday school for interfaith children there.

Bassell Crowe's three daughters are now in their twenties. "All three of them feel that this was by leaps and bounds far better than anything else they could have done," she says. "They all three loved that their parents were a part of it. We spent lots of dinner-table conversations talking and sharing opinions. It felt very much part of who we are as a family," says Bassell Crowe. "It wasn't just didactic, it was very participatory. They also fiercely identify with being interfaith kids. That's who they are, and they're quite proud of that."

The Crowes testify to the lasting effect of the community they helped to create. Rabbi Familant officiated at the funerals of both of Bassell Crowe's parents. The Crowes still host a seder each year for the interfaith families from their Sunday school years. And the group continues to exist in the form of a community service organization. For almost twenty years now, every December this circle of California interfaith families chooses two needy families—one Christian and one Jewish—and raises funds for holiday gifts in a giant bake sale. The children help to bake Christmas and Hannukah treats, staff the sale, and purchase and wrap the gifts. Bassell Crowe concludes, "Lifelong friendships have been formed through this effort, both for adults and kids."

THE WASHINGTON MODEL: CLERGY ON STAFF

Building on the experiences in New York, Chicago, California, and elsewhere, the Interfaith Families Project of Greater Washington (IFFP) in Washington, D.C., has grown into what may be the most "full service" interfaith group, providing many of the elements of a traditional religious institution. The program meets nearly every week during the school year and charges enough to fill multiple leadership positions, including an executive director, a minister, a rabbi, and a religious education director. There's a nursery and teen group in addition to Sunday school for 130 students, preschool through eighth grade. While the children are in Sunday school, adults have as many as three different options each week, which may include discussion groups; bible study, Judaism 101, and Christianity 101 classes; grieving groups; meditation and yoga classes; community service projects; and invited speakers from across the religious spectrum.

Uniquely, and perhaps most radically, IFFP begins each Sunday morning meeting with what is called a "Gathering" filled with reflection and song. To critics, the Gathering veers dangerously close to worship in some kind of third religion with a new interfaith liturgy. To members, Gatherings provide a fulfilling and empowering opportunity for families to reflect together in a space where neither parent is a guest. For program teachers, the Gatherings ensure that children have a chance to hear and participate in the prayers and songs they learn in the classroom. "I don't think you can do religious education without the experience of the practice. It's more than flipping latkes," says Ian Spatz, a former IFFP board chair. Finally, the Gatherings allow children and adults to experience the transcendence we call spirituality—to go beyond intellectual classroom discussions of comparative religion.

The four "founding mothers" of IFFP did not originally set out to create a full-service community with a spiritual component. When Stacey Katz (raised as a Conservative Jew) met Irene Landsman (from a Unitarian and Catholic background) in a pregnancy exercise class at the YMCA, they were drawn together by their shared experience of being pregnant and being intermarried. They recruited Laura Steinberg (Jewish) and Mary Joel Holin (Catholic), and through the early years of motherhood and growing friendship, they researched their options for raising children with both religions.

Katz recalls, "I just assumed that we could find a group, that we couldn't be the first people to invent this—that somewhere in the great big city of Washington, D.C., there was some sort of program for interfaith families. Because when I looked up and down my block, every other family was an interfaith family. So when you see the numbers like this, you have to believe there's some group out there."

In 1990, they opened the phone book and began calling houses of worship. As Landsman recalls, "There were a lot of false leads. A synagogue would say they had many non-Jewish spouses and a group for them, but the kids had to be raised Jewish. And then we found some churches that had many Jewish spouses and would be quite welcoming, but they certainly weren't going to provide Jewish education. A lot of them said, 'Well, we talk about Passover at Easter time,' and that would be it."

"I can't remember when it came to us that we were going to have to invent an interfaith community, but that was a powerful experience—kind of appreciating that we were the adults, this was our generation, and that we could do it," recalls Landsman. "It was very, very child-focused at first. That was the one thing that we could all agree on: that we wanted some religious education for our kids. The thing we weren't so sure about is what we wanted for ourselves, except to have a community, to have other people with whom to celebrate holidays. What really didn't get addressed back then was individual spiritual life. We were pretty intellectual about it."

The founding families assumed that the adults' spiritual needs would be met outside of IFFP. Katz recalls, "What we were thinking was that we would seek out what we called 'sister congregations.' We wanted to organize it so that we weren't all just spread out to different churches and synagogues."

But this idea of partnering with a specific church and synagogue proved difficult to implement. On the Christian side, the problem was the diversity of denominations. Would IFFP partner with a Catholic church? A Methodist church? A Unitarian Universalist community? All of the above? On the Jewish side, at first the idea seemed more feasible. Katz had "wonderful discussions" with a local Reform rabbi, who invited the interfaith families to attend services at his synagogue. But ultimately, the partnership never moved forward. Katz recalls, "This rabbi was very involved with the Reform rabbis, and he was beginning to tell me that the Reform congregations were getting more strict about what they were demanding of their membership in terms of commitment to Judaism."

Meanwhile, after three years of rapid growth in the interfaith education program, in 1998 IFFP hired its first staff member. Reverend Julia Jarvis was raised as a Southern Baptist, is ordained in the progressive United Church of Christ, and practices Buddhist meditation. Although she was originally hired to direct the Sunday school, Reverend Jarvis immediately sensed that the adults in this new community needed spiritual care, and organized the first Gathering in a classroom hallway. Some members, staunch secularists, remained uncomfortable with singing and reflecting as a community and skipped the Gathering, arriving just in time for bagels and coffee, followed by Sunday school and adult discussion group.

But pushed by adults who needed and wanted more, the IFFP Gatherings quickly expanded. Each prayer or song was carefully labeled so that children (and adults) could understand the historic origins. A house band played songs from Jewish, Christian, and folk traditions. Marci Shegogue, a Jewish woman who met her Catholic husband doing musical theater in college, sat at a keyboard directing the band and led the *Hamotzi* (the Jewish blessing over bread, in this case recited before the bagel snack rather than challah) each week. And her husband, Rich, led the group with his gorgeous tenor voice each week in singing the Lord's Prayer.

In order to provide a sense of balance and bring Jewish resources to the group, the community next hired longtime Georgetown University chaplain Rabbi Harold White in 2004 as a Jewish spiritual adviser. Jewish in-laws who had steered clear of the community began to attend Gatherings in order to hear this legendary teacher. And in 2011, the group began full-fledged High Holy Day services, open to the Washington-area community, led by Rabbi White. Rabbi White and Reverend Jarvis, after co-officiating for many years at weekly Gatherings and life-cycle ceremonies, have become close friends as well as work partners. Says Reverend Jarvis, "I love Judaism. There've been times when I've thought about converting."

INTERFAITH GATHERINGS

Why should the idea of Jews and Christians singing, reflecting, and, yes, praying together, be so controversial? Recently, I attended a Thanksgiving interfaith service in a Long Island town. This event has been held each year since 1940. It falls squarely in the "interfaith cooperation and appreciation" tradition: intermarried families were not mentioned. A dozen different Christian clergy members and a half-dozen representatives from three different Jewish congregations participated. Townsfolk in yarmulkes and townsfolk in red and green holiday sweaters packed the service. We all felt warm and fuzzy and progressive and patriotic, reading prayers and singing songs from both Jewish and Christian traditions, as well as *America the Beautiful*.

I loved it. But I also kept thinking that for our family, the service felt very familiar. Every week throughout the school year at IFFP, we sing Christian and Jewish songs and say Christian and Jewish prayers, led by Christian and Jewish clergy in a community filled with Christians and Jews. What's the difference? At such annual services, sponsored by towns or interfaith dialogue groups, Jews and Christians unite but still clearly retain their separate identities. In our community, a large proportion of the children and a growing number of the intermarried adults *identify themselves as interfaith*: a label that can provoke curiosity, concern, or even alarm.

As a logo, IFFP uses the Venn diagram of two overlapping circles to represent the three spaces that members experience together. The common ground—the intersection of the two circles—is a space that feels good, feels safe. But interfaith families journeying together aim to explore all three spaces: Jewish, interfaith, Christian. Sometimes, venturing away from the center into the rocky terrain of religious particularities feels difficult. But just as often, it feels exhilarating. "I think a lot of people don't know what we're doing," says Reverend Jarvis. "They think we're Unitarians or that we're starting a new religion. You have to come and experience it to understand it."

At the beginning of every Gathering, the IFFP community recites a responsive reading written by Oscar Rosenbloom, who served as cantor for the Interfaith Community of Palo Alto.

READER: We gather here as an Interfaith Community
               To share and celebrate the gift of life together
ALL: *Some of us gather as the Children of Israel*
               Some of us gather in the name of Jesus of Nazareth
               Some of us gather influenced by each
READER: However we come, and whoever we are
               May we be moved in our time together
               To experience that sense of Divine presence in each of us
               Evoked by our worship together
ALL: *And to know in the wisdom of our hearts*
               That deeper unity in which all are one.

On any given week, the Gathering may center on a Jewish holiday or concept, a Christian holiday or concept, or a shared value such as compassion or service or peace. No matter the theme, the Gathering includes the central Jewish prayer known as the *Sh'ma*, the Lord's Prayer, the Interfaith Responsive Reading, the Interfaith Benediction and Charge, and the *Hamotzi* blessing over snacks. These constant elements serve as rituals threading through the different Gatherings, and help children to memorize fundamental prayers: my two teens know all these prayers by heart. The idea of commingling these liturgical elements may upset people who grew up in a single-faith environment. But for me, as an interfaith child, and for many of the couples in this thriving community, the disparate Jewish and Christian elements in these Gatherings create synergy rather than dissonance.

Recently, after more than a dozen years of Gatherings, IFFP designed a "Yom HaShoah," or Holocaust Remembrance Day. For me, this day marked a new level of maturity in the community, a moment when we dared to address a very charged topic, one that is still painful and of deep importance to both Jews and Christians. In my experience, remembering together as interfaith families transformed Yom HaShoah into a day to remember our specific ancestors lost in this tragedy but also the need for universal education about the Holocaust for both Christians and Jews and the reality that any community can become a victim or a perpetrator.

As at many Yom HaShoah gatherings around the world, we read from Elie Wiesel and Anne Frank, we sang the haunting "Eli Eli" by martyred war hero Hannah Senesh in Hebrew and English, we sang the "Hymn of the Partisans" in Yiddish and English. But we also sang the Christian hymn "How Can I Keep From Singing," a standard for Quakers, Baptists, and Catholics (as well as Pete Seeger!). This nineteenth-century hymn speaks of "earth's lamentation" and the "tumult and the strife," reminding us not only of the Holocaust but also of contemporary genocides in places like Sudan and Syria and even the desperate worldwide struggle with climate change. When community board member André Parraway, an African American Episcopalian married to a white Jewish woman, read the words of German Lutheran theologian Martin Niemoller, "First they came for the communists, and I didn't speak out . . ." they took on new resonance for me. As intermarried couples and as interfaith and interracial children, we represent Hitler's worst fears. And yet here we are, in a country that allows radical freedom of religion and the intermarriage that Hitler tried to stop.

At our Yom HaShoah remembrance, community member Fredie Adelman spoke about her father's memory of being liberated by a squadron of African American soldiers who gave him chocolate.

Adelman noted, "We are all very fortunate to belong to IFFP, a community that tells truths about who we are." And when Rabbi White made mention of the Armenian genocide, which predated the Holocaust, I saw Adelman's Armenian American Christian husband, Mark Gulezian, nodding in appreciation.

At the end of each Gathering, we read a Benediction and Charge composed by Oscar Rosenbloom, which incorporates elements of a Presbyterian charge to the congregation and the traditional Jewish priestly benediction:

ALL: *May we go out into the world carrying with each of us the love and blessing of this Interfaith Community*

READER: May we continue to hold on to what is good and to stand as beacons of light and understanding for all people.

ALL: *May God's spirit and peace be with us each now and forever.*

READER: May the Lord bless you and keep you and bring you peace. Amen.

As we marked Yom HaShoah together as Christians and Jews, this interfaith charge took on added significance as we vowed to work to try to prevent any and all such future tragedies.

REPLICATING AN EXISTING PROGRAM

Starting an interfaith families school or community from scratch may sound daunting. But in recent years, young couples have been able to build on the New York, Washington, and Chicago models to create new communities. The Catholic/Jewish curriculum created by Patti Kovacs in Chicago is available for sale. Meanwhile, the IFC headquarters in Manhattan supports six chapters in four states, providing nonprofit status, curricula, and Christian and Jewish educators. And the IFFP in Washington is inspiring the formation of new groups in Philadelphia and elsewhere.

Kate Hornstein encountered IFC while living in New York in 2003 and then founded a new a chapter after her family moved to Boston. She is also an active member of her Episcopal church. Her husband grew up in Conservative Judaism. Hornstein's daughters are now sixteen and twelve, and her older daughter has traveled to New York for retreats with the teenagers from the IFC chapters there. IFC Boston holds interfaith classes and programs at Hornstein's church, and also holds events at a progressive Jewish community in the Boston suburbs. Hornstein feels she is filling an important niche: "The people who show up at our group are mostly people who weren't doing anything, or were doing both religions, but piecemeal."

When Pam and Steve Gawley moved from Manhattan to Long Island, they also took IFC with them. IFC Long Island actually meets in a synagogue, which, Pam Gawley says, has "been very supportive of what we do, and we're very respectful of them." The rabbi will even refer couples to the interfaith group, and the interfaith group refers couples to the synagogue. Gawley describes the growth of the group as organic: "It's a very personal decision and I don't like to get involved with trying to convince people to be a part of it. If you can make a decision to be one religion, I think you should. If you can't, and you need a place to come, we're here."

Felise and Mark Shellenberger fall firmly into the category of an interfaith couple who both come from strong religious backgrounds. Mark is the son of a Methodist minister. Felise was the head of her college Hillel. When their oldest child was three, they joined IFFP in Washington.

When the Shellenbergers moved to the Philadelphia area years later, they took the IFFP concept with them. Because the group is too small for single-grade classrooms, they have adopted a small family co-op system, similar to the California interfaith groups, with parents attending alongside their children in a one-room schoolhouse model. "With the parents all staying together, we've learned so much from each other, about each other's religions, or even how within the same religion we all do things differently," Felise Shellenberger says. Children and parents are learning Hebrew together, with some friendly competition between kids and adults.

NEED FOR INTERFAITH COMMUNITIES IN THE FUTURE

Will independent communities for interfaith families be necessary if Jewish communities become more fully welcoming? Today, many Jewish institutions are trying hard to welcome interfaith families. The Jewish Outreach Institute and InterfaithFamily.com work full-time to encourage a more inclusive Judaism and to provide support to non-Jewish spouses helping to raise Jewish children. Nevertheless, they draw the line at encouraging the "doing both" pathway or providing access to Christian clergy, and they discourage interfaith families from formally educating their children about Christianity.

Jewish institutions are still struggling to overcome the sense of exclusion felt by interfaith families. In my survey of parents who joined interfaith communities, one mother of two, a Baptist married to a Reform Jew, wrote, "We researched and visited a few Reform congregations, but never felt we 'fit' as a family. For example, one Reform congregation would not allow me, the non-Jew, to hold or touch the Torah. At another, the religious education director was cold and unwelcoming. Also, my husband was not comfortable joining a congregation where the sitting rabbi would have refused to marry us."

Other families cite the importance of having both parents equally engaged and involved in the religious education of their children, and credit independent interfaith communities with helping to achieve that balance. One Conservative Jewish mother of two married to a Christian explains that when they belonged to a synagogue, "I was not getting any support from my husband for making the kids go to Sunday school and Hebrew school." Some spouses are willing to throw themselves into the partner's religion for the sake of the children, as my mother did. But many others cannot make this sacrifice, and do not feel it is necessary to do it for the children's sake when there are benefits of raising the children with both religions.

About a quarter of the families in my survey had tried affiliation with a Jewish congregation. No matter how warmly a non-Jewish spouse is welcomed by a Jewish institution, there often remains a sense of separation, a difference that marks this parent as a "guest" of the community rather than a full member. Families that choose an interfaith community are seeking full membership for both spouses, and they are seeking to give their children the reassurance that both parents are equally valued and equal members of the interfaith tribe.

TODAY, THE ORIGINAL FOUNDERS OF the first interfaith family communities all have grown children. IFC founder Lee Gruzen now lives at the tip of lower Manhattan. Gazing out her window toward the Statue of Liberty, she muses, "Where the land meets the sea is the exciting part, the littoral. It's where the new life happens: for me that's where the action is. The coast for me is more interesting than the ocean."

The littoral, the shore, the edge. As interfaith families, this is where we live, and where we thrive. The creative power, the fertility, of the space sustains us.

CHAPTER THREE

The Case for Choosing Both

Benefits of Dual-Faith Life

In the face of resistance or skepticism from family, friends, and religious leaders, why do families consider choosing both? It is clear that, despite the difficulties, many in this growing movement see being both not simply as a compromise or negotiated settlement but as a positive, and even inspirational, choice. In this chapter, I catalog the specific benefits of raising children with both religions, discovered in my own journey and in my research with these families. Some of these benefits are inherent in raising children with both religions, and some are specific to raising children in a community with a formal interfaith education program and support for interfaith families.

PROMOTING TRANSPARENCY ABOUT DIFFERENCES

Neither parent, neither religion, is suppressed in an interfaith family that chooses both religions. The children appreciate that one parent has not been assigned a dominant role in the family's religious practice. And while they must learn to integrate two worldviews, as rebellious teens and young adults, they often appreciate the respect their parents show them by allowing them to make their own decisions. "No one is dictating to me what to believe and what not to," reports a thirteen-year-old girl in the Washington interfaith group.

The stress some children may feel in eventually allying with one parent or the other must be balanced against the stress children may feel if they perceive that a parent is suppressing his or her own religion on behalf of the child. A child may observe a Christian father, no matter how devoted he is in driving the kids to Hebrew school, glance longingly at a neighbor's Christmas tree. A child being raised solely as a Catholic may observe the discomfort of a Jewish mother around a crucifix. These observations can cause the children to feel confusion, guilt, and even resentment on behalf of the "out-parent." In a family where both religions are cause for celebration, this situation can be largely avoided.

Meanwhile, interfaith children trying to formulate an identity as solely Jewish or solely Christian often struggle against society's assumptions about their religion, based on physical characteristics, name, and extended family. An interfaith child raised Jewish may be presumed otherwise because of brown skin or even blond hair. An interfaith child raised Catholic, but whose last name is Cohen, will be presumed to be Jewish. Such physical or cultural obstacles to a single-faith identity may well be surmountable, and even character-building. On the other hand, children allowed to identify equally with both sides of the family may more easily integrate the reality of their hair, their name, and even their grandparents.

ENCOURAGING FAMILY UNITY

Many interfaith parents are nostalgic for their own upbringing in a family where everyone practiced the same religion together. In an interfaith family where one parent converts, this unity may be achievable. However, short of conversion, *complete* unity in religious practice is not going to be possible in a family in which two parents already represent two religions. Choosing one religion for the children strengthens their alliance and identification with the parent of that religion, inevitably leaving the other parent out, to some extent. This occurs even when the out-parent participates in the designated family religion. My mother went to Hebrew classes and virtually dropped her own religious practice. However, I was always conscious that she had not converted; and if I forgot, there was always someone from the Jewish community there to remind me. In another example, one mother, raised as an Episcopalian and married to a Reform Jew, tried taking her son to synagogue and church before joining IFFP. She says of the synagogue and church, "They weren't enough because they didn't provide a community in which we were both equally members."

Families who choose to raise their children in an interfaith community often cite unity as one of their reasons for doing so. In my survey, 48 percent of adult respondents, over one hundred of them, responded that one of their reasons for joining an interfaith community was that they didn't want one spouse to feel left out. In an interfaith setting, both parents have equal status; neither parent feels like the out-parent. Both parents can sit at a gathering or holiday celebration with the children, and neither will feel like a guest. There is never a question of who can hold the Torah, who can say a blessing.

Ideally, when a family chooses both, it means parents also take on equal responsibility in transmitting culture and beliefs to the children. If a Christian wife is toting the kids to Hebrew school, at least she knows she can also tote them to Mass. It also means that while both parents may be sacrificing some of their traditions because of time and logistical constraints, neither parent is being asked to sacrifice everything.

GIVING EXTENDED FAMILY EQUAL WEIGHT

Choosing one religion can strain relationships with the extended family celebrating the "out-religion." Parents feel they must be on guard against grandparents from the "other side" proselytizing or lobbying in more subtle ways. There may be pressure to minimize contact with the "wrong" side during school vacations, which often coincide with religious holidays.

Grandparents may not understand what it means at first to choose both religions, since interfaith family communities did not exist when they were raising children. Often, they become less skeptical when they visit the community or when they see the results of dual-faith education in their grandchildren. "My husband's parents (Jewish) have attended High Holy Days and love Rabbi White," says one Washington parent. "They were afraid this was a 'Jews for Jesus' type of group and were relieved that it was not. My parents (Roman Catholic) have never been, but seemed glad that our daughter knew the 'Our Father' prayer recently when we attended church with them." And a Jewish father in Washington writes, "I think my brother's family was somewhat skeptical until they attended my daughter's Coming of Age ceremony and liked it very much."

In the survey, about 30 percent of parents indicated that grandparents and extended family were "mainly enthusiastic" that their children were part of an interfaith community. About 16 percent chose, "They're just glad we're 'doing something.'" Of course, some grandparents are simply struggling to be diplomatic and suppress concern; about 30 percent of parents reported, "They don't say much about it." Less than 2 percent reported their parents and extended families as upset. But respondents wrote in to record "disinterest," "sarcasm," "disapproval," "finds it strange," and "still hoping we'll be more Jewish as time goes by." A woman in Chicago married to a

Reform Jew wrote, "My conservative Catholic parents are supportive but concerned. They mostly keep their concerns to themselves,
and I'm sure many Rosaries are said for us."

Nevertheless, one of the benefits of choosing both is that both
sets of grandparents may transmit beliefs and rituals more freely. A
Catholic grandparent can teach a grandchild to say the rosary, even
while a Jewish grandparent can teach a grandchild to say the Kaddish (the traditional Jewish prayer for mourning). In fact, extended
family members on both sides can be appreciated as guardians of
religious lore and family history. A mother of two young children
in Washington, Veronica Sholin was raised Catholic; her husband
was raised in Reform Judaism. When asked about the greatest benefit of raising children with both religions, Sholin replied, "Both
sets of holidays are celebrated in our home, and our kids can identify with both parents and the grandparents."

Of course, whether parents choose one religion or both, an extended family member (or friend) may make anti-Semitic or anti-
Christian remarks, or tell the children that they must accept Jesus
or they will burn in hell or that they are not really Jewish. In the
end, those of us in interfaith marriages cannot completely protect
our children (whether they are raised with one religion or two)
from intolerance, and from the exclusivity of fundamentalist religious institutions, but an interfaith families community becomes a
safe space in which to process this intolerance.

SIDESTEPPING THE MATRILINEALITY CONFLICT

In interfaith families choosing one religion for their children,
the issue of whether it is the mother or father who is Jewish can
have a tremendous impact on the children. Children raised as Jews
with a Christian mother will not be accepted by Conservative or
Orthodox Jews unless they undergo conversion, no matter how
scrupulous the family is in raising the children as Jews. Children

raised as Christians with a Jewish mother will hear from these same quarters that they are Jews, no matter how they were raised or how they feel.

As I've noted, Reform Jews have ruled that children can be Jewish if either the mother or father is Jewish. However, these families must "prove" their adherence to Judaism as their sole religion by jumping through certain hoops (baby-naming ceremonies, bar or bat mitzvahs). Children born to two Jewish parents do not need to pass these tests. And many of these hoops (including baby-namings for girls and even bar mitzvah ceremonies) are relatively modern traditions, not ancient rituals. So the standards of required practice end up being completely different for families with two Jewish parents and interfaith families. The hypocrisy inherent in this situation is a turn-off for many interfaith families, and in particular for rebellious teenagers.

And sadly, despite the historic decision by Reform rabbis to allow patrilineal Jewish children into the fold, even many Reform Jews continue to reject them. Generations of tradition and tribal consciousness are not easily erased by a rabbinic recommendation. As a patrilineal Jewish child whose parents did everything by the book to raise me as a Reform Jew, I can attest to this. For instance, once I was at a party talking to a Jewish man about his grown interfaith son, who was on a journey of discovering and nourishing his Jewish roots. The father, after marrying a Catholic woman, had raised his son without religion. Meanwhile, a friend of mine was listening to our conversation. She belongs to a Reform synagogue and knows that I was raised as a Jew, learned Hebrew, and became a bat mitzvah. She turned to this Jewish man and said, "Unfortunately, your son has the same problem that Sue has, which is that neither of them is a Jew." When I pointed out that this is not the policy of her own Reform synagogue, she was insistent in denying the legitimacy of patrilineal Jews.

In an interfaith community, children are raised to believe that they have a right to claim both their Jewish and Christian heritage, regardless of which parent is Jewish. In my survey of grown children, I asked, "Is it important to you whether it is the mother or the father that is the Jewish parent in an interfaith family?" Less than 7 percent answered that it was important to them. One young man, age twenty, raised at IFFP, said, "It seems to be important to other people, but I have never felt that it is."

Of course, when interfaith children go out into American society, they must face these issues. A woman raised in the New York group, now twenty-five, wrote, "It's important to others, because whether or not you believe in the passing of Judaism through the mother, everyone wants to pigeonhole you like that anyway." Another New York woman raised in the group, and now twenty-seven years old, concurs: "I do sometimes resent it when others (of any faith) tell me that just because my mother is Jewish then I am. Too easy an answer, I think."

But as we've seen, choosing one religion does not solve this problem. And even those who have converted formally sometimes find that they are not wholly accepted by the tribe. In the end, since the different Jewish communities have different opinions on the heritability of Judaism, and these opinions are still in a state of flux and conflict, it seems difficult and rather fruitless to try to conform to them.

PROVIDING LITERACY IN BOTH RELIGIONS

The most common reason parents in my survey cited for choosing an interfaith community was a desire for their children to be knowledgeable about both religions. More than 90 percent of parents chose this as one of their reasons for joining. Whether or not a family also belongs to a church or synagogue or both, a dual-faith religious education program gives children the freedom to compare and contrast in a way that is rarely condoned in a single-faith educational setting. And an interfaith education program provides practical advantages over shlepping children to two different religious schools. One Washington parent explains, "We didn't feel competent to be the sole religious teachers for our child, but sending him to both church and temple religious school was not realistic or appealing."

Even if your child chooses not to practice a religion as an adult, or to embrace a non-Abrahamic faith, our culture—American literature, music, politics—was forged in a Judeo-Christian context. A familiarity with Bible stories, rituals, and holidays from Judaism and Christianity makes a child more culturally literate. "Judaism, Christianity, and even Islam on some level, are part of popular culture, common parlance," says Reconstructionist Rabbi Nehama Benmosche, who taught at IFC in New York and helped to write some of the Jewish curriculum. "You need to get some kind of religious education to really be able to know what's going on in our world. It's part of what we do to give our kids a sense that religion is part of American culture."

PROMOTING CULTURAL HARMONY

In adulthood, interfaith children have a chance to become a part of the solution to the problems of religious intolerance, rather than accepting that they are part of some problem. "This is where the world is heading," says Reverend Allan Ramirez, a minister who works with the IFC on Long Island. "No one is going to stop love. No one is going to stop two people from loving each other and marrying each other."

There have been dark moments indeed in the history of Jewish-Christian relations. But that is no reason for Jews to remain ignorant of the tenets of the dominant religion in our culture, nor for Christians to remain ignorant of Judaism as the origin of Christianity. One mother from New York explains, "My children are in the unique position of being able to experience the joys of two sets of traditions, cultures, and teachings and ultimately will gain a greater understanding of the interrelationship between the two religions without the 'tunnel vision' and intolerance which can sometimes accompany being raised in one faith alone."

While interfaith parents sometimes worry about putting too much pressure on their children to be role models of peace and reconciliation, their very existence is beneficial in the world, according to Reverend Ramirez: "It may not change the world next year or the year after, or the year after that. But they are the seeds of love that are being planted, for some future generation to learn from and be inspired by."

Interfaith love and interfaith families have already played a quiet but essential role in fostering interfaith dialogue, though this is rarely acknowledged. Jewish philosopher Martin Buber (1878–1965) is perhaps best known for his description of the "I-Thou" relationship, in which two people communicate on a deep and mystical level, beyond words. He saw the relationship between humans and God as the ultimate form of "I-Thou."

Buber's love for his wife, Paula Winkler, who converted from Christianity to Judaism, clearly informed his development of the I-Thou philosophy, often popularized in interfaith dialogue as "embrace of the other." In Buber's obituary, the *New York Times* wrote that he was "regarded as a pioneer bridge-builder between Judaism and Christianity." Rabbi Harold White at IFFP loves to quote Buber, his former teacher, who wrote: "The world is not comprehensible, but it is embraceable: through the embracing of one of its beings." I would argue that Buber's literal embrace of Winkler was fundamental to much of his work, not incidental.

Some of the most important writers on American religious pluralism have also been inspired by their interfaith relationships. In *American Grace: How Religion Divides and Unites Us*, academics

Robert Putnam and David Campbell describe how their own families "illustrate the social and familial networks that knit together people of many different religions." Campbell's parents were born Protestant and Catholic, but both eventually converted to Mormonism. Putnam, raised Methodist, married a Jewish woman and converted to Judaism himself, and their family tree now includes Catholics, Evangelicals, and secularists as well. "It would be hard to rouse anti-Jewish or anti-Evangelical or anti-Catholic or anti-Methodist or even anti-secular fervor in this group," they write. They go on to make the leap from interfaith families to interreligious peace: "And that personal pluralism means that America is graced with religious harmony."

Similarly, in Eboo Patel's memoir *Acts of Faith*, he describes the women he dated—a Mormon, a Jew, and a Hindu—before meeting the Muslim woman who became his wife. These relationships were not incidental—he describes how they informed his voyage of self-discovery as a Muslim and the impetus to found the national Interfaith Youth Core, an organization devoted to interfaith cooperation on college campuses. And in his book *Without Buddha I Could Not Be a Christian*, Paul Knitter writes of the impact his Buddhist wife has had on his own connection to both Christianity and Buddhism.

Nonetheless, the unique potential of actual interfaith youth—that is, the grown children of interfaith families—to contribute to the interfaith movement has yet to be recognized or fully appreciated. Many such programs recruit a specific number of Jews, Muslims, and Christians, in rough or precise balance. A young adult claiming more than one religion does not fit these given categories. Moreover, interfaith identity or multiple religious belonging may challenge the premise that interfaith dialogue will strengthen, rather than muddy, singular religious identity.

Reverend Heather Kirk-Davidoff discovered this irony while studying at Harvard Divinity School, when she was already married to her Jewish husband. In her experience, official interfaith dialogue "absolutely does not" want to hear from actual interfaith families. She recalls participating in a yearlong program with other Jewish and Christian seminarians. "The whole big model was, you find your place to stand, you stand firmly in your location, claiming it, and then out of that location, you enter into dialogue," she says. But as she got to know the other participants, she gradually realized "they all had some interfaith family connection."

One Catholic seminarian was the child of a Jewish and Catholic marriage. A Protestant seminarian had previously dated a Jewish man and completed almost the entire Jewish conversion process. Many of these students had been motivated to join the dialogue precisely because of their personal experience with interfaith families. And yet, they each felt forced to represent one, and only one, religion. Reverend Kirk-Davidoff explains, "The conversation would have been so much more real and rich and full if the kid who had grown up in a Jewish/Christian home talked about it through his own experience and identity." She found herself wondering whether people from interfaith families should actually be leading the discussion.

Similarly, when asked to attend an interfaith dialogue event, interfaith families pioneer Ned Rosenbaum told me that the speakers at such events always remind him of "parallel lines in Euclidean geometry, never meeting." His response was that they should invite him, a Jewish man, and his Catholic wife, who raised their children with both religions, to speak "if they ever wanted to see what happens when interfaith paths cross like strands of DNA."

JOINING THE LIMINAL REVOLUTION: INTERFAITH PRIDE
In the 1960s, anthropologist Victor Turner used the term *liminality*, derived from the Latin word *limina*, meaning "thresholds," to describe a boundary state between two spaces, times, or identities.

Since then, academics and popular writers have seized on this idea of living in liminal space—where rules are suspended, creativity flourishes, and the obsession with boundaries and binary *either/or* thinking gives way to a *both/and* synergy. The positive characteristics associated with liminality lend strength and validity to individuals who want to build an identity out of drawing on qualities society has long considered mutually exclusive—black and white, male and female, or Christian and Jew.

In choosing to raise our children with interfaith identities, we join a growing societal rebellion against being forced to choose one race, one culture, even one gender. This rebellion is evident in a number of recent literary novels: Zadie Smith's novels *White Teeth* and *The Autograph Man* depict children of mixed race and mixed religion; the protagonist in Yann Martel's *Life of Pi* insists on celebrating Christianity, Islam, and Hinduism simultaneously; and Jeffrey Eugenides's Pulitzer prize–winning *Middlesex* portrays an intersexual, someone born with both male and female characteristics, who claims the right to a nonbinary gender identity.

Meanwhile, queer theorists have been rejecting false binaries and embracing a plethora of new labels beyond gay and lesbian: transgender, bisexual, pansexual, asexual, omnisexual, pomosexual (a label for people who refuse labels). A number of clergy who have been willing to reach out to interfaith families raising children with both religions come from the LGBTQ community. The willingness to work with families who are very much outside the mainstream may not be coincidental. "I wonder if it comes from a queer perspective: that kind of marginality or education on the margin appeals to me," says Rabbi Nehama Benmosche of her passion for working with interfaith families.

As an interfaith child, I feel sympathetic resonance with mixed-race and multiethnic people, gay and transgendered people, immigrants raised with two cultures, and what are known as "third-culture kids"—those who have been raised overseas in diplomatic or military postings. All of us can draw strength and creativity from our liminal status and from each other. Maria Root, a multiracial psychologist, has written a Bill of Rights for People of Mixed Heritage that I find holds great power and relevance for interfaith children. When the word *religion* is substituted for *race* and the word *interfaith* for *multiracial*, her manifesto translates perfectly. The words I added, with Root's permission, are in parentheses and italics below:

The Bill of Rights for People of Mixed Heritage (*or Interfaith People*)

I have the right:

- not to justify my existence in this world
- not to keep the races (*or religions*) separate within me
- not to justify my ethnic (*or religious*) legitimacy
- not to be responsible for people's discomfort with my physical or ethnic (*or religious*) ambiguity

I have the right:

- to identify myself differently than strangers expect me to identify
- to identify myself differently than how my parents identify me
- to identify myself differently than my brothers and sisters
- to identify myself differently in different situations

I have the right:

- to create a vocabulary to communicate about being multiracial or multiethnic (*or interfaith*)
- to change my identity over my lifetime—and more than once

- to have loyalties and identify with more than one group of people
- to freely choose whom I befriend and love

I use this Bill of Rights in leading discussion groups with interfaith teens on identity formation. It is hard to imagine a Jewish, Catholic, or Protestant teen group willing to tackle this document. An independent interfaith group creates a neutral space for teens to address identity issues head-on. They need opportunities to be surrounded by kids experiencing the same benefits and drawbacks of interfaith family life.

An interfaith community provides a forum for children and adults alike to work out religious issues without pressure to convert or make forced choices. Beyond developing a defense, these communities help point to the truly positive aspects of an upbringing in two religions. Interfaith children represent a love that transcends boundaries, and they should be able to claim their birthright as bridge-builders and peacemakers with pride. Among parents in my survey, the third most common reason for joining an interfaith community was a desire for their children to develop positive self-esteem as interfaith.

No matter how they have been raised, interfaith children must eventually leave their parents and encounter a world that may misunderstand them. An educational program that explicitly addresses identity will allow children and teenagers to prepare to meet friends *and* critics with confidence.

CHAPTER FOUR

Facing the Objections

"But You Can't Be Both!"

Clearly, choosing both religions is not the right decision for every interfaith family. It is equally clear that choosing both requires a certain comfort level with the road less traveled. This chapter is for those who are seriously considering dual-faith celebration and want to anticipate the arguments they will face, as well as fully explore their own reservations about this pathway.

Below, I address some of the common concerns parents have about choosing both. My responses are based on a lifetime of experience as an interfaith child, as a parent who celebrates two religions with my children, and as a leader of a thriving interfaith group, as well as the interviews with or survey responses from over three hundred parents, children, teachers, and clergy members in interfaith communities around the country.

THE CHILD WILL BE CONFUSED

One November, the first night of Hanukkah fell on the day after Thanksgiving. Two weeks later, I was making pasta sauce with my five-year-old son, and we were adding olive oil. Suddenly, he piped up, "Mom! This is a great dish for Thanksgiving because the oil makes it sacred and holy!" My eager sous-chef was conflating Hanukkah (the holiday celebrates holy oil that miraculously lasted eight days) and Thanksgiving. My son's confusion stemmed in part from the fact that he had just studied both of these holidays in quick succession, in his public kindergarten, along with Kwanzaa and Christmas.

The point is that not all religious confusion in our children stems from their interfaith condition. Children (not to mention adults) often find religion confusing, whatever their upbringing. For very small children, religious identity is built primarily on the concrete observance of holidays, with the attendant smells, tastes, and memorable rituals. Thus, the toddlers who ask, "Are we Jewish or Christmas?" Beyond Hanukkah and Christmas, many of us who are living in increasingly diverse urban areas want our children to learn about the Hindu, Buddhist, and Muslim holidays celebrated by friends and classmates. A bit of confusion is bound to ensue.

Parents often panic when a small child confuses Moses with Jesus. But after years of interaction with the teens and young adults who grew up in interfaith communities, I believe that the best course of action is to stay calm and carry on with teaching and explaining. As we give our children an ever-deeper and more consistent experience of the two specific cultures rooted in their families, the confusion eventually yields to an appreciation of their entwined histories.

Adults raised in single-faith families, even if they are intermarried themselves, may underestimate the ability of children to tolerate ambiguity and live with the reality of interfaith identity. "Children can handle ambivalence, can handle complexity," says social worker and therapist Susan Needles, who works with interfaith couples in New York City. "It's only adults who want it tied up in a neat package. Children are going to tear open the package anyway." In other words, interfaith children do not passively accept a simple religious label bestowed on them by parents.

My husband's cousin, Reverend Rick Spalding, the Presbyterian minister who co-officiated at our wedding, was also the first Christian religious educator in the very first religious education program for Jewish/Christian children, in New York City in the 1980s. The children he taught there are now in their late twenties and thirties, and he subscribes to the "complex, not confused" mantra of many clergy who have actually worked with interfaith communities.

"It's not a question of simplifying anything," insists Spalding. "You can't simplify it except by nailing it in the closet forever and never going into or acknowledging that closet. It's a complex world, and I don't think we do our children any favors at all by pretending it's simpler than it is." Part of the goal of interfaith religious education is to help children address this reality and to remind them of all that is positive about being part of an interfaith family. Spalding adds, "I think this particular complexity is a lot less scary and a lot more life-giving than a lot of other complexities."

Granted, teaching two religions can be a daunting task. To take just one example, young children are often amazed that Jesus was Jewish. Many parents, both Christian and Jewish, tend to avoid emphasizing this fact. But for interfaith children, this fact, while initially confusing, is an essential point of historical connection between the two religions. For many, Jesus the Jew is deeply resonant, almost as if he were a fellow interfaith child. Like them, Jesus embodies a bridge between Judaism and Christianity, whether or not he is seen as a savior or as the Messiah.

Few Jews or Christians grow up thinking about Jesus as a Jew, but for parents who are truly teaching both religions, rather than just celebrating two sets of holidays in a secular fashion, there is really no way and no reason to avoid the conundrum. Interfaith children will struggle to understand it at an early age and to articulate their thoughts around it. Interesting questions, many of them on the cutting edge of theological and historical debate, will naturally ensue. Did Jesus think he was departing from Judaism in his teachings? How was Judaism practiced at the time of Jesus? When, and how, and why did Christianity split off from Judaism?

By the time they have graduated from religious education programs, the majority of teens raised in dual-faith communities say they do not find the two religions confusing, according to my survey. With support from parents, teachers, and interfaith peers, they have explored the historical and theological points of divergence and intersection between the two religions. As one teen from IFFP says, "It was confusing in the early years, but not now."

Clergy opposed to raising children with both religions (and often, pushing for families to choose their religion) often cite their own anecdotal experiences of confused interfaith children raised with two religions. In my experience, these accounts, on closer inspection, usually illustrate what happens when intermarried parents, rejected by religious communities, end up without any community in which to raise their children. And for every such child these clergy cite, I can produce an eloquent, happy, well-adjusted, and spiritually-fulfilled child raised in an interfaith community.

"Kids can handle a multiplicity of identities," says Rabbi Nehama Benmosche. "They do it all the time. They're students, siblings, grandchildren, soccer-players. They act differently in each of those roles. They can have a Jewish role and a Christian role." One twenty-five-year-old woman who was raised in New York's IFC said she did not find learning about both religions confusing "because I never knew a life without both of them." Children raised with both religions experience this understanding as part of their identity, whereas interfaith parents may never have an intuitive understanding of what it means to be both, simply because they are not both. A twenty-eight-year-old woman, also raised in IFC, says, "I remember being in kindergarten and identifying myself to my classmates as 'both Jewish and Christian' and understanding what it meant."

Others do label their experience confusing, but are not troubled by it. They take intellectual pleasure in the freedom to cross boundaries. As a twenty-seven-year-old IFC alumna states, "I don't think that learning more is ever confusing. Or rather, I think that questioning and perhaps being confused (or knowing that there are options) is never a bad thing."

MYTH: THE CHILD WILL BE STRESSED BY HAVING TO CHOOSE BETWEEN PARENTS

It is important to ensure that young children will not feel pressured to choose one religion over the other. Parents who have made a unified choice to raise their children with both religions should explain that the choice *has* been made for the children—a choice to celebrate both religions. This should reassure children that their job as a child is to study and appreciate and celebrate, not to choose. Although in adolescence, when some children do begin to ponder the possibility of choosing a single faith, the intent is that when and if they do so they have been thoroughly and nonjudgmentally educated about the choices, which takes many years.

Instead of stressing eventual choice, we reassure these children that they have the right to learn about, and participate in, both of their family religions. When they begin to understand how the two religions diverge theologically, we continue to emphasize that they may or may not ever choose one path or the other. They have the right to continue to identify with both religions, or to choose a third religion, or none.

By adolescence, interfaith children often reach the practical realization that their eventual choice of religion may have more to do with the religion of their future spouse, or with the religious communities available to them geographically, or with personal preference, than it does with choosing one parent over the other. And we reassure our children that because we as parents have total mutual respect for the two religions, we both will support a child who does eventually choose one religion or the other or neither.

Reverend Ellen Jennings, the director of religious education at IFFP for seven years, did not observe children in the community feeling pushed to choose between religions. She says, "By the time they're ready to make a choice, presumably they're at least in college." She also points out that all adults go through this process of choosing a religious pathway, even those from single-faith families. "Look at my family of origin," she adds. "My mom, who was raised Catholic, married a Presbyterian, became Episcopalian, and ended up with four children who each have substantially different religious views—a United Church of Christ minister, a homeschooling Pentecostal, a "Christmas and Easter" Episcopalian who reads the Dalai Lama, and an oil executive who sometimes stops off at the local Catholic church for a moment of silence before work."

In any case, choosing one religion for your child does not erase the possibility that the child will feel torn between two parental religions. Children may be drawn to the religion that was not chosen for them. Sometimes, this is a form of rebellion against the choice made by the parents. Sometimes, children are drawn to one religion for their own mysterious reasons. And sometimes, the out-parent has not completely suppressed or hidden the religion, and is waging a subtle, or even subconscious, campaign to win the child over.

Many children being raised with both religions announce their allegiance to one religion at some point during childhood. This could stem from a subliminal desire on the child's part to stir up family psychodynamics, a transient urge to belong to a group of peers who are having a First Communion or becoming bar/bat mitzvahs—or a sincere expression of an aesthetic or theological preference.

Whatever the reason, I advise parents to encourage the child to explore his or her feelings about religion and the reasons for the choice. If the choice is sincere and informed, the parents can rest assured that they have done their job well. If your child has chosen your religion, you may feel some sense of pride or victory. But keep in mind that many teenagers and adults, interfaith or not, shift their religious affiliation more than once in a lifetime.

MYTH: INTERFAITH CHILDREN WILL NEVER CHOOSE

Many children keep their interfaith identity as their primary religious identity: apparently, they find this identity has more advantages than disadvantages. Some find a different way of embracing inclusiveness; they may find that Unitarian Universalism offers the community they seek, or will end up secular humanists, often following in the footsteps of their secular parents. But it is a myth that all interfaith children will be paralyzed or unable to choose a single religious home unless raised with a single religious identity. Some do choose a singular religion, and some of their stories are told at length in chapter 10.

Raised at IFFP by a Jewish mother and Catholic father, one young man had both a bar mitzvah and a Catholic confirmation ceremony. At seventeen, he identifies himself as a Quaker and subscribes to the Quaker belief in "God in everyone." One woman raised in New York's IFC by a Presbyterian mother and a Jewish father chose an Episcopalian identity by age twenty-seven. She feels comfortable in both a church and a synagogue, but has chosen to join a church she attends on a weekly basis and has married a Protestant. Nonetheless, she states that her interfaith education was an advantage overall. And while she intends to "share the experience of church" with her children, she also says, "I don't want to force them into anything. I'd like them to learn about other religions as well."

MYTH: THE CHILD WILL NOT BELONG IN ANY ONE COMMUNITY

The argument that children who claim two religions will not belong to a community no longer holds power for those of us in vibrant interfaith families groups. As a community, we support each other in times of joy and sorrow. We bring food to families with new babies, drive members to cancer treatment appointments, sit shivah (the Jewish ritual of visiting those in mourning) with members who have lost loved ones. My two children sing, dance, study, light candles, and eat ritual foods with our community. With this community, they cook and serve meals in a homeless shelter, harvest farm produce and donate it to food pantries on the Jewish agricultural festival of Sukkoth, and buy and wrap Christmas presents for families in need. And on Sunday mornings, my children are surrounded by over 130 other interfaith children. Not only do they have a community, but it is a community in which they do not feel "odd" in any way.

Reverend Jennings is not concerned that the children in these programs will be spiritually homeless. "There are probably four different tracks," she says. "Some will decide they aren't interested in being part of any faith community. That's not because they're interfaith; it's just a choice some people make. Some are going to go out and replicate what they've experienced, and hopefully that will result in more interfaith communities being created. Some are going to choose Judaism or Christianity because of the person they marry, or because there is no interfaith community available, or because they feel more strongly called to one tradition. And then there are going to be those drawn to Unitarian Universalism, Quakerism, or the Ethical Society—post-Jewish, post-Christian communities—traditions that are much broader and more inclusive of different theological perspectives."

As adults, some remain satisfied with their interfaith identity and do not feel the need for acceptance by religious institutions. A twenty-eight-year-old from New York's IFC explains, "I prefer to learn about different religions, including those I have had little contact with, and let aspects of those faiths inform my own beliefs.

I have a hard time with the idea that every Jew believes every tenet of Judaism, etc. My cultural identification with that religion is enough 'belonging' for me."

Others may feel the need to find, or create, more interfaith communities to support them. A growing number of adult interfaith children have joined such communities to educate their own children, and many teens and young adults raised in these programs say that they want their children to have the same education in both religions that they did. As one parent in New York's IFC says, "There are going to be lots of them, and they're going to feel good about being both, and they're going to lead the way."

Interfaith children who want to practice Judaism but resist the idea of conversion since they already feel Jewish are increasingly likely to find progressive Jewish institutions willing to accept them as self-defined Jews. Rabbi Rami Shapiro has written a "Simply Jewish Manifesto" which includes the words, "We recognize as a Jew a person who identifies as a Jew." The most progressive Jewish communities are turning this manifesto into policy by accepting members as self-defined Jews, regardless of heritage or conversion status. As interfaith children come of age, the demand will grow for congregations with such policies, in which these children will feel accepted, without litmus tests, should they choose a Jewish pathway.

The body representing the Reform rabbinate has specifically advised that formally educating children in a second religion disqualifies them from being considered Reform Jews. Yet even this barrier is breaking down. In Chicago, the Jewish Renewal congregation Makom Shalom welcomes members whose children are learning about both Judaism and Catholicism in an interfaith Sunday school, as do some other Chicago synagogues.

In part as a result of the active communities formed by Jewish and Catholic couples intermarried in Chicago, Rabbi Michael

Sternfield of Chicago Sinai Congregation now urges acceptance of the existence of the interfaith movement. "As much as the formal institutions of Jewish life push for a single resolution concerning religious identity, more and more interfaith couples are creating their own path," he told his congregation in a Rosh Hashanah sermon. "We would be well advised to stop pretending that these families are marginal. They are not."

MYTH: THE CHILD WILL NOT FEEL COMFORTABLE IN A SYNAGOGUE OR CHURCH

Whether or not an interfaith child feels comfortable in a house of worship stems from at least three factors—familiarity with the rituals, comfort with the underlying theology, and an atmosphere that welcomes interfaith children. Individuals who grow up in a particular Reform synagogue may find the traditions in a neighboring Reform synagogue unfamiliar: different melodies, different customs, different rhetorical style. And the same is true for churches. So raising a child in one synagogue or church does not automatically make that child comfortable in every synagogue or church.

The children in an interfaith religious school learn the basic prayers and rituals of both faiths, and attend services in multiple synagogues and churches, so they find these settings generally familiar. A majority of the teenagers who went through the Washington, D.C., interfaith program report that they feel comfortable in both a synagogue and a church. Familiarity with the rituals enables them to be participants, rather than alienated observers. In the fall of his freshman year at Wesleyan University, Izaak Orlansky ended up going to High Holy Day services organized by a friend at Hillel, and found himself holding the Torah. Despite being raised with both Judaism and Christianity, he felt comfortable enough stepping forward at the moment when his friends needed him to help out in the service. And while he was aware that some in the room might not accept him as a Jew, he also felt that he had the right to participate.

Feeling comfortable is also dependent on self-confidence. Our children will feel more self-confident in a synagogue or church, or anywhere they go, if they feel comfortable in their own interfaith skins and take pride in their important role in our diverse society. And if they are rejected by people in these houses of worship, at least they will understand why.

MYTH: THE TWO RELIGIONS ARE CONTRADICTORY

If one or both interfaith parents believe in the Bible as revealed truth, whether they are Jewish, Protestant or Catholic, this will probably make "choosing both" very difficult. Indeed, a marriage in which one parent is fundamentalist or literalist and the other is not, poses challenges even if both parents are Jewish, or both are Christian. In this case, the two sets of religious beliefs would indeed be contradictory. However, many intermarried American adults interpret the Torah or Bible not as literal truth but as inspirational mystery or metaphor, culture-specific literature written to convey moral teachings, or political and social commentary.

Many who do not see the Bible as revealed truth still see it as a powerful guide, while others see it as anachronistic and relevant only as a cultural artifact. Some see it as a mix of both. Our interfaith group welcomes believers, spiritual seekers, agnostics, and atheists. We encompass parents who are eager to transmit the religious rituals of their childhoods to their children and parents who are fleeing from these rituals but are willing to have their kids learn about them. Accommodating all of these viewpoints inspires our community toward greater creativity, inclusiveness, and tolerance. Dogma is not possible in this context.

MYTH: BOTH RELIGIONS WILL BE WATERED DOWN

The truth is that many of us who are choosing both are not coming from churches or synagogues but from the vast ranks of the unaffiliated. According to the American Religious Identification Survey, of those who declared a religious identity in 2000, 40 percent reported that no one in their household belonged to any church, synagogue, temple, or mosque. In the 2008 survey, 27 percent of Americans reported that they do not expect a religious funeral at their death.

So, for many of us, giving our children both religions may be an alternative to giving them nothing. When this is the case, these children are getting infinitely more instruction in each religion than they would if the parents had steered clear of religion altogether. They will recognize religious references in literature and the media, and can compare and contrast the beliefs and practices of their two religions.

And it is not necessarily true that children who are given both religions are getting more superficial religious educations than those raised exclusively as Jews or Christians. Even without a local interfaith group, it is possible, though tremendous effort and with supportive clergy, for parents to give children a very deep knowledge of both religions. And with interfaith groups growing and now offering structured education in both religions, more families can give their children substantive interfaith educations. For instance, my children are learning Hebrew and studying and celebrating less familiar Jewish holidays, including Tu Bishvat and Shavuot. Their knowledge of Judaism easily outstrips that of many of their "fully Jewish" friends who are secular or "High Holy Day" Jews. At the same time, they can recount the life of Jesus, find wisdom in his parables, and have more knowledge of Christianity than some "Christmas and Easter" Christians.

From a cultural point of view, of course, it is true that straddling two cultures is not the same as total immersion in one. Often, this is what people are referring to when they fear that teaching two religions will "water down" the experience. Being raised in one religion does have benefits—the main one being the strength and depth of identification with that faith. Those of us choosing both recognize that our children will not have this experience.

Izaak Orlansky was raised as part of the first class of students in the Washington, D.C., interfaith community, when the education program was just getting started. At age eighteen, he described his regret at not having this immersion experience as the lone drawback of his interfaith education: "Because I haven't been immersed, I haven't been able to feel deeply faithful about either religion. I haven't ever felt like I can say I'm a devout Christian, or Jew. I'm a devout interfaith person, but I don't really know what that means. That's the only part I feel we're missing out on. You kind of have to weigh it. On the one hand, we're getting all this openness and knowledge. And the part you're losing, maybe not completely, is the ability to say, 'I know what I am and nothing's going to change the way I feel about it.'"

However, my own experience has taught me that when parents choose a single religion, it does not automatically provide an interfaith child with the sort of clarity that Orlansky describes. I recognize his wistful feelings, despite the fact that my parents raised me exclusively as a Jew. But my husband and I made the choice to "withhold" from our children the experience of total immersion in a single faith because we feel the benefits of celebrating both religions outweigh this drawback. I feel most comfortable celebrating religion with other interfaith families and giving my children that sense of comfort is of paramount importance to me. And in this era of the rise of the religious nones and the large percentage of people changing religious affiliation, even those immersed in one religion cannot realistically claim that "nothing's going to change the way I feel."

I like to use the metaphor that we are giving our children two roots, not leaving them rootless. The children of two Italian Catholics have one deep, thick cultural root to stabilize them. An interfaith child has at least two religious or cultural roots, by definition. If parents choose to nurture them, there will be two substantial roots the child can draw nourishment from. Many of us who have grown this way feel well grounded. We even dare to imagine that it gives us a certain type of stability better suited to this multicultural world, which people with a single root do not have.

MYTH: JESUS IS AN INSURMOUNTABLE PROBLEM

My sister in Brooklyn is raising her children with a Jewish identity. One day, while playing with my five-year-old son Ben, his four-year-old cousin Charlie became frustrated and sputtered "Jesus!" Immediately, my sister, who is after all an interfaith child with a sensitive ear, reprimanded him.

"Is 'Jesus' a bad word?" Charlie asked.

"No," my sister explained. "But you shouldn't say the word like that, because it might hurt someone's feelings."

"But what is Jesus?" Charlie asked.

My sister replied, "Christian people believe that Jesus was the son of God. Jewish people don't believe that."

Then my five-year-old chimed in, "And we're both, so we sort of believe it!"

There was an uncomfortable pause, followed by laughter from the adults. After a moment of panic, I realized that I did not find my son's comment to be "confused" at all. In fact, I believe he was expressing a rather sophisticated viewpoint. It is a viewpoint that his Jewish mother and his Christian father might agree on. I believe that Jesus was the son of God, in the sense that we are all children of God—meaning that all human beings should aspire to tap into the goodness within themselves. Mahatma Gandhi was the son of God. Mother Teresa was the daughter of God. As an adult who has benefited from years of interfaith adult education in Judaism and Christianity while my children attended interfaith Sunday school, I am comfortable discussing the "godliness" and goodness of Jesus, even if I don't believe he is my personal savior.

The ambiguity of my son's response may disturb some parents. My generalization of the phrase "son of God" may sound heretical to you. If so, then choosing both religions for your interfaith child may not be the right pathway for you. Or it just might be, once you get used to the idea.

Many adults raised as Christians believe that Jesus was a great leader, a teacher, a political renegade, a rebel rabbi. Some do not believe in the Virgin Birth. A 2000 poll by Barna Research found that 40 percent of all Americans and one-third of American Protestant clergy did not believe Jesus was physically resurrected.

At the same time, a growing number of Jewish intellectuals now believe that Jesus should be included in the study of Jewish history as a Jew of great historical importance and as someone who influenced, if indirectly, the evolution of Jewish practice. In truth, Jewish scholars have studied Jesus and his ideas ever since his lifetime, but the topic seemed to be reserved for mature and learned men, just as the study of the mysticism of the Kabbalah was traditionally reserved for Jewish men over the age of forty, who alone were deemed able to handle such powerful knowledge.

But efforts to include Jesus in Jewish education have until recently met with strong resistance. In my library, I treasure a first edition of *Jesus of Nazareth*, written by Jewish scholar Joseph Klausner, first published in English in 1925. A sentence from the introduction jumps out at me: "I am quite aware that the method of this book will provoke abundant hostile criticism from Jews and

Christians alike." And in the 1960s, Rabbi Maurice Eisendrath, the president of the Union of American Hebrew Congregations, proposed that Jews regard Jesus as a champion of social justice, in order to "serve as a bond between Christians and Jews." Rabbi Michael Sternfield of Chicago Sinai Congregation, in a pioneering Rosh Hashanah sermon in 2002, pointed out not only that "the way many Christians regard Jesus is not necessarily that incompatible with Judaism," but also described Eisendrath's efforts as going over "like a proverbial 'lead balloon.'"

In the twenty-first century, numerous authors, both Christian and Jewish, have written books on Jesus the Jew. Many of these are helpful to interfaith families in figuring out how to address "The Jesus Question." In *The Jewish Annotated New Testament*, editors Amy-Jill Levine and Marc Zvi Brettler write, "It is difficult for Jews to understand their neighbors, and the broader society of which Jewish citizens are a part, without familiarity with the New Testament." Some synagogue religious schools are even beginning to teach Christianity to older Jewish students, acknowledging that learning about Jesus can only improve Jewish-Christian dialogue in a country dominated by Christianity.

The Jewish adults in my Washington interfaith community, once they have gotten over the feeling that the "J word" is a forbidden topic, tend to agree that Jesus—God or man or myth—is an important topic of study, especially for interfaith children. In adult education sessions at all of the interfaith groups across the country, one important goal is to help the Jewish partners feel comfortable discussing Jesus without feeling pressured, as they might in a Christian context, to view him as the Messiah.

In an IFC discussion group on Long Island, one intermarried Jewish mother described how the "Jesus issue" drove her to seek out and join the local chapter of the IFC: "We'd done all this stuff for Passover and I thought, 'Well, now I should get some books on Easter.' So I go into Barnes and Noble, and I'm literally sitting there in tears, crying, because every book has Jesus in it, and I can't bring Jesus into my apartment. So how am I gonna find a book about Easter that doesn't have Jesus in it? That's when I sort of realized I had a problem."

So is it possible to believe and not believe in Jesus at the same time? What does "believe in" mean? As an interfaith child, I believe that Jesus existed. What does it mean to be the son of God? To be the Messiah? As an interfaith child, I do not see these as questions with clear-cut answers, nor do many of those who study the history of the evolution of Judaism and Christianity. Talmudic scholar Daniel Boyarin writes in his most recent book of the Jewishness of the Messiah concept. In the centuries just after the death of Jesus, a time before religious labeling, he writes, "Many people, it would seem, thought that there was no problem being both a Jew and a Christian." For me, understanding the religious fluidity of this historical era has become key to my identity as an interfaith Jew embracing my Christian roots.

I should make clear that if you consider yourself a Jew and also consider Jesus to be your personal savior, then you may either be, or be confused with, a messianic Jew or a Jew for Jesus—Christian sects that practice Jewish rituals while proclaiming Jesus as the Messiah. They are reviled by most Jews, and by many Christians, as proselytizers (though not all of them evangelize) using the Jewish context to convert Jews—and in particular, Jews from interfaith families—to belief in Jesus as the Messiah.

In differentiating our interfaith group in Washington from these messianic movements, I often describe our group as "the opposite of Jews for Jesus." Rather than Jews and Christians getting together to agree that Jesus was the Messiah, we tend to be Jews and Christians getting together to affirm his role as a teacher and his importance in religious history. However, we also have parents in the group who have more traditional Christian beliefs, who attest to Jesus as their personal savior but still manage to stay happily married to their Jewish partners.

In an interfaith education program, children are offered a whole spectrum of ways of looking at Jesus—as literary fiction, as an important historical figure, as a mysterious inspiration, or as the literal son of God. They come to realize that they cannot use group labels to make assumptions about the beliefs of an individual. Not all Reform Jews see Jesus the same way. Not all Presbyterians see Jesus the same way. In turn, this makes it easier for children to accept Judaism and Christianity as equally valid and connected religious pathways, which happen to use different central metaphors. And it helps them to understand that developing their own set of religious beliefs is not a particular burden imposed on interfaith children alone but a universal condition.

MYTH: ONLY PEOPLE WHO DON'T CARE ABOUT RELIGION RAISE KIDS BOTH

Not all Christians in successful interfaith marriages have become post-Christians. In Chicago, hundreds of practicing Roman Catholics married to Jews have joined the Jewish Catholic Couples Dialogue Group and enrolled their children in the Interfaith Family School to learn about both religions. Some of these Catholics describe themselves as "devout" or "ardent." My survey found that more than a third of parents from interfaith communities raising children with both religions are also churchgoers. And a third of those who go to church report that they have been going to church more often since joining an interfaith community. At the same time, about a third of the parents in the survey attend synagogues or other Jewish community services, and more than a quarter of them say they are going more often since joining an interfaith community.

The myth that interfaith families practicing both religions are all secularists and agnostics may have come from the first great wave of intermarriage, when those who intermarried often were forced to leave their cradle religions, and even their families of origin, in order to intermarry. At the same time, it is certainly true that those who had already left the religious institutions of their youth—atheists, secular humanists, cultural Jews—were more willing to intermarry since they did not risk losing the support of communities they had already left. The feedback loop—"Why would I want to be part of a church or synagogue that would reject or try to convert my spouse?"—has driven generations of couples away from religious institutions, no matter their personal beliefs or desire for spirituality and ritual. More recently, though, interfaith couples determined to maintain religious identity and practice have found more support from their extended families, interfaith families communities, and religious institutions accepting the reality of intermarriage.

Catholic academics, in particular, have begun to recognize what they call "multiple religious belonging." Theologian and former priest Paul Knitter has devoted an entire book to exploring how and why he claims both Christianity and Buddhism. Catholic theologian Peter Phan at Georgetown University notes that, in Asia, "multiple religious belonging is a rule rather than an exception, at least on the popular level." And Catholic theologian Catherine Cornille, at Boston College, has written, "More and more individuals confess to being partly Jewish and partly Buddhist, or partly Christian and partly Hindu, or fully Christian and fully Buddhist." But most of these academics have focused on multiple belonging by religious scholars and mystics, and they often warn that complex identities may be "shallow" if claimed by "dilettantes." Also, the academic term *multiple religious belonging* puts the emphasis on institutional membership. Those of us who do not necessarily belong to religious institutions prefer the labels dual-faith, interfaith, multifaith, or complex religious identity. Karla Suomola, a religion scholar at Luther College, explores the colonial roots of the theological disapproval of terms like "syncretic" and "hybrid" to describe complex religious identity and describes how these terms, as well as the playful French term "bricolage," are being reclaimed by those of us with complex identities.

Perhaps the strongest anecdotal evidence that those raising children with interfaith identity are not shallow religious dilettantes comes from the subset of intermarried clergy. Jews who are intermarried or in a "committed relationship" with a non-Jew cannot be admitted to or ordained by the rabbinical seminaries of the Conservative, Reform, or Reconstructionist movements. The only intermarried rabbis I know of are in the smaller Jewish Renewal movement. But a 2009 exposé in the national Jewish student publication *New Voices* profiled rabbinical students deeply involved with Christian partners and forced to keep these relationships under wraps. Some felt they had to push their partners to convert to Judaism by the time of their ordination.

On the other side of the aisle, Reverend Donna Schaper and Harvard theologian Harvey Cox (a minister) have each written books about their interfaith families. Both have Jewish spouses. Cox writes of his decision to raise a Jewish son while maintaining his identity as a Christian. In contrast, despite the pressure to raise Jewish children, Schaper raised her children with exposure to both religions. A full profile of another pioneering intermarried minister raising interfaith children, Reverend Heather Kirk-Davidoff, appears in chapter 6. It would be hard to accuse these intermarried clergy of not taking religion seriously.

MYTH: THE UNDERDOG SHOULD ALWAYS "WIN"

Judaism exerts a powerful magnetic force on most of us who stand anywhere in its range. In their book *Between Two Worlds*, writers

Robin Margolis and Leslie Goodman-Malamuth, both daughters of interfaith marriage, compare the persistent effect of even one distant Jewish ancestor to a red sock in a load of white laundry, permanently coloring all the descendants, however faintly.

Why is this effect so strong? Judaism is a tradition rich with history and ritual. And it has the appeal of the underdog—the outsider perspective may seem more progressive, more clear-eyed, more global, more just. Despite the pale skin of many Jews with European origins, and the fact that some Jews were themselves slave-owners and slave traders, the case has even been made by some academics that Jews can claim "non-white" status as a minority in American society. For many interfaith children, claiming Judaism as a cultural identity provides a compelling alibi when they are faced with the alternative of being cast as a white oppressor.

Judaism is appealing for other reasons as well. For atheists, agnostics, scientists, and skeptical intellectuals in general, Judaism can seem like an "easier" religion than Christianity. It does not require belief in the Virgin Birth, the Trinity, God appearing in the form of a man, or resurrection. While supernatural events also abound in the Torah, one can live as a "good Jew" through ritual observance without believing in these events, or even, as in the case of Secular Humanistic Jewish congregations, without believing in God at all.

Choosing Judaism for your children because of its streamlined theology, of course, works better for the Jewish partner in an interfaith relationship than it does for the Christian partner. Christianity traditionally requires belief not just in God but in Jesus as the Messiah. The lopsided theological demands create tension, which interfaith communities handle by tackling it head-on rather than ignoring it. "Christians can confirm everything in the Jewish liturgy. But the poor Christians can't have anything affirmed by the Jewish liturgy," says interfaith couples therapist Susan Needles, who is Jewish. "We leave them by the side of the road."

The simpler Jewish theology may explain in part why many grown children raised with both religions end up leaning toward Judaism. "Christianity is more complicated: it has all these creeds and beliefs," says Reverend Julia Jarvis of Washington, D.C.'s IFFP. However, this apparent preference for Judaism among children raised with both does not necessarily imply that these children should not be given a chance to be educated about Christianity, to interact with Christian clergy, or to grow up in a family that experiences religious balance. Many parents join the interfaith community with the belief that allowing their children access to both Jewish and Christian theology will serve them well, even if they end up choosing one religion.

When both parents are completely agreed on choosing to practice only Judaism in the family, and the Christian partner does not feel unduly pressured by a Jewish partner, the in-laws, or a rabbi, then I say, "Mazel tov!" However, after interviewing parents from over one hundred interfaith households, Brandeis University researcher Sylvia Barack Fishman found that some non-Jewish parents eventually grew to resent their children's Jewish upbringing, although they initially had agreed to it. The resentment stemmed from a longing for their own traditions, as well as a general discomfort with organized religion. My conclusion is that for some of these families, choosing both religions might have been a better choice.

The appeal of Judaism should not be used to override the attachment that Christian partners may continue to feel to their own religion or culture. For instance, someone brought up in the Roman Catholic or Ukrainian Orthodox Church may value his or her connection to a vibrant minority culture. And ultra-progressive Christians who view Jesus as a powerful metaphor rather than the literal son of God can argue that appreciating the Christian Bible does not necessarily require more leaps of faith than appreciating the Hebrew Bible.

Interfaith families who choose both for their children do feel concern for the survival of Judaism in the world. But many of us also feel that we are "making a Jewish choice" by giving our children access to both cultures, rather than choosing nothing, choosing only Christianity, or choosing a third religion. Families with only one Jewish grandparent, or with Judaism on the patrilineal side, may feel they are making an extra effort, in choosing both, to keep Judaism alive.

But why wouldn't an interfaith family with a Jewish mother choose Judaism? In my survey, more than a third of the intermarried women respondents were Jewish. It may be particularly difficult for an extended Jewish family to understand a Jewish mother who chooses to raise her children with both religions, when Jewish tradition holds that the children of a Jewish mother are Jewish.

And yet, some Jewish mothers feel that equality between the parents is of paramount importance. "I can't imagine having taken any other pathway," says Stacey Katz, intermarried Jewish mother of two grown children and a founder of IFFP. "I feel that it was exactly the pathway that was right for our family. I think kids feel conflicted when they feel conflict from their parents. And when clearly both parents are comfortable with this route, the kids feel it. For us, that harmony has worked and has been very comfortable."

For some people, the idea that Judaism passes through the mother, not the father, has feminist appeal. However, in Biblical times, membership in the Israelite tribe was passed on through the father, as described by Harvard historian Shaye J. D. Cohen and many others. Many of the heroes in the Hebrew Bible, including Moses and Joseph, took wives from other tribes and their children were clearly defined as Jews. Matrilineality was only fully codified in the Jewish legal writings known as the Mishnah around 230 AD.

Biblical patrilineality persists in Judaism to this day. Most practicing Jews are aware of their ancient "class" status as a Kohen, a Levite, or an Israelite—a status conferred by the Jewish father on his children and sometimes discernible by the last name. For instance, Jews aware of these class distinctions probably have correctly surmised that my father's family, Katz, makes him a Kohen. These distinctions still have meaning in traditional synagogues, where the Kohens, those from the priestly class, have the privilege of performing certain blessings.

I often return to the cemetery where my German Jewish ancestors are buried in rural Pennsylvania. The sign of the priestly blessing of the Kohens—two outstretched hands with the fingers separated to form two V's—is carved into the tombstone of my great-great-grandfather there. For me, this serves as a reminder of the patrilineal Judaism passed down from Biblical times. Judaism continues to have both matrilineal and patrilineal aspects, even in the most traditional settings. Thus, I reject the idea that my children have no right to learn the religion of these ancestors, to feel connected when we say Kaddish at this cemetery.

Often the most gut-wrenching arguments in favor of choosing a Jewish identity for children is the powerful survival instinct of the Jewish people as a tribe. The tribal or "racial" aspects of Judaism were central to Jewish identity centuries before the rise of eugenics and Nazism, reinforced by centuries of outsider status, diaspora, ghettos, pogroms, the dislocation to the New World, and the supreme trauma of the Holocaust. Having one Jewish grandparent, either grandmother or grandfather, was enough to mark an interfaith child as a *Mischling* under the Third Reich. Knowing this, how can we children of interfaith marriages not identify ourselves as Jews? It seems cowardly. Politically, we feel we must ally ourselves with our oppressed ancestors, as many African Americans continue to identify themselves as black when they could "pass" as white.

But for many of us, being absorbed wholly into Judaism has proved impossible, for myriad reasons. If being Jewish were simply a matter of theology, one could choose to be Jewish or not. But Judaism is also a culture: an ethnic identity. Often, when interfaith children point out that they, too, were targeted by the Nazis, Jewish people will retort that we should not let Hitler dictate (from the grave) who can be a Jew. This argument is infuriating to the heirs of intermarriage, who feel that neither does Hitler have the right (from the grave) to deprive them of their (however partial) Jewish identification, simply because Nazism recognized mixed Jewish heritage and we are thus leery of this classification system.

Personally, I avoid using the term "half-Jew" to describe myself, although there is a concerted movement, particularly among young adults, to claim this term and own it in a way that is proud and rebellious. (Just as there is a movement to reclaim and celebrate the term "mixed" for biracial or multiracial people.) I resist "half-Jew" because I am a whole person, with an extended interfaith family. I resist the implication that I am somehow fractured, and the use of fractions makes me feel diminished. But I also resent being defined only in terms of my Jewishness, leaving my Christian half as somehow unmentionable.

In terms of family lineages, we are half-Jews and quarter-Jews (as well as half-Christians and quarter-Christians). There is no way around this. While race is now understood as a social construct without biological validity, there is no avoiding the fact that we have inherited characteristics, through both nature and nurture, from both our parents. People who are half Irish American and half Italian American do not generally go about choosing to be only Irish, or only Italian. Nor, on this cultural level, can half-Jews choose to be only Jews or to be non-Jews. By definition, we are rooted in both.

MYTH: DOING BOTH IS THE SAME AS UNITARIANISM OR SECULARISM

For generations, and since long before there were interfaith communities, interfaith families have found homes in Unitarian Universalism, or in Ethical Culture or Secular Humanistic Judaism. These movements can offer successful experiences for interfaith families seeking a "third way." Unitarian Universalism (UU) is nondogmatic, and many UU communities teach children lessons based on a multitude of world religions. UU communities vary greatly from one to the next in terms of their approach and the extent to which they might "feel" Christian to a Jewish partner. The Ethical Society teaches moral behavior based on the Judeo-Christian tradition, without belief in God. Meanwhile, Humanistic Judaism serves the needs of atheist Jews but is also radically inclusive of what it defines as "intercultural" couples (since "interfaith" is not an apt term for a couple that shares atheism or secularism).

For some interfaith families, these communities are a perfect fit, but not for all. About 12 percent of those I surveyed in interfaith family communities had tried a UU community for their family, and about 7 percent had tried a secular community. One interfaith couple who tried a UU church vetoed it as "unfamiliar to both of us." A Conservative Jewish woman married to a Methodist said, "Unitarian felt too 'churchy' to me."

Some couples found that a secular community was not a good fit because God was one point on which the Jewish and Christian parent could agree, so joining a secular group was not "spiritually satisfying," as one parent explained. A Roman Catholic woman found that in a Humanistic Jewish community, perhaps understandably, "members were not welcoming to those that believed in a God."

Another issue in Humanistic Judaism can be that without a common theological bond, these communities sometimes emphasize Yiddish and Ashkenazi culture (from France, Germany, and

Eastern Europe) instead, which can alienate interfaith couples, converts, and others of non-Ashkenazi backgrounds. One Catholic woman married to a Reform Jew found that "the [Humanistic] Jewish synagogue was intent on educating my young child about famous Jews like Levi Strauss, Ben and Jerry, and an astronaut on the *Challenger* space shuttle. Both my husband and I were appalled at this method of trying to create Jewish identity."

While many early interfaith couples were more secular, many younger interfaith couples want to preserve the rites and rituals of both religions. An independent interfaith group devoted to a deep appreciation of two specific religions will give children more knowledge, flavor, and practice from both religions than a UU or Ethical Society group. By specifically emphasizing the two religions in the child's family, rather than all world religions, an intentional interfaith group addresses head-on the condition of being an interfaith child. And it allows for a wide range of beliefs, or lack thereof, in God.

MYTH: INTERFAITH MARRIAGES ARE DOOMED TO FAILURE

Contemplating whether or not they are at greater risk for divorce is not particularly relevant to an interfaith couple already in the process of determining how to raise children. However, I want to address it here because all interfaith couples must be prepared to respond to this statement, oft-repeated in the media.

Historically, interfaith marriages may well have been at greater risk for divorce. In the past, such marriages encountered opposition from family, clergy, friends, and community. These couples faced a choice to avoid religion, or to celebrate their own religions separately and alone, or to join a spouse as a guest in church or synagogue. (Or to convert, but in that case, they would not be considered an intermarriage.) It seems logical, then, that intermarrying under such conditions would stress the marriage.

But when I interviewed Barry Kosmin, lead researcher on the American Religious Identification Survey, he confirmed that there are absolutely no current, robust statistics on divorce among intermarried couples. First, he notes, all surveys of the Jewish community are complicated by Jewish disagreement on the definition of who is a Jew. Many of these studies are funded by Jewish institutions with an agenda. Plus, Kosmin points out that 40 percent of children are now being born to parents who are not married, making divorce a less useful measure of success in relationships. Kosmin suspects that divorce must still be more common in interfaith marriages than in same-religion marriages, but we do not have the statistics to know whether the difference is dramatic or dramatically declining.

Even in a recent book that attempts to portray interfaith marriage as risky, 'Til Faith Do Us Part, journalist Naomi Schaefer Riley conducted a survey that found "no discernible difference" in the likelihood of divorce when comparing Christian/Christian and Christian/non-Christian couples. And while she found that Jews were more likely to be divorced if they had been in interfaith marriages, she also found that Jews reported greater marital satisfaction if they were intermarried, although her sample was small and the difference was not statistically significant.

Most of the studies on divorce that have been done have been very small, and the definitions of "interfaith marriage" vary from study to study. One study found a 14 percent divorce rate for intermarriages, versus 12 percent in same-faith marriages. A 2009 study led by sociologist Margaret Vaaler found that differences in theological beliefs had "little effect" on the likelihood of divorce over time. Others have claimed to find hugely increased rates of divorce in intermarriages.

We do know that even the most current data, of which there appears to be very little, would reflect the conditions from marriages of a generation ago. Since studies of currently divorced people are looking at marriages that occurred years or decades before, it is difficult to extrapolate about the success rate of marriages occurring now. I suspect the divorce rate among intermarried couples will decline as couples experience less opposition from family, clergy and culture and progressive Jewish and Christian communities welcome these couples more warmly than they did in the past.

What is remarkable to me is that, of the hundreds of families who have been part of our interfaith families community in Washington, Reverend Jarvis says she only knows of three divorces in the history of the group. In New York, the Interfaith Community's president, Sheila Gordon, reports a similarly low divorce rate. Meanwhile, nationwide, some 50 percent of all marriages are said to end in divorce (though again, there is much debate over this figure).

How do we account for the anomalous happiness of couples belonging to interfaith family communities? Interfaith couples actually enter marriage with advantages, even if they face opposition. Through their choice of partner, they have demonstrated open-mindedness and a willingness to listen and cooperate, important skills in remaining married. Says Reverend Jarvis, "Interfaith couples work much harder and more intentionally on their marriages." Then, if they choose to affiliate with an interfaith community, they benefit from adult discussions with other interfaith couples, and access to supportive clergy and counselors. Therapist Susan Needles, who works with the IFC in New York, says, "I love interfaith couples. They are among the most intense, thoughtful, and successful couples I have worked with."

One of the few relatively recent studies of interfaith couples, from 2010, provides some support for these positive observations. Patricia Fishman at Northern Illinois University compared Catholic/Catholic, Jewish/Jewish and Catholic/Jewish couples. She concluded: "The findings of this study do not support the findings of researchers who argued that the differences in religious customs and beliefs may cause misunderstandings or strain in the marital relationship as well as greater risk of marital discord." Instead, she found "an indication that interfaith couples can effectively communicate and negotiate, which may be related to greater marital satisfaction."

Researchers have found that couples that pray together stay together—in that those who attend religious services together, or who share the same degree of religiosity, are more likely to stay together. An interfaith community may help couples stay together by providing a forum for shared religious experience, though it also seems probable that couples who choose an interfaith community already share certain characteristics—such as making decisions as a unit and a stronger loyalty to each other than to extended family and the culture at large—that would help them to be more successful in marriage. In the next chapter, we meet several of these couples and learn how they found their way to interfaith communities.

 CHAPTER FIVE

Meet the Parents

"Both of Our Religions, Both of Our Histories"

Who chooses to raise children with two religions? Why do couples ignore the explicit advice of clergy and the urging of worried parents or grandparents to choose one religion? Why do families sign on to a strategy that lacks support from religious institutions?

Some couples will join an interfaith community the minute they discover it exists and never look back. They immediately grasp the benefits, the liberation, the intellectual satisfaction, or the creative spirituality of claiming both religions. For others, doing both feels like the only viable option when other doors have closed—an alternative to doing nothing. Some cannot tolerate the overt or tacit expectation of conversion they sense in church or synagogue. Others have been so deeply offended by rejection of their intermarriage or by perceived religious coercion or other institutional offenses that they are unwilling to affiliate themselves with established churches or synagogues. As one Jewish woman married to a Baptist man explains, "Following a bad experience with trying to find a rabbi to co-officiate at our wedding, my partner was never fully comfortable in the synagogue setting."

For another subset, some of them couples made up of two strong believers, interfaith education complements participation in both Jewish and Christian institutions, providing a third space—a neutral arena—for reflecting on interfaith identity and issues specific to the intertwined histories of the religions. This works best when local Christian and Jewish institutions agree to allow the participation of families educating their children in both religions. Since all three of the largest Jewish movements (Reform, Conservative, and Orthodox) officially reject the education of children in more than one religion, this double-belonging (or triple-belonging—to a church, synagogue, and interfaith community) remains rare, although it does occasionally occur, most notably in the Chicago interfaith groups.

For still other couples, the countercultural nature of choosing both—the idea that it is a grassroots movement and not a religion with creed and dogma—is part of the appeal of this pathway. These individuals may respond to Margaret Mead's statement: "Never depend upon institutions or government to solve any problem. All social movements are founded by, guided by, motivated and seen through by the passion of individuals." Some of these interfaith parents are cerebral agnostics, humanists, secularists, or atheists who delight in the intellectual opportunity to compare and contrast two religions without subscribing to either. Others might agree with the fiery words of Thomas Paine: "All national institutions of churches, whether Jewish, Christian or Turkish, appear to me no other than human inventions, set up to terrify and enslave mankind, and monopolize power and profit."

While sometimes critical, not to say jaded, about the role of religious institutions, many parents who choose interfaith education programs are nonetheless seeking some of the elements traditionally provided by religion: spirituality, culture, ritual, and community. "I am a Christian culturally, but I do not regularly attend church," explains parent Alicia Torre. "I believe spiritual life is very important, but I don't think that organized religion always fosters it. Religious institutions are human, not divine, and have accounted for much evil in history as well as fostering much good."

A SNAPSHOT OF PARENTS CHOOSING
INTERFAITH COMMUNITIES

To create a composite portrait of the families who choose both religions, I surveyed 256 parents who took this path about why they did so and the effect it has had on them. All are members of independent interfaith communities with dual-faith education programs for children. As expected, about half of these adults were raised Jewish, with those raised Christian fairly evenly divided between Roman Catholics and Protestants, plus a handful of others, including Unitarians, Quakers, and Greek Orthodox Christians.

Note that I am careful to specify that they were raised in these traditions. One of the most thought-provoking questions on the survey was open-ended: "How would you describe your religious identity at this point?" The answers revealed what I believe to be the powerful effect that belonging to an interfaith community can have on adults, as well as on children. The shifting religious identities may also reflect the general shift in the United States away from religious affiliation.

About 6 percent of these parents, all born into one religion, chose labels of either "interfaith," "Jewish/Christian" or "Christian/Jewish." We might expect these labels from children raised with both religions but not necessarily from their parents. For some intermarried adults, simply living together as an interfaith family, or perhaps being part of an interfaith families community, seems to have changed the way they see themselves. Sarah Cirker, an intermarried Long Island woman, raised Lutheran, who leads one of the IFC chapters, now describes herself as an "Interfaith Protestant." And a Chicago woman, raised Catholic and married to a Conservative Jew, calls herself "Jewish Catholic, and Spiritual."

Often, clergy vying for the membership of interfaith families or worrying about the fate of interfaith children posit that labels such as interfaith or Jewish/Christian are somehow immature—that the mature way to behave is to settle down with one true religion, perhaps after a *rumspringa* of experimentation. (*Rumspringa*, literally "running around," applies to a sanctioned period in adolescence during which Amish teens can experience the outside world before choosing baptism and a spouse.) As someone who has spent half a century contemplating religious identity and has shifted from one religious identity as Jewish to a more complex Jewish/interfaith identity, I do not believe I am becoming less mature. Nor do I believe these other parents who describe the increasing complexity of their identities, and often the deepening spirituality, are becoming less mature.

In the survey, it appears that it is primarily, but not exclusively, people raised Christian who are adopting the interfaith label, reflecting the theological reality that it is easier for a Christian to embrace all that is Jewish, than vice versa. However, Lis Maring, a Washington mother of two, raised Jewish and married to a man raised as a Lutheran, self-identifies now as "Jewish/interfaith." Other responses from parents raised Jewish included "Reform Jew, leaning toward interfaith" and "Jewish, but with a Christian flavoring."

An additional 20 percent of parents claimed identities requiring entire sentences or paragraphs to describe. Scott Paul, raised Lutheran and married to a woman raised as a Conservative Jew, describes himself now as, "Evolving. Incorporating elements of Christianity, Judaism, and Buddhism."

Some of those who have intermarried and have shifted in their religious identities clearly feel both a frustration with today's Roman Catholic Church and a nostalgia for the Church of the Vatican II era. Their current identities reflect data from the American Religious Identity Survey of 2008, showing a notable decline in the numbers of Catholics in the northeastern United States. In Washington, a woman raised as a Catholic, with a spouse raised Reform Jewish, explained her current religious identity as "Non-practicing Catholic. I still feel Catholic culturally and love various aspects of Catholic ritual and teachings, especially regarding social justice and liberation theology. But I am appalled at many of the Catholic official pronouncements over the past years and have become isolated from the church."

While interfaith families are often accused of being shallow in their religious beliefs, some of the detailed identity descriptions testify to a deepening of religious thought and engagement that belies the charge. One New York man raised as a Conservative Jew, married to a woman raised as a Christian, writes, "I am dedicated to learning and teaching as much about Judaism as possible. I am beginning to bring faith into my religion (it did not exist growing up, it was just ritual) so that I can help raise children in a faithful household."

Many Jewish partners enter interfaith marriage uncomfortable with the very idea of faith, which sounds vaguely Christian. Being part of an interfaith community forces them to contemplate faith, ritual practice, culture, and the interplay of all three in both Judaism and Christianity. One parent raised as a secular Jew, with a spouse raised Catholic, described himself as "Much more open to and interested in faith and religion than at any other time in my life."

Even many of the lifelong secularists in these groups are open to the idea of their children exploring faith—and faiths. Asked her religious identity, Heidi Friedman, raised as a secular Jew with a spouse raised Baptist, wrote this lament: "Oy! Honestly, I am an atheist who wishes she were not. I believe we are biologically hard-wired for religious experience, and maybe faith. I have seen the power of faith. I want my children to have a religious education because religion is so central to our civic lives and in literature, etc. And I want them to have the option of faith."

The survey data support this anecdotal evidence of intensifying spiritual or religious practice. When asked how their relationship to their own religion or religious heritage had changed since join-ing an interfaith group, about a third of the parents chose, "I have a deeper knowledge of my own religion/religious heritage." And almost a third agreed that they have more *interest* in their own religion. About 20 percent said they feel a greater spiritual connec-tion to their own religion. Only 6 percent said they felt more alien-ation from the religion in which they were raised. A Washington man raised as a Conservative Jew wrote, "Growing up, so much was handed down as 'that's just the way it is.' It is very liberating to be able to question, and to understand to not feel bound to rules."

Perhaps less surprisingly, more than half of the respondents said their knowledge of their partner's religion had deepened. More than a third said they were more interested in their partner's reli-gion, and more than a quarter felt a greater "spiritual connection" to their partner's religion. Sarah Cirker of Long Island, raised Lu-theran, wrote, "I'm not threatened by Judaism. It's now something I feel a part of, instead of alienated from." In the same spirit, Rachel Franklin in Washington, raised as a secular Jew, wrote that the in-terfaith community had been "extremely important for me in help-ing to ameliorate the underlying sense of threat that always came with any discussion of Christianity."

Couples choose interfaith communities for many reasons, both for their children and for themselves, and these communities meet their needs in varying ways. The stories of specific couples reveal some of the nuances of both the joys and concerns they have experienced.

Jen and Rob: Two Strong Faiths

One of the myths about interfaith marriage is that only people who don't really care about religion intermarry. A related myth is that only people who don't really care about religion would try to raise children with both religions. Yet many interfaith couples today come from deeply religious backgrounds and come to interfaith communities precisely because both of them are religious, and neither spouse would ever ask the other to sacrifice his or her own practice. Jen and Rob Liebreich are one such couple.

Jen grew up going to Mass every Sunday and attended Catholic schools right through high school. "There were no synagogues in my hometown, and I only knew one Jewish person in high school," she recalls. Meanwhile, Rob grew up as a practicing Jew. But when it came time for college, both Jen and Rob immersed themselves in the culture of the "religious other": Rob went to Georgetown, a Jesuit university, and Jen went to Boston University, a private college with one of the largest Jewish populations in the country. The couple met while working on Capitol Hill. Even before they became engaged, they came to IFFP in Washington to see if raising children with both religions was a realistic strategy. "We both felt very strong in our faiths. We both felt religion was important," explains Jen. IFFP's Reverend Julia Jarvis offered Jen and Rob the opportunity to get to know the children being raised with both religions firsthand, by inviting the young couple to be Teen Group leaders at IFFP.

"We joined IFFP to see if the kids were screwed up. That's literally why we joined," laughs Jen. "After working with the teens, we felt, if our kids turned out like this we'd be lucky. These teens can talk about both religions. They educated us and made us feel confident that we would love to have our kids grow up like this."

Reverend Jarvis co-officiated at their wedding with a rabbi, and challah was used for the Communion, which was offered to all in attendance, regardless of religion. "We had the longest wedding in history, with everything that would be in a full Mass and all the Jewish rituals," Jen recalls. Their plan for the religious education of their future children was spelled out in their *ketubah*, the traditional Jewish wedding contract. Rob says, "It says we're going to raise our children with both religions, and that's what we're doing."

After having three children, Jen and Rob moved to the West Coast, closer to his family but far away from IFFP. Jen says, "Both of our families are pretty much begging us to start a group here." Rob says that they feel confident about teaching their children both religions through home rituals, for now. He says, "One of the things that IFFP taught us was the importance of rituals. We prioritize Shabbat, and we make a really big effort to celebrate all the holidays. We have bedtime prayers. All of that will carry us forward."

Fredie and Mark: Two Strong Cultures

For other interfaith families, religious belief is less important than the ability to pass on both sets of traditions and cultures. These families might fit theologically into an Ethical Culture or Secular Humanistic Jewish context. But they want their children to learn the history and stories and traditions of both parents: they want both depth and balance in religious education, whether or not they are believers.

Fredie Adelman is both the daughter and granddaughter of Holocaust survivors. Her father and grandfather survived years in the camps together. As is not uncommon among survivor families, their experience drove the Adelmans away from Jewish practice and theology but not away from Jewish culture and identity. "My father said he had fasted enough for himself, for us, for our children, and our children's children and all the generations beyond during his years in prison," recalls Fredie. "So on Yom Kippur we would go out hiking and mushroom hunting. It was not about organized religion for us. We were a very secular family."

And yet, Jewish culture played an integral role for the Adelmans. "My father and mother spoke Yiddish to each other," Fredie recalls. "My grandparents spoke only a little English. It was all part of the environment." Every year, the Adelmans hosted a huge Passover seder. "Invariably after a few hours of conversation it would get to—who had a worse time in which camp? 'You had a potato? We didn't have a potato, just potato peelings.' It was their way of working it out."

In college, Fredie majored in anthropology and helped to organize a multilingual Passover seder on campus. Students brought a tremendous variety of *haggadot*, the books used to lead the seder, from all over the world. And Fredie had an epiphany about the joy of Passover: "It finally occurred to me that the seder didn't have to be about concentration camps."

She went on to get a graduate degree in museum education and helped to plan the Holocaust Museum in Washington. While working for the Smithsonian on *Precious Legacy*, an exhibit of Judaica collected by the Nazis in Prague, she met Mark Gulezian, a photographer who traveled to Prague to take the images for the exhibit.

Mark had grown up in Massachusetts, a center of Armenian diaspora culture. "My grandparents were all survivors of the Armenian genocide," says Mark. He and Fredie were drawn together by their museum work, but also by their parallel ancestry. Fredie remembers visiting her grandmother shortly before she died. "I told her that I was going to marry Mark and that he was Armenian," recalls Fredie. "She said, 'The Armenians suffered, we suffered. They're good people.'"

For their wedding, they were able to locate an Armenian Protestant minister and a rabbi to co-officiate. And the klezmer band learned Armenian circle dances for the reception. After their children, Jacob and Amye, were born, they began to celebrate both sets of holidays. "I think it's because we weren't religious that we weren't going to try to impose one or the other," says Mark. "But at the same time, we both felt there was value in having knowledge about both of our religions, both of our histories."

Eventually, they began to question whether homeschooling in the two traditions was adequate. Fredie recalls, "When Jacob got to first grade, he had a friend whose family was very involved in a church. Jacob asked why we weren't going to church. Me saying 'Well, you're both' wasn't enough."

Then they discovered IFFP. "We found all these other kids who were both and grappling with it, and it was okay," says Fredie. "This is a place where we can be both and talk about it. Up until that point, Jacob could only have the 'both' conversation with us, and we weren't his peers."

For Mark, who grew up attending church, the structure of formal religious education was appealing. "For me, it was, Do you want your kids sleeping late and watching cartoons on Sunday morning? Or do you want them to learn something they're not going to learn any other way: the stories, where they came from, things that will help them?" he asks.

Both Gulezian children went through IFFP's group Coming of Age ceremony and claim both religions. Jacob, now twenty and an architecture student at Drexel University, speaks to the importance of both family cultures: "I can't lose my Judaism because it traces back to the Holocaust, that's extremely important to me. And my Christian side traces back to the Armenian genocide. I don't think either should be forgotten, ever."

For the past decade, Fredie has taught in the IFFP religious education program and has shared her family's Holocaust stories with every eighth-grade class of students in IFFP's two-year Coming of Age program. She guides the students through the Holocaust Museum and then shows them the photos of her parents and the records of transit through the camps of her father and grandfather. At the museum, they see the Nazi charts describing *Mischlings* and come to the realization that whether or not they are considered Jews by Orthodox Judaism, interfaith children were not safe from the Nazis.

"I feel like I have a responsibility to pass the story and the responsibility on to kids. To give the next generations a thread of connection to people who lived the experience," says Fredie. She sees this message as intimately tied to the messages of compassion, inclusion, and social justice they learn at IFFP. "The kids look at the *Mischlings* charts with the eye and hair comparisons, and they get it in very visceral ways," she says. "They begin to understand how precarious every life is in a society that is intolerant."

Amy and Steven: "A Long, Difficult Journey"

In some cases, interfaith families spend many years struggling to find a path that works for them. Amy (this couple asked to be identified by first names only) grew up in a kosher Conservative Jewish home in Queens, going to Hebrew school three times each week and Jewish camps in the summer. "Judaism was a very, very prominent part of my childhood," she says. "I never in my life would have even considered marrying someone who wasn't Jewish." And if a non-Jewish boy dared to call her, her father would say that Amy wasn't home.

Meanwhile, Steven was growing up Catholic on Long Island. When he met Amy after college, he was the head usher for the 7 p.m. Mass at his Catholic church, and one of his closest friends was a priest. "It was almost like love at first sight," says Amy. "But it was also almost like an 'Oh no' kind of thing, because it wasn't anything I ever thought would happen." Steven's family did not oppose the union, but Amy's family struggled—her father refused to even meet Steven.

The two were forced to face their religious differences. "We knew from the beginning that we wanted to do both," says Amy. "I knew I could never leave Judaism. He knew he could never leave Catholicism. We were both so involved in our religions. We knew faith was important to us, we knew we wanted a home with faith and a spiritual sense, but we didn't know how to navigate that path at all."

Before even approaching Amy's parents, they met with a young rabbi, a friend of Amy's. "You cannot be both religions, you're going to have to pick one; it's not possible to raise your children with both," Amy recalls him telling them. "Steven and I left kind of panic-stricken. We thought, maybe we can't do this."

Steven then proposed that they go to see his friend, the priest. "I was really scared of going to see a priest," admits Amy. "I had never set foot in a church my whole life until I met Steven." What happened next surprised her. "The priest said, 'Right now, we have to concentrate on making Amy's family okay. You're going to need her family someday.' His advice was to get married by a rabbi, in a temple. At that point we were planning to have either a priest and a rabbi, or a justice of the peace. I didn't think my parents were coming to the wedding."

The priest agreed to get a dispensation so that Steven would be married in the eyes of the Catholic Church. Says Amy, "Both of us were just blown away by how open-minded he was." As for raising children, the priest did not oppose their plan to raise them with both religions. "He said, 'I want you to make an agreement that someday, if your child chooses to be Jewish, or Catholic, you're okay with that.' That's something that always stuck with me," says Amy.

While their four children were still small, Amy, a professional teacher, felt confident teaching them religion. "We were buying up every book, every tape, thinking we were going to homeschool them on religion," says Amy. "I would make *hamentaschen* [a traditional holiday pastry] on Purim. I would buy CDs and play the music I grew up on. But I was feeling guilty that they were getting too Jewish. I knew so much more about my own religion."

When she attempted to get advice or resources online, she encountered intolerance from people opposed to raising children in both religions. "Just when I felt like I was making progress, there would be such hatred. As much as you can say, 'Well, it's just some crazy person,' it would upset me," Amy says. The couple also felt that homeschooling their children in religion was not providing spiritual support for them as adults. "I felt like we were missing something. We needed something for when times are tough, a place to go," says Amy. "For us, who had been so involved in our religious institutions, it was hard."

Then, in 2011, *Long Island Newsday* ran a feature about the local chapter of the IFC. Amy and Steven immediately signed up, even though they live forty-five minutes away. "We went for Rosh Hashanah to the first service, and I cried through the service. I turned to my husband and said, 'Our children have a place to get married, a place to celebrate things, a place to go when things aren't going well.' We have a rabbi in front of us who's okay with us. We have a priest sitting next to us at Rosh Hashanah who's okay with this. We were so thirsty for this, for so many years, that we cannot get enough of it now."

An interfaith community has provided Amy and Steven with spiritual experience, formal religious education for their children (now eleven, nine, seven, and five years old) and community. "Steven and I have realized that it's not really important to give yourself a label," says Amy. "What's important is to know that there's something that's greater than you, a spirituality, something you go to in the good and bad times. We're teaching our children to have that, even though people may have turned up their noses at us along the journey."

Susan and Lisa: Two Women, Two Religions

The growth of the interfaith families movement parallels the increasing diversity of American families. Some interfaith gay, lesbian, interracial, or adoptive families seek a single religious identity for their children because they fear adding any additional complexity to their families. On the other hand, some of these families seek out the sense of balance and radical inclusivity represented by interfaith family communities.

Susan Mathis grew up as a practicing "Conservadox" Jew: Conservative but leaning toward Orthodox. She attended Hebrew school three days a week and was elected to youth leadership in her synagogue. Then, at some point in her teens, she began reading from the English side of the prayer book and contemplating some of the more troubling passages. "I was like, 'Who smote whom? What?'" she recalls. "I became very cynical." In college, she stopped going to services.

By the time she met Lisa Henderson at a dinner party in 1992, "religious difference seemed like a complete nonissue," Susan recalls. Lisa had been raised in a churchgoing family with roots in the South, in the conservative Church of Christ denomination. But in college at Cornell, she found herself gravitating to Jewish girls. "I was drawn to all that was East Coast, funny, sarcastic, edgy; it seemed more my personality," she says. At the same time, she was struggling with her experience of Christianity. "I think I was uncomfortable with people who were too Christian, who reminded me of my extended fundamentalist family," she recalls. "I was coming out; I was becoming a feminist. I couldn't stand all the talk in church about 'God the Father.'"

When Susan brought Lisa home to introduce to her parents, they knew she dated women, but she warned them ahead of time, "She's not Jewish and she's blonde." Her father replied, "Nothing wrong with that!" During the brunch meeting, Susan went upstairs with her mother who commented, "She's very nice, but such a *shiksa* [the Yiddish word for a non-Jewish woman]." Susan recalls, "She would have been much, much happier if Lisa was Jewish. I remember my mother saying mixed marriages never work; it's not fair to the children; they don't know who they are."

But Susan and Lisa were undeterred. They settled down, bought a house, and began talking about adoption. By then, Lisa was open to the idea of raising kids Jewish. It was Susan who was deeply ambivalent: "I had some real problems with the us-versus-them mentality of Judaism, as I experienced it growing up, especially the idea of the chosen people, which I viewed as, I guess, hypocrisy. It's a strong word, but I didn't want to indoctrinate my kid the way I was indoctrinated."

Part of Susan's issue with Judaism stemmed from the fact that they planned to adopt from China. "Everyone in the congregation I grew up in looked the same. Not that Lisa and I would have been welcome as a gay couple there, anyway. And that was a part of it too. I didn't feel I could raise this kid Jewish because I was not really welcome where I felt most comfortable."

After adopting two girls, Lisa and Susan fell into a pattern of celebrating Jewish holidays with Susan's nearby family and Christmas with Lisa's mother. But Lisa's mother remained troubled. Lisa recalls, "What she observed was that there wasn't much religion in our lives, and that pained her. We were raising them with both, but in a sort of de facto way."

Then, when the girls were six and eight years old, Lisa's mother died. In mourning, Lisa felt a longing for her children to understand her roots in Christianity. "Suddenly, I wanted a community where I felt comfortable," she recalls. "It's crazy, because it's nothing to do with faith, but it's to do with identity. I just wanted my children to know where I came from."

At that point, Lisa and Susan decided to join IFFP. Eight years later, their second daughter is finishing up the Coming of Age program. "At IFFP, we feel validated as a family," says Lisa. "I was just looking for maybe a structure for them, a little bit of support for my heritage. Who knows what they're going to be doing down the road? Hopefully, they will understand and remember the Kindness Prayer, some good things about Christianity. And the fact that neither Susan nor I are guests in this community is an amazing thing."

Meanwhile, after her father died, Susan began accompanying her mother to Conservative synagogue each week. "Over six or seven years that I went with her, I started to feel part of that community," she says. And when her mother died, she spent a year saying Kaddish for her at the synagogue. But while Susan continues to feel the pull of the Conservative Judaism she grew up with, she still cannot picture her family there: "The rabbi told me, 'We did just have a gay couple join, but they're both Jewish.' Lisa would be a fish out of water."

And IFFP has also changed her: "I've loved the adult group at IFFP. I love the discussions about religion and interfaith issues. One thing IFFP has done is opened me up to learning about Christianity." She has always wanted to study the Talmud, but now she could also see herself studying the new edition of the New Testament with Jewish commentary.

Susan still seeks out Jewish ritual practice and Lisa still craves a more contemplative and peaceful religious space on Sunday mornings. But they both acknowledge that an interfaith community has provided a home they could both accept, preserved a sense of balance and mutual respect, and benefited their children. "What I hope is that the kids stay on the path they seem to be on," Susan concludes. "They are really thoughtful people. It would bum me out if they became super religious in any religion, even Jewish. I couldn't see them becoming fundamentalist anything. It would be a hard thing for me to get over."

André and Gayle: Two Races, Two Religions

Growing up, André Parraway's family life revolved around St. Luke's Episcopal Church, a historically black church in the District of Columbia dating back to the 1870s. His mother was a director of religious education there, his sister taught in the Sunday school, and André spent a decade as an altar server. While his church attendance trailed off in his mid-twenties, he assumed he would go back to raise a family. "I always knew that whomever I married, I'd want to raise my children in a religious structure," he recalls.

Gayle grew up Jewish in New Jersey, though religion did not play a strong role in her family. "I remember saying to my mother, 'I'm not into religion, I don't need to raise children with religion,'" she recalls. "And my mom, who's not religious, said, 'Don't do that! The kids are going to be completely left out, because everyone else has some religious foundation.'"

Gayle and André met at work. At first, their racial differences overshadowed any discussion of religion. Their religious differences just didn't seem to be a big deal, and in fact, they haven't been. Around the time they got engaged, an article about IFFP ran in the *Washington Post*. As André recalls, "That was kind of it. Basically, there was an answer presented to us before we even began to deal with the question."

The first rabbi they approached refused to marry them because they were planning to raise their children with both religions, but they stuck with their plan. Eventually, they found a Humanistic Jewish rabbi to co-officiate with an Episcopal priest from André's church. After their daughters were born, they joined IFFP: the two girls are now eight and ten years old. André, who experienced being one of only two African American students in his high school class, comments: "You want them in a setting of kids who are in similar situations. At IFFP, they're all in the same boat. It makes them feel very comfortable."

While most couples can articulate the challenges as well as the benefits of the interfaith education pathway, Gayle and André say that they have yet to encounter a downside. As much as anything else, this may reflect their easygoing attitude. Says André, "We don't see any disadvantages. Every December, when they talk about the December dilemma, we're like, 'What dilemma?' I remember to buy Hanukkah candles; Gayle can't wait to decorate the Christmas tree."

André and Gayle have an advantage in that both families accepted their relationship. But André also points out that he thinks some of the success of their interfaith family has to do with their strong commitment as a nuclear family to this pathway. "Regardless of whether we had the family support or not, we were going to do what we were going to do," he explains.

As for the double complexity of two races and two religions in the Parraway family, they have confidence that this new generation is growing up with different attitudes toward both race and religion. "They're comfortable in their skin," Gayle says of their daughters, "because we've helped make them that way. Maybe they accept that they're Jewish and Christian because they also know that they're black and white."

Eileen and Steve: Through Thick and Thin

As the earliest members of interfaith communities reached middle age, they began to appreciate the benefits of community in the years beyond child rearing. Eileen O'Farrell Smith's commitment to the interfaith community has steadily deepened through the illness and death of her husband and into a period of intense spiritual discernment.

Eileen grew up Irish Catholic on Long Island. She went to Catholic high school, then Catholic college, and ended up in Chicago, where she met Steve Smith. Steve came from an Orthodox Jewish family in Boston, though he had stopped practicing the religion after his bar mitzvah. Eileen had had a brief early marriage to a Catholic man; Steve, a brief early marriage to a Jewish woman.

"When we met, religion really wasn't an issue," says Eileen. "He was a Red Sox fan, I was a Mets fan—that seemed more important at the time." Nevertheless, Eileen was a "card-carrying Catholic" who went to Mass every week. When they did discuss marriage, they did not see an easy solution. "I didn't know anything about Judaism, and from his perspective, he couldn't see having Catholic kids, because he would feel left out," recalls Eileen. But they were not going to let that stop them from being together. "The bottom line was, I was thirty-five," she says. "What if we couldn't even have kids? Should religion be a dealbreaker? So we just let it go."

Just weeks after marriage, Eileen was pregnant, and the couple proceeded to have three children in four years. On Sunday mornings, Steve would stay home with the babies, and Eileen would go to sing in the choir at Mass. In 1991, while pregnant with their third child, Eileen says that "all hormones broke loose" and she began to mourn the fact that none of their children had been baptized or would be part of any religious community. "It was breaking my heart that we had done nothing," she recalls.

That spring, the *Chicago Tribune* ran a front-page story about the Jewish Catholic Couples Dialogue Group, the discussion group for intermarried couples, under the guidance of Father John Cusick and Rabbi Allen Secher. Steve called Father Cusick, initiating a friendship that would sustain Steve until the end of his life. Father

Cusick and Rabbi Secher convinced Eileen and Steve to join other Dialogue Group couples at Sunday Mass at Old Saint Patrick's Church in downtown Chicago, and at Friday night Shabbat at Makom Shalom, the Jewish Renewal community nearby.

By the time all three children were in grade school, Catholicism and Judaism had become "a huge piece of our family fabric," says Eileen. They eventually joined Chicago Sinai, a Reform temple, and Steve ended up serving for years on that board. Eileen also served on committees there and would be invited up to the *bimah* (pulpit) to light the Shabbat candles. "Steve had been married to a Jewish woman, but he hadn't been to shul in twenty-six years when I met him," says Eileen. "I brought Steve back to Judaism. The power of our love brought him back."

Meanwhile, they also took the children to the Interfaith Family School at Old Saint Pat's on Sunday mornings, then filed into the front row pew for Mass at 11:15 with Father Cusick. The three kids took it all in stride, according to their mother. "Nobody was confused. What were they going to be confused about?" asks Eileen. "They were able to integrate their own sense of, 'Mom believes this, and Dad believes this.' The kids seemed to be able to speak to the 'both,' to own it. It was celebrated, it was a glorious thing." The only drawback, says Eileen, was practical: "The downside was, well, they got shlepped a lot."

Over the years, Father Cusick continued to arrive at the Smith house for dinner and then disappear into Steve's basement office to drink Scotch and discuss Chicago politics. "He was Steve's best friend," says Eileen. And when Steve became very ill in the last two years of his life, after a fourteen-year battle with brain tumors, the extraordinary friendship between a Jewish man and a Catholic priest only deepened.

When the end came, in the summer of 2008, Eileen drew on all of the family's overlapping religious networks to plan Steve's funeral service. "I knew that he wanted John to preach, and that it had to be at Old Saint Pat's," says Eileen. "The church was thrilled and honored that this Jewish funeral was going to be there." Rabbi Secher led the service, two friends from the Chicago Symphony played the Kol Nidre (the central prayer recited on Yom Kippur), the Saint Pat's choir sang the *Shehecheyanu* (a blessing for new experiences), and there were some five hundred people crowded into the pews. At one point, Rabbi Secher invited all ten clergy members in attendance to come up for the traditional Jewish blessing of Aaron. "We turned the place into a tremendous temple of the presence of God," recalls Father Cusick.

To this day, Eileen continues to light candles for Shabbat, for Hanukkah, and for Steve's *yahrzeit*, the anniversary of his death. She goes to synagogue on the High Holy Days and again on Steve's *yahrzeit*. With all three of her children out in the world, Eileen also continues as the executive director of the Interfaith Union, a group she founded to bring support and interfaith education to families in the Chicago suburbs.

Just before Steve died, Eileen told him that she had been accepted into a graduate program at Catholic Theological Union in Chicago. That fall, she began her formal study of theology and graduated with a master's degree in 2012. "Steve transformed and enriched and deepened my life in such profound ways that I become speechless," says Eileen. "I am so deeply in love with Judaism as it informs my Catholicism. My God is a limitless God, a boundless God."

Ethan and Dana: Interfaith, the Next Generation

As a growing number of adults have multireligious backgrounds, it makes sense that more families will seek out multireligious communities. Each of the interfaith programs I've described in these pages now attracts adults who grew up in interfaith families. While most, like me, were raised in one religion, or no religion, they are, in effect, raising second-generation interfaith children.

Ethan and Dana (not their real names) represent two different permutations of the modern American interfaith family. Dana grew up very close to her only Jewish grandparent, her grandfather. When he intermarried, two generations before it became common, his Jewish family sat shivah, as though he had died. So his daughter and granddaughter Dana were raised Protestant. "But I always knew Judaism was part of my family," says Dana. "All my mom's cousins were Jewish, and I was always curious about Judaism. I always felt this pull."

When Dana met Ethan, they sensed interfaith symmetry. Both of Ethan's biological parents had been Catholic, but he is very close to his Jewish stepfather. Dana says, "When I met him, it brought up all those feelings of how I had always been drawn to Judaism." So after marrying and starting a family, she and Ethan began celebrating Shabbat at home, put their children in a Jewish preschool, and decided to join a synagogue. At the same time, they continued to celebrate Christian holidays with Dana's family.

When they joined the synagogue, they were living in a college town in the West. "There weren't that many people who were Jewish there," says Dana. "So to them, we were very Jewish. They were happy to have us. They didn't even question us about it when we joined the temple." The family also joined a Unitarian Universalist congregation, and their older children were officially named and welcomed in that community. "I just can't see us as one or the other. We thought about it, but I just can't see us as a Jewish family. We are both," says Dana. "I couldn't be just Catholic either. I couldn't be one thing."

However, when they moved to the New York area with three kids in tow, they did not sense the same acceptance. Dana explains, "We found this idea in New York of, 'How are you Jewish? I mean, are you kidding me?' Our only claim is patrilineal, and then it's one generation removed on my side, and not biological on Ethan's side. It's very tenuous." They quickly found their way to an IFC chapter.

Dana feels that Christianity would have been a more obvious, and easier, choice for her family. She feels her desire to also teach her children Judaism rattles the world. "And yet it calls to me, and it's part of us," she sighs. "It's hard because in our particular culture there's so much emphasis on authenticity, and if you try to raise your kids with both, you're somehow offending people who are authentically either one and that what you're doing is somehow false."

In the context of an interfaith community, nobody questions Ethan and Dana about their right to connect to Judaism or Christianity. At Passover seder, their young daughter recites the traditional four questions (a central part of the ceremony) not in English but in Hebrew, thrilling her Jewish step-grandfather. Says Dana, "I know that if they learn these things young, it's going to stick with them more: the prayers they memorize they will always know, the feelings that they have that are positive about religion, the songs that will bring tears to their eyes."

CHAPTER SIX

Radically Inclusive Clergy

FOR MANY INTERFAITH COUPLES, finding supportive clergy
remains one of the greatest challenges of raising children with
both religions. It may feel hard to trust a rabbi or pastor, knowing
that official institutions and policies often discourage intermarriage
and the teaching of two religions. Some couples cannot accept clergy
who refuse to witness their wedding yet want them to join a church
or synagogue. Others, coming from secular backgrounds, may not
be convinced they need a minister, priest, or rabbi, never having
experienced the benefits of a pastoral relationship.

The daring clergy who work with families who have chosen
both religions are a distinct minority. Like the families, they must
weather the skepticism of their peers: why would they agree to
"share" these families with other clergy? Do they, by definition,
"dilute" their beliefs in order to do so?

In spite of the criticism these clergy face, they testify to the
tremendous fulfillment they gain from meeting the needs of families who have struggled to keep faith, spirituality, ritual, or culture
in their lives. Many of these rabbis, ministers, and priests feel a
particular empathy with marginalized or disempowered groups,
having worked with the civil rights movement, immigrants, the
gay and lesbian community, youth, or the poor. This social-justice

calling weaves through the lives of most, if not all, of the clergy who have worked with interfaith groups.

Reverend Allan Ramirez: "Let Our Love Drive Us"

When the Long Island chapter of the IFC first approached Reverend Allan Ramirez about acting as a Christian resource, he was not the least troubled by the idea. "I thought it was very natural and in many ways admirable," he recalls. "Here are families with two different religious traditions, but they are very committed to both of those traditions. I thought, 'Hey, I wish we had more of that kind of commitment in our churches.'"

Reverend Ramirez, an Ecuadoran American, served a mostly white, affluent congregation at the Brookville Reformed Church, a Protestant congregation dating back to seventeenth-century Dutch settlers. But for over thirty years, he had led this congregation on an unusual program of progressive activism, from organizing flu vaccines for day laborers to advocating for legislation to protect domestic workers. Until his retirement in 2012, he was widely considered one of the most influential advocates for Latinos on Long Island.

And yet Reverend Ramirez sees his support for interfaith families over the past decade as the high point of his career. "If I can be so presumptuous as to say there is a jewel in my crown, it is my having had the privilege to work with the interfaith families," he says. "Interfaith families are pointing us in new directions, challenging our limited orthodoxy and pushing us in a way that is so much more visionary."

Working outside the strictures of religious identity labels energizes Reverend Ramirez: he is unconcerned about the disapproval of institutions. "I think they need to stretch theologically a little bit," he says of those who criticize religious double-belonging. "I think God is doing something wonderful with these interfaith families, which is to say, 'I'm going to take you out of that single box that you've been in. As love brings you together, I'm going to have you see me from a bigger, panoramic view.'"

Reverend Ramirez worked closely with a rabbi on Long Island, advising and supporting the IFC chapter there and co-officiating at life-cycle ceremonies. He invited the rabbi to speak from his church pulpit in Brookeville, and Reverend Ramirez spoke at the rabbi's Shabbat services. But he recognizes how unusual this is. "The problem is really us, the members of the clergy," he says. "We're looking out for our own members, our own church. It's part of our measuring success by the standards of Western society, how many heads we can collect. Instead, I say I will measure success by the spiritual richness of this community."

Reverend Ramirez traces his own radical inclusivity to his experiences with feeling marginalized as a Latino American. "I am very suspicious of establishments, organizations," he explains. "At the end of the day, if they want to argue doctrine—to me, it comes down to a very simple, straightforward idea. I'm presented with the situation of these interfaith families, I say to myself, 'What would a loving God do? Would a loving God look at the regulations, all the dos and don'ts? Or would God simply look at these families, love and embrace them, and welcome them? If somebody wants to argue about their creeds, regulations, their theological whatever, knock yourself out. But I've got a lot more important things to do."

Reverend Ellen Jennings: "No Cognitive Dissonance"

Many Christian clergy drawn to working with interfaith families either come from interchurch families, with parents from two Christian denominations, or have been in interchurch or interfaith marriages themselves. The interchurch experience of striving for faith and spirituality despite doctrinal and ritual differences sensitizes them to the challenges and possibilities of interfaith family life.

Reverend Ellen Jennings's mother grew up Catholic, her father grew up Presbyterian, and her husband grew up Ukrainian Orthodox. Deeply involved in the youth activities at her Episcopal church as a girl, she became a religion major at Dartmouth, studied biblical Hebrew and spent time on a kibbutz. After college, while dating an "adamant atheist," she experienced a classic crisis of faith and went off to spend three months at a Buddhist retreat center. She ended up at Harvard Divinity School without a specific religious denomination and uncertain where this journey would take her. "I felt okay about having become what I then considered to be post-Christian. I was a seeker."

After several years working at Bread for the World, a Christian antihunger organization, she felt drawn to find a church community in which to raise her children. At the local United Church of Christ congregation, she found a progressive theological home. Then, in 2001, she was recruited by IFFP in Washington to become its director of religious education.

"There was no hesitancy on my part," she recalls. "I have little patience with anybody on the Christian side who has a problem with interfaith communities." On the other hand, she was sensitive, as are most Christian clergy, to the concerns of Jewish clergy about Jewish continuity. Jennings says, "When I heard those arguments from the Jewish side, I could empathize and understand. I actually don't know what to do about that argument except to say that I don't want Judaism to die out, and at the same time, I don't think we should restrict these kids from having opportunity to see the world more broadly."

Reverend Jennings ran IFFP's religious education program from 2001 to 2007, developing much of the curriculum. Her three young sons, though they have no Jewish heritage, grew up with IFFP as their primary religious community. In 2007, she was ordained in the United Church of Christ with the entire IFFP community in attendance and with IFFP's Rabbi Harold White, speaking at the ordination. She now serves as pastor at Cleveland Park Congregational United Church of Christ in Washington, D.C.

In her years at IFFP, Reverend Jennings arrived at a deep appreciation of the merits of an interfaith community. She says, "In most of the interfaith families I had met up until that point, either one parent really didn't care, which was fine, or one had to decide that they didn't care enough, or as much. And I think that's too bad, because both traditions are rich, and I think it's important for both parents to be able to share what they've grown up with."

Reverend Jennings believes there are specific benefits for students learning two religious systems. She likens it to learning two languages and, as with languages, believes the earlier the child is exposed to both, the better: "I've observed that their brains are not just capable of but, as with learning languages, are actually much more ready to receive and accommodate a variety of perspectives, the younger they are."

She adds, "There doesn't seem to be any cognitive dissonance for children at IFFP in terms of the fact that there could be more than one way to understand God, or to reach God, or to talk about God, or more than one set of rituals. This is in direct conflict with all of people's fears about raising children in more than one tradition, or exposing them to more than one early on. People assume kids cannot handle that. I think they are absolutely capable of handling it, and that, sadly, the older we get without having that exposure, the less able to handle it we become."

Reverend Rick Spalding: "You Don't Have to Give Up Your Religion"

Reverend Rick Spalding was the first Christian educator hired by the IFC in New York City. But very quickly, he became a key support to the parents, as well as the children in the program. "What caught me by surprise and really catalyzed my commitment to the program was the sense of need among the families," he recalls. "They were really asking each other, and the universe, for help."

Reverend Spalding felt moved by the plight of families struggling against the idea that one or both parents must abandon their own religious practice for the sake of having a peaceful interfaith family. "What was so poignant to me was that there were all these people who loved their religions" and yet had somehow become convinced "that in marrying out of their faith they had to leave their religion behind," he says. "A lot of people really had figured that the only way to deal with difference was to not deal with it: that the only way through it was around it. I had this dawning and deepening conviction that you absolutely don't have to give up your religion when you marry someone of a different religion."

Reverend Spalding has now served for more than a decade as the Chaplain to the College at Williams. "I'm a monofaith person in terms of my family background and practice," he explains, noting the growing presence of interfaith children on campus. "But I see that the world has been getting steadily more and more interesting in a multifaith sort of way for the past thirty years."

Reverend Julia Jarvis: "The World Will Move This Way"

Of all the clergy who have worked with families celebrating two religions, Reverend Julia Jarvis has perhaps the deepest experience, having spent more than a dozen years on staff at IFFP. She now serves as spiritual director and community leader in partnership with IFFP's Jewish spiritual leader, Rabbi Harold White.

Reverend Jarvis grew up the daughter of a Southern Baptist Minister of Music and graduated from the Southern Baptist Theological Seminary in Louisville, Kentucky. After she had taken many religious twists and turns, her passion for social justice fueled her search for a religious home open enough to embrace her deconstructed and reconstructed theology. Eventually, she was ordained in both the Disciples of Christ and the progressive United Church of Christ, and she continues to be active in that denomination, as well as in a Buddhist meditation group. While providing pastoral care in the neonatal intensive care unit at Georgetown University Hospital, she met Rabbi White, the longtime Georgetown chaplain, who would later become the other half of the dynamic duo of clergy leading IFFP, as well as her dear friend. They traveled to Israel together and to see Vietnamese Buddhist monk and peace activist Thich Nhat Hanh. Reverend Jarvis officiated at the funeral of one of Rabbi White's family members and recently attended a whole string of parties for Rabbi White's eightieth birthday. Their interfaith friendship inspires the IFFP community.

Reverend Jarvis sees the benefits of community as key for interfaith children but equally important for the adults. "I'm a huge cheerleader of interfaith marriages," she explains. "When I work with young couples, often, they don't know they can do this. I just keep telling them how brave they are, that they are standing on the shoulders of other people. People have been forging this road for a long time, and the road is there for them. It's a dirt road, maybe it's not paved yet, but there are signposts for them, there are lots of resources for them."

Reverend Jarvis believes that interfaith education for adults is essential to a successful intermarriage. "I ask my couples to start an interfaith library. A lot of people don't know that much about their own traditions, let alone their partner's traditions," she explains. "I have them talk to each other about what they imagine their children knowing, and learning, and ritualizing. I have them meet other interfaith couples, ones that have been through a life of interfaith marriage, because they need support, they need resources, and they need community. And if they live where there's no community like ours, that's tougher. I encourage them to look at the Unitarian church, to look at religious homeschooling, or to find at least four other interfaith couples and start their own community."

Jarvis is still in touch with many of the IFFP students who have gone out into the world, and she is proud of the ways they have benefited from growing up in an interfaith community. "They know how to embrace the 'other,' as Martin Buber would say," she explains. "They don't pass judgment: they are very open and receiving. The world has to move this way. It's good for the Jews, and it's good for the Christians."

Reverend Heather Kirk-Davidoff: "Judaism Is a Very Deep Part of My Life"

Reverend Heather Kirk-Davidoff occupies the unique position of having led an interfaith community as a minister while also being an interfaith spouse and parent raising her children with Judaism and Christianity. She served as the spiritual director of IFFP from 2003 to 2006.

Reverend Kirk-Davidoff herself comes from two generations of interchurch marriage. Her mother was born to an Irish Catholic father and Protestant mother. "At that time, neither group saw the other group as Christian, or as going to heaven. So it was a source of tension," she explains. Her mother grew up as an Episcopalian, then married her Quaker father. In what could be considered destiny or irony, the Kirk family settled in the Jewish neighborhood of Highland Park in Saint Paul, Minnesota. "During the year I was thirteen, I probably went to a dozen bar or bat mitzvahs," she recalls. And in high school, she started dating Jewish boys.

While at Yale, she met science major Daniel Davidoff. "Sometimes people ask me, 'How can you be married to a Jewish guy and be a Christian minister?' Part of it is that the relationship predated me being me, me being a grown-up," she explains. "My adult self was formed in the context of being in a relationship with Dan."

Dan Davidoff had grown up in a secular Jewish household in Brooklyn. "Their religion was left-wing politics," says Kirk-Davidoff. "On that level, we were raised in households with identical ideologies. Politics drove the bus in both of our households."

The winding path taken by the Kirk-Davidoffs became the classic story of a secular Jew who returns to religious Jewish practice through the influence of a Christian spouse. "The first time Dan went to High Holy Day services was with me, on my suggestion, because I wanted to go," she recalls. And in her last year at Harvard Divinity School, they were married under a chuppah, the Jewish wedding canopy.

By the time the couple had twin boys, they were active in an egalitarian Jewish community, Havurat Shalom, in Somerville, Massachusetts. At the same time, Reverend Kirk-Davidoff was working as a minister at a nearby Congregational church. Their plan all along was to raise their children with both religions. "That is the exact thing that I read, over and over again, that you're not supposed to do. And I actually wholeheartedly disagree," she says. "I think that children navigate all sorts of complexities. Parents have different personalities; they have different political views. Kids grow up in households where they're forming a sense of self with different parents. I guess I just have a lot more confidence than some families have in my children's ability to navigate difference."

While immersing her own children separately in both Judaism and Christianity, Reverend Kirk-Davidoff was at first skeptical about a community that tries to bridge the two traditions. "I became persuaded over the course of working at IFFP," she admits. "We found an enormously strong sense of personal identification with those other couples. There was an element of just what the doctor ordered—we really didn't even know we needed it until we had it."

And while outreach efforts by Jewish congregations now provide discussion groups for interfaith couples and families, Reverend

Kirk-Davidoff sees a clear distinction. "I don't have any interest in an interfaith couples group in a synagogue context," she admits. "There would be constant self-monitoring about, 'Are you Jewish enough?' whereas IFFP was an incredibly accepting place about what variation on this theme you wanted to have."

She also experienced the power of an interfaith community to help couples through crises of faith and marriage: "I remember one family where the Christian husband had a major religious experience at a family funeral. He started going to church. His Jewish wife was like, 'I did not sign on for this.' It was not easy. IFFP saved their marriage."

Reverend Kirk-Davidoff has coauthored a curriculum on "relational evangelism," entitled Talking Faith, and has been active in the national "emergent church" movement. She says, "I am a convinced Christian." Nevertheless, she disagrees with the idea that the divinity of Jesus is the defining difference between Judaism and Christianity. "To say that the real dividing line is, 'Do you think Jesus is the Messiah or not?' strikes me as false," she says. That is not to say that she only sees the common ground, or ignores the particularities of each religion. "Do I believe that the religions are the same? Absolutely not. They're different languages and stories," she explains. "The languages and stories and traditions are not irrelevant, they're what give life texture and meaning and color."

These days, Reverend Kirk-Davidoff serves as the minister at the Kittamaqundi Community Church, an ecumenical Christian church in Columbia, Maryland. The three Kirk-Davidoff teenagers go to their mother's church on Sundays. But the family also belongs to a Reconstructionist synagogue, where Dan plays fiddle in a klezmer band, and the children recite the Hebrew blessings when they celebrate Shabbat together on Friday night.

For Reverend Kirk-Davidoff, the depth of her family's connection to Judaism serves as testimony to the power of choosing both religions. "Judaism lost Dan's family a couple of generations ago," she says. "He's actually one of the most religious Jewish people in several generations of his family. Being involved with religious life with me made him value it more." And their religious life together has had a profound effect on Reverend Kirk-Davidoff as well: "I'm not Jewish, but on some fundamental level, I'm not 'not-Jewish" either. Judaism is a very deep part of my life after all these years."

Nor does she believe that her children are stressed about choosing a religious pathway: "I've always said to them, 'This is who you are. You're the children of an interfaith family. This is always going to be your story; this is what we're giving you. But you're going to take your own journey with this.'"

Rabbi Harold White: My Rabbi

One of the most profound benefits for me of being part of an interfaith community has been my relationship with Rabbi Harold White. For more than a decade after my intermarriage, I had no rabbi and did not expect ever to have one again. Now, I have the friendship and support of an elder statesman, a rabbi who studied with Abraham Joshua Heschel and Martin Buber. Rabbi White has been immersed in the intellectual Jesuit context of Georgetown University as a chaplain for over forty years, teaching alongside both priests and an imam. He brings all of his deep understandings of the connections between Judaism, Christianity, and Islam to IFFP.

Since 1976, Rabbi White has been both adored and shunned in the Washington, D.C., area for his willingness to witness interfaith marriages. When he first took this step, he knew it would mean being ousted from the Conservative movement in which he was ordained. (Conservative and Orthodox rabbis are not even allowed to attend interfaith weddings as guests.) With the support of Georgetown president Tim Healy, who promised Rabbi White a perpetual job as chaplain, he went ahead and eventually switched his affiliation to the Reform rabbinate. "I knew that there would be recriminations, that I would be ostracized," he recalls. But he also knew that he would be helping couples that otherwise would be alienated from Judaism.

Despite his pioneering role supporting interfaith couples, Rabbi White at first questioned the wisdom of raising children with both religions. "Ten years ago, I would have been opposed to IFFP," he admits. "It was very clear in my mind that I thought you should raise the children and educate the child in one religion. I came into IFFP with a great deal of skepticism."

Ultimately, he felt drawn to the idea of providing Jewish history, liturgy, ritual, and philosophy to these parents seeking to connect their children to Judaism. After ten years on the IFFP staff, he rebuts the argument that these interfaith children will be stressed by religious choice. "You're not telling the child 'You have to choose one or the other,' because you are providing an interfaith identity," he explains, "with the understanding that when they mature, they may meet someone of a different religious tradition and go that way."

He also finds that the skepticism of the Jewish community about raising children with both religions has begun to wane. "Before, I was the renegade, I was 'responsible for Judaism dying,'" he says. "Now, I have respect for this community from the Jews that I never had before. There's a clear understanding that I work with these couples because I care about the survival of Judaism."

He refuses to see interfaith communities as a threat to Jewish continuity. "There's something mysterious," he muses. "Why have we as a Jewish civilization continued to exist, when Rome, Greece,

Portugal, Germany tried to exterminate us? I have a mystical faith in our survival. IFFP might even increase the numbers of Jews."

Rabbi Nehama Benmosche:
"Each Kid Is on an Individual Faith Journey"
The newest generation of rabbis often has more direct personal experience with interfaith relationships. Nehama Benmosche grew up in a Reform Jewish family she describes as "culturally Jewish, not very religious." By the time she was in high school, she was the most religious person in her family. She even skipped her senior prom to attend a synagogue event. "At that point I had decided I wanted to become a rabbi," she recalls.

As a Middle East Studies major at Emory University, Rabbi Benmosche actually became Orthodox for a while. She stayed on for a master's in Jewish Studies and found a spiritual home in a gay and lesbian Reconstructionist community. However, she also found herself in a serious relationship with a Christian woman. "You can't be in an interfaith relationship and study to be a rabbi," she says. So in 1991, she put aside the dream of ordination and instead began a doctoral program in religious education at Jewish Theological Seminary (JTS), the Conservative Jewish seminary in New York.

While studying at JTS, she went to work as a Jewish educator at the IFC. "I always thought that interfaith education for interfaith families was a great idea," she says. At the IFC, she helped to develop and expand the Jewish curriculum, interweaving classroom and experiential learning. Rabbi Benmosche waves off concerns over stressing children with choice. "It's not about what we give kids access to that's going to confuse them," she says. "What's going to be confusing is to try to direct a journey that's not to be directed by us, as parents. We can give them tools for the journey, but we can't give them direction."

Eventually, Rabbi Benmosche left her IFC teaching role to start Reconstructionist rabbinical training, though she remains on the IFC board. Now raising children with a Jewish partner, she was ordained in 2010. She remains convinced that she is contributing to Jewish continuity in working with an interfaith families community. However, she understands that it may be difficult for people who have not worked with these programs to understand her perspective. As a rabbi now, she says she would welcome a family that was educating a child in both religions to her own congregation, but she's not sure the families in her congregation would feel the same way.

Rabbi Benmosche is happy to see many Jewish communities becoming more welcoming to interfaith families. But her own experience as part of a marginalized group leads her to believe that the need for independent interfaith communities will remain. "From a queer perspective, I know there's a difference between being accepted by the majority and being in a position where you *are* the majority," she says. So she envisions that families educating children in both religions "are still going to want spaces where you are the majority."

Rabbi Allen Secher: "The Most Important Work I've Done"

Rabbi Allen Secher remembers the precise moment when he decided to begin officiating at intermarriages. As a Reform rabbi, his movement allows him to make his own decision on this issue, even while discouraging intermarriage. "I was a standard, run-of-the-mill rabbi saying 'no, no, no' to interfaith marriages," he recalls. He was approached by a young woman who had been a youth group leader in his congregation, in the San Fernando Valley in California. She asked him to officiate at her marriage to her Christian fiancé. Rabbi Secher said no but agreed to attend. "So I went to the wedding," he recalls, but he was stunned by the spiritual emptiness of the civil ceremony. "It was like the judge was reading from a telephone book. I was incensed." Feeling deep regret that he had turned this couple away, he made his decision. He called the bride's parents, who were active in the congregation, and asked them to attend Friday night services to hear his announcement. He remembers, "So I stood up in the pulpit and I told the story of the girl coming to see me. And I described my reaction to the wedding. I said, 'I should have been there.' And I said, 'I want to tell you, from here on in, if a couple wants a rabbi as part of the ceremony, I will be there for them.'"

After moving to Chicago, Rabbi Secher co-officiated at a wedding in 1990 with Father John Cusick, Catholic adviser to the Jewish Catholic Couples Dialogue Group. At around the same time, David Kovacs, one of the founders of JCDG, asked Rabbi Secher to become their Jewish adviser, working with Father Cusick to care for the interfaith flock. Rabbi Secher invited interfaith families to be full participants in his Jewish Renewal congregation, Makom Shalom, even while they attended the interfaith Family School and Mass at Old Saint Pat's on Sunday mornings. Although Rabbi Secher has now retired to Montana, he continues to return to Chicago to officiate at interfaith life-cycle rituals.

Reflecting on his long career involving everything from civil rights activism to producing Jewish children's television programming to becoming a circuit rider as the only rabbi in the state of Montana, Rabbi Secher says that working with interfaith families "is probably the most important work I've done in the rabbinate, because it's been to embrace these couples, rather than send them away. To show them that Judaism can be a positive thing in their lives, without saying Judaism is the only path."

His rabbinical colleagues have not always appreciated Rabbi Secher's interfaith work. "I'll tell you the image I use," says Rabbi Secher. "I go to a meeting of the Chicago board of rabbis, and the meeting is on the eightieth floor of the Sears Tower. When I walk into the room, suddenly the Sears tower tilts at 20 degrees, because every rabbi in the room moves to the far side so they won't be infected by me."

Those who dare to approach him often tell him what they think in no uncertain terms. "I've been asked to back off. I've been told, 'Look what you're doing to Judaism,' and so on," sighs Rabbi Secher. He recalls mentioning the Interfaith Family School to a rabbi known as an expert in the sociology of American Judaism: "He said to me, 'You can't do that.' I said, 'What do you mean you can't do that?' He said, 'A child can't be raised in two traditions.' I said, 'Why not?' He said, 'They'll be confused.' I said, 'Why do you think that?' He said, 'Statistics show it.' I said, 'Show me the statistics. There are no statistics at all.'"

Father John Cusick:
"Why Don't We Look at It as a Double Blessing?"

Almost twenty-five years ago, two young couples came separately to the Reverend Father John Cusick, director of the Archdiocesan Office of Young Adult Ministry in Chicago, to inquire about starting a support group for Jewish and Catholic couples. Father Cusick and Father Dan Montalbano, archdiocesan director of Catholic-Jewish Relations, provided Catholic guidance, along with Father Bernie Pietrzak. A steady stream of intermarried couples discovered the Jewish Catholic Couples Dialogue Group when they were referred by the Catholic Church's required Pre-Cana counseling for engaged couples.

Jewish and Catholic couples often must contend with family and friends who have outdated information about Catholic restrictions on intermarriage. In fact, intermarriage is allowed, and only the Catholic partner is now asked to sign a commitment about raising children. That commitment is worded very carefully, explains

Father Cusick: "No non-Catholic can be asked to promise anything. The promise is asked of the Catholic. And the promise is, Will you do all in your power to baptize and share your religion with your children? Well, of course people are going to do that."

In other words, this promise does not preclude Jewish partners from also sharing their religion with the children. Father Cusick maintains that he is not unduly worried about the identity of the children given this interfaith education. "Why wouldn't we look at it as a double blessing instead of a problem?" he asks.

Father Cusick admits he knew nothing about Judaism, growing up in an era of religious and racial segregation in Chicago. "There was no diversity in my life growing up: I lived in a 98 percent Catholic neighborhood," he recalls. "I never met a Jew until I was twenty years old." But through his work with interfaith families, he developed a deep friendship with Rabbi Allen Secher. "Allen and I would go out for breakfast and pick a topic: say, death and dying. He would talk about it from a Jewish perspective and I would offer my insights from a Catholic perspective," he recalls.

In advising couples and in-laws, Father Cusick and Rabbi Secher modeled their deep respect for each other. During these joint pastoral counseling sessions, "oftentimes, Secher would be the defender of the Catholic and I would be the defender of the Jew," laughs Father Cusick. "All of a sudden, out of the mouth of the rabbi, I would hear, 'Don't mess with their Catholicism.'"

Both the priest and the rabbi in this remarkable partnership insist that they are not watering down their religious practices, even while they innovate. At a First Communion for interfaith children, they sat the children at a long table, surrounding the priest and rabbi, so that they would understand the connection between a Passover seder and the Last Supper. When I asked Father Cusick the meaning or context for a Communion with interfaith children, he paused at first, taken aback. "The context is sharing the body and blood of Christ," he stated firmly. And then added, "The first time we did it, Allen Secher leans over to me, and he says, 'This is a Catholic moment, don't water it down.' That came from the rabbi. I've tried hard to celebrate and maintain Catholic moments and in a dual-faith context, I think that's very important."

Father Cusick stresses all that the two traditions share, as well as the tragic history that has kept them apart for so long. "Look at the religious symbols we have in common," he says. "We use water, we use salt, we use bread, we use wine. Once someone does not have to be the enemy and we don't have to prove we're right and they're wrong, this opens up a whole different approach."

The emphasis on the primacy of love across religious lines has had a strong impact on the clergy as well as on the families. "I had Allen Secher say a blessing at my mother's funeral," recalls Cusick. "There was a Catholic bishop sitting there, and I said, 'Keep sitting, I've got a rabbi to do this.'"

The admiration is mutual. Says Rabbi Secher: "One of the great joys of my life is my friendship with Cusick." In fact, the rabbi has asked his friend the priest to preach at his own memorial service. Secher says, "He's the best preacher in Chicago—priest, minister, rabbi—he has no peer."

Father Cusick acknowledges that not everyone experiences or responds to the deep pull that pluralism exerts on him. "My tragedy is I'm a dreamer," he says. "I believe in the continuing ongoing creation of the world. I believe God's not done with us yet. These are amazing moments when we're learning to live with diversity."

SEARCHING AND QUESTIONING

Each of these clergy members testifies to the inspiring nature of working with interfaith families. Discovering that this pathway can be more than just a "better than nothing" compromise, they have been moved and revitalized by the work and by working in partnership with clergy from other faiths. These partnerships benefit the clergy, the families, and the broader community.

Reverend Heather Kirk-Davidoff views interfaith families as embodying the essence of biblical quest: "I don't think religion is about resolution, or answers," she explains. "Religion provokes searching and questioning. An encounter with the divine, however you want to construe that, often shows up as unrest, as disturbance. When God encounters somebody, the result is movement: 'Abraham, go to this new land!' That's essentially what everyone has to do—leave where you are, go somewhere else. This is not the story of searching and searching, finding God, and then going and resting. That story is not in the Bible. The story in the Bible is: 'I'm all set, I'm good, God encounters me, and it screws my life up—I have to move, encounter challenge or difficulty, take on an insurmountable task.' That's the process, the model, of the experience of faith in the Bible."

CHAPTER SEVEN

Baptism, Bris, and Baby-Welcoming

W HEN MY CHILDREN WERE born, I had no religious community. During my first years of motherhood, we were living in Brazil, far from family and close friends. At the time, I was still trying to shake off the dominant "choose one religion" mentality. Since we had not chosen a single religion for our daughter or son and lacked the support of an interfaith community, I did not feel we had the right to religious celebration of their births. In any case, I knew that it would be difficult to find Jewish clergy to officiate at a bris or Jewish baby-welcoming celebration for children with only one Jewish grandparent. And since I had been raised without any religious instruction in Christianity, I did not feel comfortable with the Episcopal baptism service, which seemed to include a promise to raise the children solely as Episcopalians.

Now, after almost fifteen years of joyous involvement in an interfaith community, I see this issue through a completely different lens. We welcome babies into our community in a group ceremony each spring. We have clergy to support families whether they choose to have a baptism, a bris, or an independent and individual baby-welcoming ceremony drawing on both traditions. If I were to have a baby now, I would celebrate the event with gusto, drawing on all the Jewish and Christian rituals and liturgy in our family tree.

I believe that the birth of an interfaith child is cause for celebration. By incorporating both traditions into a creative baby-welcoming or by choosing to have both traditional rituals, couples communicate their intent to raise a child in two religions, while educating family and friends about the possibility and the beauty of interfaith life.

TRADITIONS FOR WELCOMING BABIES

Most religions welcome babies with some sort of ritual. In Jewish tradition, boys have a bris, the circumcision ceremony performed on the eighth day of life to affirm the covenant Abraham made with God in Genesis. (The Gospel of Luke describes the circumcision of the baby Jesus on his eighth day. This can be a total revelation to Jews who do not realize the gospels attest to Jesus's Judaism.) At the bris, a Jewish boy also receives his Hebrew name.

Jewish sacred texts do not require a welcoming ceremony for girls, but even in ancient times, the birth of a Jewish girl was announced to the community. Trees were planted in celebration of the birth of all children (cedar for a boy, cypress for a girl). When the child married, the tree would be cut down and carved into the poles that hold up the wedding canopy, or chuppah.

In the twentieth century, a ceremony for Hebrew baby-naming evolved for both genders. Boys (usually at a bris and baby-naming performed together) and girls (at the baby-naming) receive a Hebrew name that ties them to their Jewish ancestry. These ceremonies may include a blessing over wine, wrapping the baby in the tallit, touching the hand of the baby to a Torah scroll, and prayers of thanksgiving for the safe birth.

Religious historians theorize that Christian baptism (which involves immersion in, pouring, or sprinkling of water) evolved from the Jewish purification ritual of immersion in a *mikveh*, a pool or bath of natural water. Converts to Judaism immerse in the *mikveh* as their final act in the conversion process. John the Baptist (a cousin of Jesus and a born Jew) made immersion in water the central ritual of his practice, which of course predated the evolution of formal Christianity as a religion separate from Judaism.

For Christians, the intent and meaning of christening or baptism varies according to denomination. In biblical times, infants were not regularly baptized. Some denominations, including Quakers, do not baptize at all. Baptists, Mennonites, and many Pentecostal churches practice believer's baptism, in which children are baptized only once they are of an age to understand and accept faith in Jesus. For some denominations, baptism is required for salvation; for others, baptism simply marks membership in the denomination.

Denominations that practice infant baptism include Catholicism and many mainline Protestant churches (including Episcopal, Presbyterian, Methodist, and Lutheran). But the meaning of baptism varies even among these denominations. While the Catholic Church urges baptism, there is no official teaching on what happens to the soul of infants who die before baptism. The common conception that they go to "limbo," a place that is neither heaven nor hell, was never official church doctrine. And in general, the Catholic Church has shifted away from the idea that the unbaptized would be condemned to hell in the afterlife.

For Muslim newborns, welcoming rituals include the father whispering the call to prayer in the baby's ear and rubbing dates or other sweets on the baby's gums. The circumcision ritual known as Khitan is common among Muslims, although it is not mentioned in the Qur'an and is not performed on infants in every Muslim subculture. Circumcision occurs on the seventh day and may involve a naming ceremony and the sacrifice of a sheep to feed the poor.

Some Muslims and Hindus have a tradition of shaving the baby's head on the seventh day. Hindu baby-welcoming ceremonies vary, depending on the ethnic group, but traditionally also include bathing in ritual water and receiving a name. So across the religions of the world, we see common elements—the centrality of water, the importance of naming. Parents can draw on these common elements in creating an interfaith welcoming ceremony.

A CATHOLIC AND JEWISH CEREMONY

Is it possible to have both a Catholic baptism and a Hebrew baby-naming? The answer is yes, whether the rituals are separate or combined. Finding clergy to support you may be challenging, but many families have done it. Connecting to an established interfaith families community, with clergy experienced in officiating at such ceremonies, obviously helps.

For at least twenty years now, interfaith couples in Chicago have been welcoming babies with organized religious rituals combining Catholic baptism and Jewish baby-naming. In 1980, the Catholic Church issued instructions clarifying that the sacrament of baptism can be given to the child of a family if there is "any pledge giving a well-founded hope for the Christian upbringing of the children." In the Jewish Catholic Couples Dialogue Group, many parents interpret a sincere desire to raise children with both Catholicism and Judaism as fulfilling this pledge. In 1991, they began celebrating the birth of interfaith children with a Catholic priest and a rabbi co-presiding.

Rabbi Allen Secher co-officiated with Father John Cusick in those very first baptism/baby-naming rituals. Secher recalls how they developed a liturgy for the first such ceremony. "We did the world's longest baby-naming/baptism, because we didn't want to leave out anything," he says. "I must admit that at the first one, when he did 'in the name of the Father, the Son, and the Holy Spirit,' and made the sign of the cross over the baby, I had difficulty with it. But my attitude was, 'This is their child, not mine, and it's for them to make decisions as to how to raise the child. I can be there to be a comfort to them and to make suggestions, but it's their decision. I can bring to it everything that Judaism does.'"

After that first experience, Rabbi Secher and Father Cusick developed a fifteen-minute ceremony, more reasonable for a new mother to stand through. They found that in some cases, the family did not want an official baptism included, but the clergy still talked about the importance of water to life, and to both traditions.

Eileen O'Farrell Smith, founder of Chicago's Interfaith Union, has written an entire book describing how and why these ceremonies evolved in Chicago, entitled *Making Our Way to Shore: An Interfaith Guide to Baby Naming and Baptism*. Smith's book includes a sample service for a ceremony; chapters on the meaning and content of Jewish bris and baby-naming ceremonies, and the meaning and content of Catholic baptism; and a transcribed conversation between priests and a rabbi who perform these ceremonies. The Interfaith Union now schedules baby-naming/baptisms at three different houses of worship on dates throughout the year, with two priests and two rabbis on the roster to co-officiate.

THE ROLE OF COMMUNITY

For many clergy, a baby-naming or baptism is intended to welcome a child into a specific religious community. From this perspective, the idea of a private baby-naming or baptism or christening makes little sense. "The community needs to be part of the experience," says Reverend Julia Jarvis of IFFP. "When we are asked to do private ceremonies, I always ask that they include the community.

To me it means being embraced by a community in which you are going to raise this child."

And yet, interfaith families sometimes feel forced into a private ceremony, especially if they do not have the support of family or institutions in welcoming the baby into both religions, or into a religion different from the one expected by family and institutions. At speaking engagements, when I tell the story of my own secret baptisms, I am always surprised by how many other adult interfaith children experienced covert baptizing by loving and well-intentioned family members. One couple confided to me that they had given their child both a bris and a private christening, but that the Jewish grandparents had never been told about the christening.

For Reverend Jarvis, the group ceremony for welcoming babies to the IFFP community each spring has tremendous spiritual significance precisely because it takes place with the whole community in attendance. All of the babies who have been born or who have joined the community in the past year gather with their parents. Some have already had a bris, a Hebrew naming ceremony, a baptism, and/or an individual interfaith baby-welcoming ceremony with family and friends. But the group ceremony welcomes each of these babies into the community, no matter what religious label their parents have chosen for them, and in so doing, recognizes the bond they share. Someday they will enter the religious education program as classmates, and this is their first ritual as an age cohort.

The group ceremony begins with the Interfaith Responsive Reading (included in chapter 2), affirming the sense of community. Next comes the Lord's Prayer and the *Sh'ma*, the central prayer of each tradition represented by these families. Then, four community members hold up a tallit, and the babies and parents crowd underneath it, echoing the ritual of the wedding chuppah. Rabbi White recites the *Shehecheyanu*, the Jewish prayer of thanks for reaching any milestone or holiday. Next, the community reads from Genesis of the promise to Abraham to make his descendants as numerous as grains of sand on the shore.

Reverend Jarvis touches each baby's eyes, ears, nose, and mouth with a daisy. Often the fussiest babies go quiet at the tickle of the petals as the community reads:

> *Bless our children's minds with intelligence and wisdom.*
> *Bless their eyes so they will see great vistas.*
> *Bless their noses with delicious and fragrant aromas.*
> *Bless their mouths for the enjoyments of tasting and talking.*
> *Bless their hearts with deep love and a strong steady beat.*
> *Bless their arms for embracing friendship and love.*
> *Bless their feet so they will carry them happily through their days.*

Finally, both the rabbi and the minister whisper blessings into the ears of each baby. When these young families return to their seats, each baby clutches a daisy—a small reminder that each new interfaith child will be not just tolerated, or grudgingly accepted, or allowed to participate with qualifications but nurtured in this community as a creation as perfect as any flower.

SEPARATE OR COMBINED CEREMONIES

For some couples, the group ceremony is enough. But many couples also want individual interfaith ceremonies in order to give thanks for the safe arrival of a newborn without waiting for the annual group ceremony and to celebrate with family. The intent of these rituals is not to promise to raise the child in one religion exclusively, but rather to promise to raise the child with an education in both. "Of course, I believe that all faith traditions are just different languages for mysteries for which we have no words," says Reverend Ellen Jennings, a former IFFP staff member. "So, blessing babies in more than one 'language' just seems so lovely and complex and real."

Before designing an interfaith welcoming ceremony, clergy urge the couple to examine their own feelings about the traditions for newborns. "The most important thing is to find out what each ritual means to them personally and then try to support both of them," Reverend Jarvis says. " You both need to decide what a bris means, and what a baptism means, to you. If it doesn't mean you're saving the baby, or making it Christian, then that relieves the Jewish parent. And then we can also talk about what it has meant historically, how the ritual came about."

At one welcoming ceremony I attended for the baby of a Jewish and Catholic couple in our community, Reverend Jarvis blessed the baby in the name of God, the Son, and the Holy Ghost. Then Rabbi White pointed out the similarities between the Trinity and the three Jewish aspects of God—the Redeemer, the Revealer, and the Creator. In some interfaith baby-welcoming ceremonies, the baby will be anointed with oil by a minister or priest, rather than baptized with water. And once again, Rabbi White finds ample Jewish precedent for this ritual: "It's a Jewish concept: my cup runneth over, I anoint my head with oil."

Ultimately, as interfaith children reach adulthood, they will seek out the religious rituals that they feel they need for membership, when and if they feel they need them, in order to join specific religious communities requiring these rituals. Joining certain Christian communities may require baptism, and unofficial baptisms like my own would not count. Joining certain Jewish communities may require full conversion, including not only immersion in the *mikveh* but also, in some cases, adult circumcision. Some parents want to provide these rites to prevent a child from having to undergo them in adulthood. Reverend Jarvis says she understands why interfaith couples may want to give their children this dual passport, stamped with the birth rituals for admission to both religions. She says, "If you have certain paperwork that can get you in, like a visa, and you need that to be able to get in, I don't feel judgmental about it."

Whether the baptism, baby-naming, or bris is formal or informal, public or private, it is essential that interfaith children understand that their religious identity is neither dictated nor limited by rituals performed at their birth. For some interfaith families from a Protestant background, the model of only baptizing adults or older children when they reach an age of reason and consent may make a lot of sense. However, waiting for formal baptism does not preclude having a ritual welcoming a newborn.

Having a baptism at birth does not prevent someone from identifying as Jewish and joining a Jewish community later in life. This point may seem obvious, yet I have met interfaith parents who struggle with the misunderstanding that their children will somehow never be able to be Jewish if they are baptized. Jews do not believe that baptism automatically makes a Jew into a Christian; on the contrary, they do not believe it has any effect on the child. Rabbi White explains, "So many Jews were baptized against their will over the centuries that it was decided that baptism did not negate their Jewish identity." Likewise, there is nothing to stop someone who has been given a Hebrew name at birth, or even had a ritual circumcision in the Jewish or Muslim tradition, from later choosing to identify as a Christian, or a Hindu, or a Buddhist.

THE CIRCUMCISION DEBATE

For young couples still finding their way along an interfaith pathway, the circumcision decision can be fraught with tension. Even among Jews, resistance to circumcision goes back at least to the birth of Reform Judaism in Germany in the early nineteenth century. At that time, the founders of the movement called circumcision barbaric and rejected it (along with kosher laws and the use of Hebrew in the liturgy). In the twentieth century, American Reform Judaism gravitated back toward more traditional ritual, including circumcision. Today, even as world health experts promote circumcision, a small but growing number of Jews want to replace this ritual with a symbolic recognition of the covenant called the *brit shalom* (covenant of peace), involving no cutting. Humanistic Judaism holds that circumcision is not necessary for Jewish identity, and there are even groups in Israel pushing to abolish the practice.

For an intermarried parent who is not Jewish or Muslim, it can be particularly difficult to submit infant sons to circumcision at a time when Americans are shifting away from it. On the other hand, forgoing circumcision may feel to an interfaith couple like a luxury they cannot afford if they want their child to be able to claim a Jewish identity. For a child who may someday convert to Conservative or Orthodox Judaism, it is obviously beneficial to have been circumcised as an infant, rather than face a more traumatic adult circumcision under general anesthesia. Reform and Reconstructionist Jews, on the other hand, do not require adult converts to undergo circumcision.

THE BAPTISM DEBATE

Baptism can be an equally fraught issue for interfaith couples. For Reverend Heather Kirk-Davidoff, deciding with her Jewish husband whether or not to baptize their future children created what she describes as "the biggest crisis" of their interfaith marriage. As a minister ordained in the United Church of Christ (UCC), she explains: "The reason why I really wanted to have them baptized was that, in the UCC, Communion is open to all baptized Christians." She was afraid her own children—a minister's children, at that—would feel excluded if they weren't baptized and could not come up to take Communion.

Meanwhile, Reverend Kirk-Davidoff's husband bridled at the idea of submitting infants to baptism. "Dan was like, 'Just let the kids decide. We don't need to make this decision for them. They can get baptized anytime; don't force this on a baby.'" As a result of this impasse, in her first year as a minister Reverend Kirk-Davidoff did a lot of thinking and reading about baptism. "There's a very good argument for not having infant baptism, in terms of actual historical Christianity," she decided. "Jesus is baptized as an adult."

Finally, she told her husband she would agree not to baptize the children. But as so often happens with interfaith relationships, in a twist reminiscent of an O. Henry story, her husband had worked his way around by then to agreeing to the baptism of their three children. And so they were, in fact, baptized. Around the same time, the children also had Jewish baby-naming ceremonies.

INTERFAITH CHILDREN RESPOND
TO THEIR BIRTH RITUALS

In surveying the teens and young adults raised in interfaith family communities, more than a third of them reported having a bris or Jewish baby-naming, about 20 percent a baptism in a church, almost 20 percent an informal baptism by a family member or friend, and about a quarter of them an interfaith baby-welcoming ceremony or a combination bris and baptism. Some reported having both Jewish and Christian, or formal and informal, or separate and combined ceremonies, thus the total is more than 100 percent. But almost a third of them had no knowledge of any ritual at birth.

In the survey, I asked teens and young adults how they felt about the rituals they did or did not have at birth. The only respondent who expressed regret was a sixteen-year-old atheist from Chicago, who had both a baptism and a Jewish baby-naming. She wrote, "I am not comfortable with my baptism; I wish my parents did not do it." A twenty-one-year-old from Washington who describes herself as Jewish and had no birth rituals says, "I'm fine not having had them." And a twenty-year-old from Chicago, now identified as Jewish, who had both a church baptism and a bris, wrote: "Not knowing what the future held, I am glad that I was welcomed into both religious communities at birth."

Although a child will not remember a ritual from infancy, it may have a positive effect to know, later in life, that his or her parents marked the arrival of an interfaith child into the world with community and joy. We want our children to know that they have always been a cause for celebration, a harmonic interfaith chord, rather than cause for conflict or discord.

CHAPTER EIGHT

Coming of Age

Cultures around the globe celebrate adolescence as a primal rite of passage. In this spirit, interfaith families can draw on rituals from both religions to celebrate the complex inheritance of their children as they enter adulthood as part of the extended interfaith tribe. Adolescence is a threshold, a liminal state of being both child and adult, and I am attracted to the rich complexity of this bothness. For me, that exquisite moment when an interfaith child comes of age provides a first opportunity for that child to stand up before family, friends, and community and feel the joy of creating and leading rituals that transcend boundaries. In this chapter, parents and children describe the different choices they have made to mark coming of age in interfaith families, providing inspiration for noting the adolescent rite of passage.

COMING OF AGE IN JUDAISM AND CHRISTIANITY

Most movements of Judaism now encourage all children to mark the moment of becoming a bar or bat mitzvah (literally, a son or daughter of the commandment). When they reach the age of maturity (twelve for girls, thirteen for boys), they traditionally become responsible for adhering to Jewish law (fasting on Yom Kippur, for instance), whether or not there is an official ceremony.

The idea of a bar or bat mitzvah ceremony (beyond the usual Shabbat liturgy) and the elaborate celebration that often follows do not stem from Hebrew scriptures; in fact, they are relatively recent inventions. Starting in the Middle Ages, this milestone began to be recognized by calling a boy who turned thirteen up to the bimah (pulpit) for his first *aliyah* (the blessing before and after a portion of the Torah reading). Even more recently, the tradition expanded to involve reading the Torah portion itself, reading the *haftarah* (a secondary reading from the book of Prophets), giving a speech (a *d'var torah*) analyzing the Torah portion, and leading many of the Shabbat prayers.

In the late twentieth century, a parallel celebration for girls, the bat mitzvah, became popular in America. Today, even many Orthodox Jews mark the arrival of girls at the age to assume the "yoke of the commandments," although traditional Orthodox women do not get up in front of the congregation to read from the Torah. A form of bar or bat mitzvah can also be found in Secular Humanist Judaism, although God is not mentioned and the Torah is not involved. Meanwhile, many rabbis, parents, and even teens are now rebelling against the recent evolution of elaborate themed mitzvah celebrations (think monogrammed bootie-shorts in swag-bags and hired "animators" to get the guests dancing).

In Christianity, adolescent rites of passage vary with the denomination. In Roman Catholicism, children receive the sacrament of First Holy Communion at the age of discretion, usually seven or eight. The sacrament of Confirmation at age fourteen or fifteen marks entry into adulthood in the Church. The ritual includes both anointment with holy oil and the laying-on of hands, in order to receive the Holy Spirit.

Protestant denominations vary greatly in the specific rituals performed and the exact meaning of "confirmation." For many denominations, the group rite of confirmation serves as a mature statement of faith and entry into full membership in the church as the child comes of age. However, denominations such as the Baptists, who do not practice infant baptism and instead practice believer's baptism, do not have confirmation, since anyone who is baptized is already a full member.

Catholic youth and many mainline Protestant youth take a rigorous course of study in order to prepare for group confirmation with classmates in their age cohort. Unitarian Universalist communities have developed Coming of Age programs, in which youth ages twelve and up are paired with adult mentors, culminating in a group ceremony in which they make a statement of personal belief as they enter the adult community. And many Secular Humanist and Ethical Culture communities have similar programs involving years of preparation.

GROUP INTERFAITH COMING-OF-AGE CEREMONIES

Drawing on Jewish, Christian, Unitarian, and Secular Humanist traditions, interfaith groups around the country have each developed slightly different ways of approaching coming-of-age rituals. Interfaith communities with large enrollments (including Washington, Chicago, and some of the New York programs) now have group ceremonies for students who have completed the formal interfaith education program. Surrounded by interfaith elders, the graduates acknowledge the role of both religions in their lives.

In the survey, three-quarters of the interfaith youth who responded to a question about coming-of-age rituals said they had participated in these group ceremonies. More than half also had individual bar or bat mitzvahs or individual interfaith coming-of-age or interfaith bar mitzvah ceremonies. About a quarter of them reported having a First Communion, reflecting the fact that only a portion of Christian parents in interfaith communities are Catholic, and that only the Chicago group provides clergy support for a First Communion specifically for interfaith children. Only one survey respondent had a Catholic Confirmation (though many other interfaith children raised in these groups have had confirmations).

For families who decide not to have a bar mitzvah or a Christian confirmation, the group ceremony can provide a satisfying way to welcome teens as adults into the community. These children understand that they can choose to have a bar mitzvah or be confirmed as Christians, should they so choose, at any time later in life. Jacob Gulezian, twenty, said, "I opted out of a bar mitzvah. My parents gave me the choice. I didn't have any family pressure to do it. With the [IFFP] group Coming of Age, I felt that was sufficient for me to feel like I'm now part of this community."

Clergy working with interfaith youth testify to the unique benefits of group ceremonies. "Interfaith or not, it's key for youth to know they are an important and supported part of a larger, multigenerational community," says Reverend Ellen Jennings. "And, perhaps especially for interfaith youth, it's important for them to know they have peers who are on a similar path, with similar family stories and traditions and similar challenges and blessings."

In the IFC in the New York area, twelve- to fourteen-year-olds go through a two-year program called Identity and Transition, designed specifically to explore religious identity and spiritual development and culminating in a group commencement ceremony. At IFFP as well, seventh- and eighth-graders spend two years immersed in a coming-of-age curriculum. Each student chooses a mentor and a project with a community service component. At the group ceremony each May, the community recognizes that these students have reached physical maturity, passed through the K–8 dual-faith education program and reached an age when they must draw on learned ethical principles in order to take responsibility for their own actions.

At a recent IFFP Coming of Age ceremony, each teen spoke to the community about his or her own spiritual journey. One young man described his influences in the Christian, Jewish, and secular worlds, citing Martin Luther King Jr., the Sermon on the Mount, Mother Teresa, Anne Frank, Shakespeare, and the Torah. His summation: "Both religions have a lot to teach the world." Another teen concluded: "I don't have the answers, but now I have a better idea of what the questions are." A third challenged the idea that there could be one true religious pathway: "What if you lived life as a kind person in one religion and then died and found out you should have been a Catholic? . . . If life is all about choosing the right God, then life has a few flaws."

Then, together, the community celebrated the shared ethical heart of Jewish and Christian traditions. The rabbi chanted the Ten Commandments from a torah that survived the Holocaust. The minister read the words of Jesus on the two greatest commandments ("Love God" and "Love thy neighbor as thyself"), from the Gospel of Mark. In conclusion, Coming of Age teacher Rob Liebreich explained to the assembled families that these teens, while often skeptical and oppositional in an age-appropriate fashion, still have faith. He concluded, "It may not be the faith you want them to have, but it's theirs."

INDIVIDUAL COMING-OF-AGE CEREMONIES

Both our children went through the group Coming of Age ceremony with their IFFP classmates. But for some families, this community process is more akin to Christian confirmation than it is to a bar mitzvah, and it is not enough. Each year, some of the families in our community elect to also create an individual ceremony built on the bar mitzvah framework. My family chose that route. We wanted our children to learn Shabbat prayers, to affirm a deep connection to Judaism, and to have the formative experience of standing up and leading a service. And we wanted to provide an opportunity to bring the generations of our family and friends together, to *kvell* (gush with pride) and dance a joyful hora while also sharing with extended family the powerful experience of our inclusive community.

Our intent in choosing a bar mitzvah model was not to strengthen the Jewish identity of our children at the expense of their Christian identity. Rather, we wanted our children pushed to master Hebrew literacy: a fundamental skill for both Jews and for the most learned Christian clergy members. And we wanted to counterbalance a lifetime of immersion in American Christian culture with a strong dose of Jewish learning delivered through the classical relationship between rabbi and pupil. We know that if our children choose to be practicing Christians, they can show up at almost any church and be welcomed and quickly absorbed into the community. And we also know that if they choose to be practicing traditional Jews, rudimentary Hebrew and knowledge of the Shabbat prayers gained through the bar or bat mitzvah process will prove tremendously helpful to them in advocating for themselves as Jews or in undergoing the rigorous conversion process.

Part of the joy of designing an individual ceremony is the complete freedom to make every element meaningful. The ceremony may or may not involve a Torah reading, and the young person leading the ceremony may or may not read in Hebrew from the Torah. A rabbi, minister, or priest, or any combination thereof might officiate. The ceremony might take place in a borrowed sanctuary (often Unitarian Universalist) or at home, or in a community center or hotel ballroom (as in the case of many bar or bat mitzvahs). And the family is free to label the ceremony as a bar or bat mitzvah—or not.

At the ceremonies for our children, my husband and I stood up and spoke to them in front of friends and family about who they are, our pride in them, their role in the world. Our children then stood and learned that they can be poised and articulate in front of our community. They saw that their family—their Jewish family and their Christian family—will go to great lengths to be with them at important moments in their lives. Our intention was for our son and daughter to connect to the ancient traditions of Judaism (and by definition, the Christianity that sprang from Judaism) and feel the continuity of the generations flow through them. And we wanted them to claim all this and experience the beauty of such a ceremony, no matter what we label it and no matter what others might say or think about it all.

I was an introverted child, terrified at thirteen by the prospect of getting up and leading a congregation in prayer. But I remember, precisely because it was such a stretch for me, how much I seemed to mature in the process of becoming a bat mitzvah. On the other hand, my mother has never forgotten, or forgiven, the agony my dyslexic brother went through to learn his Torah portion in Hebrew. From her point of view as someone raised Christian, learning to read a language that you cannot actually understand, and memorizing a portion you will probably never read again, seemed punitive and unreasonable.

Our daughter Aimee saw the value of learning more of the Shabbat prayers used in a synagogue, including the prayers before and after the reading of the Torah portion. If she becomes a practicing Jew, these prayers will serve her in good stead every week throughout her life, anywhere in the world. And learning these prayers would move her in the direction of "being comfortable in a synagogue," a goal we have as parents and as interfaith communities.

On the other hand, she decided not to read or recite her Torah portion in Hebrew. The academic feat of memorizing or deciphering the vowel-free handwritten Hebrew from the Torah itself is not required in order to count as a bat mitzvah. For those of us who are interfaith children with Jewish fathers, the relatively recent evolution of the elaborate bar or bat mitzvah ritual makes it all the more ironic that Reform Jewish communities now virtually require the ceremony as proof that an interfaith child is being raised Jewish.

Aimee preferred to read her Torah portion in English, a decision that felt very organic to our interfaithness. It honored her Jewish ancestors, the Classical Reform Jews who preferred English liturgy in temple. And, at least half of those celebrating with us—half of our IFFP community, extended families and friends—would be Christian. In this context, reading the central Torah portion in English felt like an act of inclusion.

We also freely adapted the bar mitzvah tradition by choosing the Torah portion. Torah readings are usually assigned according to the week of the year, since the Torah is read chronologically. But our rabbi encouraged Aimee to choose a portion that would be meaningful, looking through the weeks near her birthday to find a portion that would speak to her.

This may seem like an unfair picking and choosing. And I know that some adults derive keen pleasure from the intellectual challenge of drawing meaning from even the most "problematic" portions of the Torah, the paradoxes that Buddhists might call *koans*. And yet each of the modern Jewish movements (Conservative, Reform, Reconstructionist, Renewal) strives to make Judaism relevant and more deeply spiritual through a selective curating and reimagining of ancient traditions.

Aimee found a Torah portion that spoke directly to interfaith families: the story of Jethro visiting his son-in-law, Moses. In her *d'var torah*, she explained, "Moses was married to a woman named Zipporah who was a Midianite—therefore they were an interfaith couple. When Zipporah's father, Jethro, comes to visit, it is fascinating to find out that everyone worshipped together that night, with Jethro respecting the Jews' practices although they were not his beliefs." Aimee used the scene between Moses and Jethro as a springboard to describe her own spiritual quest: "I learn about both Judaism and Christianity without the ropes that your parents use to bind you to one or the other. I feel very free."

In my own words to Aimee at the ceremony, I made reference to the IFFP symbol, concluding: "You stand today surrounded by your many mentors from the Interfaith Families Project and your extended family. You are supported by all of these overlapping circles and by the interlocking circles of Jewish and Christian heritage. Today, you write your own history as an interfaith pioneer."

Aimee's ceremony had a lasting effect in terms of her self-confidence and familiarity with Jewish liturgy. Two years later, at a Yom Kippur service designed by our interfaith Teen Group, I watched her stand up and lead the Jewish call to prayer: "*Barchu et adonai hamvorach . . .*" Seeing her stride up to the front of the sanctuary, hearing her voice ring out with such assurance, thrilled me. On that day, I saw my own daughter made stronger by a day of fasting. I saw her as an adult endowed with spiritual insight and the gift of leadership.

Three years later, my son, Ben, chose to chant from the Torah with a tallit draped around his shoulders, flanked by two rabbis and my eighty-six-year-old father—his only Jewish grandparent. My daughter, the proud big sister, led us in the haunting melody of peace, "Oseh Shalom." Judaism's Hebrew liturgy has survived through the millennia, through the diaspora, through the Holocaust. When my children learned to decipher Hebrew and recite Hebrew prayers, they affirmed their connection to this powerful history. But all religions and rituals evolve over time, and Judaism is no different. In creating coming-of-age ceremonies that reflect the full heritage of my children, we realize that we are pushing boundaries.

We tried not to become paralyzed by the often-conflicting "requirements" for a bar mitzvah issued by various sages and authorities. I spent a lot of time fending off the "a bar mitzvah has to include such-and-such" statements. I helped each of my children craft a rite of passage best suited to their own place in their spiritual journey. Our children transitioned into adulthood at the heart of an interfaith community. So the intent in their ceremonies was to be as welcoming, inclusive, personalized, and comprehensible as possible. When my children recited the *V'ahavtah*, we not only included the English translation ("Thou shalt love the Lord . . .") but explained in the program that this is the prayer from Deuteronomy found in every *mezuzah*, which, naturally, also meant explaining that a *mezuzah* is the case, containing the prayer scroll, affixed to the door of a Jewish household.

And we pointed out that the words in the *V'ahavtah*, "thou shalt teach them diligently to thy children," have special resonance for us as an interfaith family. My father married a Christian, but he made sure I learned this prayer. I married a Christian, but I made sure my children learned this prayer. Our family may be patrilineal renegades, wild and woolly, motley and mixed, outside the box and beyond the pale. Some think we are sadly mistaken. And yet we are serious and willing to put time and considerable effort into the religious education of our children.

Ironically, it was Rabbi Harold White who practically insisted we include in our son's ceremony the reading from the Gospel of Mark about how Jesus affirmed the centrality of the V'ahavtah as the greatest commandment: "Thou shalt love the Lord thy God . . ." The rabbi sees this passage as reflecting a deeply Jewish Jesus, a Jesus coming of age as he engages in lively debates with his Jewish elders. It seemed fitting that my husband's brother, who is studying for the Episcopal priesthood, gave that reading from Mark at Ben's ceremony.

And so the words of Jesus, noticeably absent at our wedding, were printed up in my son's bar mitzvah program. In that moment I felt I was growing and learning alongside my children, coming into my own as an interfaith adult, receiving permission to discuss how Judaism and Christianity are intertwined in my soul.

Other Christian elements in the service included readings by both Christian grandmothers and three Christian hymns related to the environmental theme of Ben's Torah portion. One was a Gospel solo sung by an African American friend. "Morning Has Broken" (a Christian hymn covered by Cat Stevens before his conversion to Islam) was led by our house band of friends, including one Sufi who was raised Christian, one agnostic Jew, one Buddhist Jew, and one intermarried pastor's daughter. And my Jewish father pounded out the third Christian hymn on the grand piano.

It was my husband, Paul, who came up with the idea of asking Reverend Julia Jarvis to give her final blessing during a laying on of hands in which every person in the room connected physically to the people around them, and ultimately to our son. While this ritual may be most familiar to Christians, from the ordination of clergy and confirmation of adolescents, it has roots, like so much else in Christianity, in Judaism. In Genesis, Jacob lays hands on his grandsons as he blesses them, and Jewish parents remember this by blessing their children on Shabbat, placing hands on their heads. So what may have seemed to some like a startling Christian element grafted onto a bar mitzvah to us felt like an appropriate acknowledgement of the echoes and synergies in the sibling relationship between these two Abrahamic faiths.

How often will my son use his new tallit? Or his uncle's gift of an Episcopal hymnal? He may continue to use both, or neither. Will my daughter make more use of the sonorous Buddhist meditation prayer bowl given to her by her godmother (herself the child of

Jewish and Christian parents)? None of us can know where life will lead our children. Children grow up and make their own choices, whether they are interfaith children or single-faith children. All we can do is prepare them with love and with deep knowledge of our own traditions.

WHAT DO WE CALL THE CEREMONY?

My daughter, Aimee, and her friend Sally had a joint ceremony, and the program read "Interfaith Coming of Age and Bat Mitzvah." We consciously chose that complex title to reflect our complex families. Jared McGrath, the son of a Catholic father and Jewish mother at IFFP, learned Hebrew with a private tutor and chanted a Torah portion at his ceremony. Jared invited the entire class from his Catholic school and his Catholic schoolteachers to the ceremony his family labeled an Interfaith Coming of Age. Jared admits that the unfamiliar label, while true to his interfaith identity, confused some guests.

He recalls, "They said, 'That was cool. I don't know what you called it,' even though it was right on the invitation and program: Coming of Age. Some people called it a bar mitzvah and sent money. Some people thought it was a birthday. They just totally didn't get it. One of my friends goes, 'This is weird because at your bar mitzvah, you read from the New Testament.' And I said, 'That's because it wasn't a bar mitzvah.' And the friend said, 'But you read Hebrew from the Torah. So why did you do both?' Sigh. 'Let me explain this again. My mom is Jewish, my dad is Christian. . . . '"

Jared remembers worrying about how Jewish and Catholic guests would react to his interfaith ceremony. "I was worried about stepping on someone's toes," he admits. At the same time, he sensed an opportunity to be a bridge-builder. "I knew I was in a unique one-time situation with my audience, and I knew that I wanted to prod people a little if I could. I remember looking hard to find things from the New and Old Testament that said the same thing, to put the common thread in front of people's eyes."

In the end, he received tremendous positive feedback. He explains, "You get over the initial idea of conflicting ideologies, or what people *consider* to be conflicting ideologies, clashing. You get past that to the truth at the heart of everything, which is that you're celebrating—the maturation of the person."

Those of us who design rituals for our interfaith children in adolescence are neither forging a third religion nor hiding safely in a "Kumbaya" common ground. We acknowledge the angular differences between our two religions, in the delicate politics of including Jesus in the ceremony and in the arduous hours our children spend learning the cantillation marks to guide the chanting of Torah. Our ceremonies honor the shared space, but also the particular beliefs and cultures and histories represented by all the grandparents and elders who stand up to support the children as they come of age.

COMMUNION AND CONFIRMATION

Some intermarried Catholics and some intermarried Protestants feel strongly about having their children make First Communion. In the Chicago groups, clergy support Catholic and Jewish children in undergoing any or all of the traditional rites, depending on the desires of the child or family, to demonstrate and deepen their commitment to one or both religions: a First Communion, then a bar or bat mitzvah, then some go on for Catholic Confirmation. Although designed specifically for interfaith children, the Chicago group's First Communion is clearly a Catholic ritual, with the rabbi there to say a blessing and represent the Jewish roots of the children. The bar mitzvah is clearly a Jewish ritual, with a priest there to say a blessing and represent the Catholic roots.

Demand from interfaith families first drove Rabbi Allen Secher and Father John Cusick in Chicago to design a First Communion for Catholic and Jewish children. "I said, 'Well, we don't have First Communion in Jewish tradition, nothing even close,'" recalls Rabbi Secher. "'Well,' they said, 'but we need a ceremony wherein there's participants from both traditions.' So Cusick and myself developed a ceremony. First Communion is decidedly a Catholic event, so we developed a Catholic event with some Jewish flavor. The priest ran the Communion with occasional participation from the rabbi. A few years later the group came back and said, 'Next step, bar mitzvah.' This is a Jewish event, there's nothing like it in Catholic tradition, so it will be an event slanted Jewish with Catholic participation. And when it comes time to bless the child, it comes from the two of us."

Eileen O'Farrell Smith, the Catholic founder of Chicago's Interfaith Union, recalls that her daughter Nora was the only one of her three children to choose to have a Catholic Confirmation. Even then, Nora paid tribute to her interfaith heritage by choosing to be confirmed using her Hebrew name. "She and the bishop had a field day with that," Eileen recalls. "But it was perfect."

In interviews and in the survey, adult interfaith children from Chicago who underwent these separate Jewish and Catholic rituals testified to their meaning. A young man who had a bar mitzvah, First Communion, and Catholic Confirmation and has now chosen to identify as Jewish reports, "The coming-of-age rituals were extremely instructive. It was the preparation and completion of these that guided me to the path I am on today." A young woman who had a bat mitzvah and First Communion wrote, "I felt that both were truly wonderful ceremonies, that I was blessed to be able to participate in both. Both had real meaning to me, and I learned a great deal about myself through them." And a teenage boy who had a bar mitzvah and First Communion wrote, "I feel honored to have participated in such sacred and ancient rituals. I feel it has truly brought me closer to my faith."

HOLDING OFF ON RITUALS

Some interfaith families prefer to hold off on specific religious rites of passage for adolescents. In the New York area's IFC, families tend to have individual bar or bat mitzvahs or Catholic Communion or Confirmation only if and when the child chooses a single religion. In a geographic area with deeply rooted Catholic and Jewish cultures, interfaith children may wrestle with the conflict between the strong expectations of family and friends and the decision to put off these rituals. But the struggle itself can lead to more clarity for interfaith adolescents about their own beliefs and commitments.

At a retreat with IFC students in the Identity and Transition program, teens from the various suburban New York chapters shared their feelings about going through this period as interfaith children. They were unanimously enthusiastic about their interfaith education program. But when asked about the disadvantages of being interfaith, the group often returned to the topic of coming-of-age rituals.

One boy explained, "I asked my mom, 'When am I going to have a ritual?' And my mom said, 'Well, you're both.' That was tough for me, and my friends would always be asking me and I didn't have much guidance about how to explain it to them. Now I can explain it better. I just think I'm both. I'm not going to dedicate to one religion just yet."

Another boy told this anecdote: "My friend asked me if there were any video games coming out that I liked. And I said, 'Sure, why?' And he said, 'Well isn't your bar mitzvah coming up?' And I said, 'No.' But, I guess since 99 percent of the kids in my school are Christian, they don't think of me as both; they think of me as Jewish."

Some of these New York families have been moving in the direction of creating individual interfaith coming-of-age ceremonies, like those that are more common in the Washington group. One thirteen-year-old described how she honored both her religions at her birthday: "I didn't have a bat mitzvah or a confirmation, but I had a big thirteenth birthday party. During the party I said some prayers in Hebrew and some Christian prayers."

One of the Identity and Transition leaders, considering the meaning of such a ritual for interfaith children, says, "Each individual is considering, 'Is it that I'm choosing one or the other, is it that I can be both, and do I have to make a choice?' All those questions have to be embedded into what that ritual will be. It has to be reflective of, 'Where is it that each individual is right now?'"

Another program leader, Anna DeWeese, notes that having to think about whether or not to participate in these rituals creates thoughtful adolescents: "I think they recognize that there's a lot of doing it 'just because,' and that answer is not satisfactory to them. I think the benefit for them is, it really trains them to what I like to think of as a healthy criticism of automatic response and automatic participation."

Pam Gawley, a leader of IFC's Long Island chapter, recalls how she and her husband, Steve, worked through these issues with their middle child: "Matthew came home and said, 'You know I feel really uncomfortable. Everyone goes to Hebrew school.' And I took that as, he definitely wants to be Jewish."

She continues, "So Steve said, 'Let's sit down and talk with Matthew and see what he says.' Steve said to him, 'Look, Matthew, if you feel more comfortable being one religion, and you want to have a bar mitzvah, I'll have one too, because I want to be the same as you, and maybe we'll just be a Jewish family that's still part of the interfaith community.' And Matthew said, 'Absolutely not. I'm interfaith. That's who I am, that's what I want to be.'"

Matthew's older sister, Michaela, sixteen, did enroll briefly as a preteen in a Hebrew school program, but she, too, decided she felt more comfortable in the interfaith community and had a group ceremony with her interfaith class instead. "The bar mitzvahs here are insane," she says. "In some ways I was relieved that I didn't have to have a bat mitzvah because there was no comparison of 'Why is hers bigger than mine? Why is hers more expensive?' But it was very hard. Every weekend you have a different bat mitzvah."

In the Westchester (New York) chapter of the IFC, Elizabeth Engel, fifteen, confirms the struggle. "We live in a very Jewish area, and when bar and bat mitzvah season rolled around, I felt kind of left out," she says. "At that point, what do I have to show for what I've been learning? Now, I'm not so jealous because I'm happy that I'm getting a continued education. I feel like sometimes when people are raised in one religion they take it for granted. I don't take it for granted that I have to identify with two religions—there's never a moment where I just don't care."

Elizabeth also articulates the way her interfaith education has prepared her to appreciate both Jewish and Christian rites of passage. "I feel like my Christian friends only know about Christianity and they go to people's bar or bat mitzvahs but have no idea what's happening, and they don't get it," she explains. "And I have Jewish friends who get invited to people's confirmations and think it's great but they don't get it. I can be happy for both my Jewish and Christian friends but also understand how significant it is."

In some cases, the clergy who work with interfaith families have no issue with multiple separate rituals. Reverend Allan Ramirez, who works with the IFC on Long Island says, "I have families who have baptism, and a Jewish baby-naming, and Communion, and a bar mitzvah. All of it comes naturally, because they've done it from the get-go. Some people will say, 'Isn't that confusing them?' And I say, 'No. You're confused, not the child. The child is accepting it.'"

Should a child be ready to make a commitment to one and only one religion in order to undergo a coming-of-age rite? I feel that the answer is no. Whether or not they have chosen a singular religious identity, if children want to deepen their connection to Judaism through a bar or bat mitzvah, or deepen their connection to Christianity through Christian rituals, I see that as a good thing. If they are more comfortable staying connected to both religions through a group or individual interfaith ceremony (whether it is called a coming of age or an interfaith bar mitzvah), I see that as a good thing, too.

Dual-Faith Education

B Y THE TIME AN adolescent comes of age in an interfaith community, he or she has been educated in both religions. But what does dual-faith education look like at the classroom level? And is it working? To begin to answer these questions, I considered the perspective of parents, students, clergy, and classroom teachers. Hearing from the teachers was particularly revealing, since they are pioneering the art of teaching two religions and mentoring interfaith students.

Most of the building blocks of an interfaith classroom would be familiar to anyone who attended Hebrew school or Sunday school. The students sing songs, put on plays, make craft projects, and do community service together. They listen to Bible stories, celebrate holidays, learn prayers and rituals and religious history, talk about how to do good in the world, and ponder the meaning of God and life.

The essential difference between dual-faith education and traditional single-faith education is that interfaith teachers do not insist that children affiliate with any single identity or believe in any specific creed or dogma. Instead, they point out both the commonalities and the differences between the two religions and guide interfaith children to feel positive about finding their own place in the religious universe.

THE GOALS OF INTERFAITH EDUCATION

Interfaith family communities around the country share many philosophical and educational goals. In the Washington, D.C., program, the stated goals include helping students appreciate their Jewish/Christian identity; supporting parents as primary religious educators; exploring student ideas about faith and God and prayer; celebrating holidays while teaching the history, stories, prayers, and rituals that go along with them; learning about the different denominations and branches of Judaism and Christianity; identifying values and developing the tools for ethical decision-making; and highlighting the importance of social justice in each tradition while giving students the opportunity to engage in acts of community service.

Each of the programs also has unique aspects. In Washington, all students begin Hebrew literacy in pre-kindergarten, and a dedicated music teacher visits each classroom in the younger grades. In New York, seminary students designed the curriculum and serve as teachers, deepening and enhancing theological discussions. In Chicago, the programs are designed specifically for Catholic and Jewish children and put special emphasis on understanding the historical tensions between Catholicism and Judaism.

For example, in Chicago, a description of the Interfaith Family School's seventh-grade curriculum, entitled A Time to Heal, covers history including medieval interfaith relations, the Holocaust, the creation of the state of Israel, and the Second Vatican Council. The curriculum notes, "By this point the students know that there have been problems between the two faiths in the past and in the present, but they do not fully know why." In a classroom with a Jewish and a Catholic teacher, interfaith students can attempt to understand this history in a safe and neutral space.

In New York, the IFC education goals include respect for religion in general, an appreciation of what is distinctive in Judaism and Christianity, encouragement for children to pursue their own spiritual journeys and develop their own concept of "the Divine," development of the values, ethics, and commitments that grow out of their Jewish and Christian heritages, and finding joy and delight in these heritages and practices. The emphasis on "joy and delight" serves as a powerful antidote to the usual pessimistic fretting about the fate of interfaith children.

HOW DO YOU TEACH TWO RELIGIONS AT ONCE?

A body of knowledge on how to teach interfaith children is just beginning to emerge. Reverend Ellen Jennings, former director of the education program at IFFP, writes, "there are as many ideas as there are human beings" when it comes to religious concepts such as miracles, the afterlife, or the human soul. "The truth is," she writes, "we're *never* going to reach agreement!" In response to this reality, she suggests that methodology is far more important than theology in the interfaith classroom.

Jennings counsels a three-step process, based in part on the "Godly Play" religious education curriculum derived from educator Maria Montessori's work. First, tell the story. "Stories do not have to be literally true or false," she reminds teachers and parents. Next, acknowledge that there is more than one answer, and always give the child a chance to share what he or she believes. Finally, answer questions with questions in order to "get the child to begin thinking for him/herself rather than being 'fed' answers by an authority figure."

Children are encouraged to ask their parents to describe their own beliefs, since, due to the diversity of actual beliefs even within a single movement or denomination, teachers cannot accurately state "If your mother is Jewish, she believes X" or "If your father is Christian, he believes Y." There is simply no way to generalize about the beliefs of a parent community that may include

Reconstructionist Jews, Greek Orthodox, and Buddhist Unitarian Universalists, among others.

In order to better understand the diversity on the Jewish and Christian spectrum, the sixth-grade students at IFFP spend the entire year investigating the various Jewish and Christian movements and denominations. They visit synagogues, Quaker meetings, gospel churches, and Catholic churches. They explore the specific religious traditions in their own family trees and share their findings with their classmates.

When my son was in this program, I encouraged him to do a report on the passionate Hasidic sect of Judaism. At the time, the popular reggae rapper Matisyahu was deep in a Hasidic phase. My son pulled up the music video of the hit song "King Without a Crown" for his classmates on a laptop and explained the messianic imagery for them. For months afterward, whenever he was in an adolescent funk, he would climb out his bedroom window onto the roof of our house with his guitar and strum Matisyahu's "One Day," a song filled with yearning for religious unity. I felt thankful that his interfaith education had pushed him to discover useful religious inspiration even in this rebellious period.

OPTIONS FOR ACCESSING DUAL-FAITH EDUCATION

For families that want to educate children in both Judaism and Christianity but do not live anywhere near one of the thriving interfaith education programs, the news that such programs exist may be inspiring but also frustrating. One alternative, albeit a time-intensive one, is homeschooling in two faiths. The importance of community may drive some families to seek interfaith education in a UU congregation or to start up an intentional interfaith community. Another option is to enroll children in two separate religious education programs, in a church and synagogue. However, not only does this approach require double the time and financial commitment, it may prove impossible to get cooperation from local institutions. Some families simply attempt to fly under the radar when enrolling children in two different programs. But even if they manage to gain acceptance for double enrollment, some children (and their parents) may find it difficult to interpret what may sound like two conflicting dogmas, without the help of teachers devoted to interfaith education.

Most Jewish communities will not educate children who are also being formally educated in a second religion, by policy. In 1995, the Union of American Hebrew Congregations (now the Union for Reform Judaism, or URJ) passed a resolution recommending that congregations draw up policies that offer enrollment in religious education programs at Reform synagogues and full-time day schools "only to children who are not receiving formal religious education in any other religion."

Ten years later, in an analysis of this resolution's effect, a URJ committee acknowledged that only some congregations had written the prohibition into their membership policies. Others were allowing interfaith children in the early grades to "try out" Judaism before asking the family to make an exclusive commitment. And still others adopted what the committee described as a "Don't Ask, Don't Tell" attitude toward children being educated in two religions. The committee urged congregations to make the prohibition of dual-faith education more explicit, noting, "If a congregation does not have a clearly articulated policy, many interfaith families may enroll in synagogue schools under the assumption that they can raise their child as both Christian and Jewish."

The update on the resolution quotes Proverbs: "Train a child in the direction to take, and when he is old, he will not depart from it." The choice of this verse ignores the reality, documented by the Pew Forum on Religion and Life, that almost half of all American adults change religious denomination at least once. It also ignores the complexity of familial, social, cultural, and institutional influences on the religious identity of adult interfaith children. Families that want Jewish education for their children will get it, whether they have to create interfaith communities, or homeschool, or "forget" to mention that they also take their children to another Sunday school. Refusing to allow children a Jewish education seems short-sighted, given the demographic rise of interfaith families.

DEVELOPING INTERFAITH CURRICULA

Over the years, the various interfaith education programs have cross-pollinated and drawn from Unitarian Universalist, Episcopalian, Reform Jewish, and Ethical Culture curricula, as well as a curriculum produced by the Jesus Seminar, an ecumenical group of scholars who study the historical Jesus. At the fifteenth anniversary celebration of IFFP, when parent Fredie Adelman wrote a reflection on her decade of teaching interfaith Sunday school, she quoted from nineteenth-century Unitarian theologian William Ellery Channing on the purpose of religious education:

> The great end in religious instruction, whether in Sunday school or in the family, is not to stamp our minds irresistibly on the young, but to stir up their own; not to make them see with our eyes, but to look inquiringly and steadily with their own; not to give them a definite amount of knowledge, but to inspire a fervent love of truth; not to form an outward regularity, but to touch inward springs . . .

It is no coincidence that interfaith families have for generations gravitated to Unitarian Universalism, with its embrace of theological diversity and absence of dogma, and have felt welcome there. The architect of much of the IFFP religious education program, Reverend Ellen Jennings, was hired away from IFFP to become a director of religious education at a UU community. Sharron

Mendel Swain, the godmother of my own daughter, and a Jewish and Christian interfaith child and former teen leader at IFFP, also now works as a UU director of religious education.

And yet, interfaith communities provide all content specifically tailored to interfaith children in a way that a UU community could not. Reverend Jennings explains some of the differences. "Unitarian Universalism tries to cover more," she says. "In my UU community, we had a three-year rotation of curriculum themes: one year on UU identity, one year on world religions not including Judaism and Christianity, and one year on Jewish and Christian heritage. So in one out of three years, the UUs were doing what IFFP is doing every single year."

Reverend Jennings points out the perhaps obvious fact that the amount of content one can teach about a particular religion in a finite period of time is in inverse proportion to the number of religions being taught. "At IFFP, are you getting the depth of Jewish education that a Hebrew school is able to provide? No. But are you covering a lot more in both Christianity and Judaism than the UUs typically do? Yes," she says.

Nevertheless, many interfaith couples feel drawn to the inclusivity of Universalism. Families that don't feel a strong need to pass on the specific and complex Jewish and Christian rituals of their ancestors and, in particular, those who want to primarily stress social justice themes shared by Judaism and Christianity may find a UU congregation to be a comfortable theological home.

WHO TEACHES INTERFAITH EDUCATION?

All major interfaith community education programs pair Jewish and Christian educators in the classrooms to provide both perspectives. These teachers together can access knowledge of both traditions while simultaneously modeling a collegial or even loving relationship across religious boundaries.

In Chicago, Washington, and California, parents teach the classes. There are many advantages to this: Since the teachers are themselves in interfaith families, they are acutely attuned to the benefits and challenges of interfaith life and they arrive convinced of the legitimacy of interfaith education since they have chosen this pathway. In some cases, married couples teach together, providing both religious perspectives while also being able to speak from their experiences as co-creators of an interfaith family. Parent teachers also increase the interconnectedness of the community, as children bond with adults who may become mentors in adolescence. And, the adults learn alongside—or just ahead of—the children, creating a more educated parent community. "We've had hundreds of Christian parents in our school who've learned a lot about Judaism, and that's cool," says David Kovacs, a founding member of the Chicago group. And the same is true for Jews learning about Christianity. Finally, when parents teach, it prevents the "drop the kids off and run errands" phenomenon. While "drop-off" religious education may be better than nothing, parents engaged in the classroom send a message to their children that they value religious education themselves—that it is not just something to be tolerated for eight years and then left behind.

One notable disadvantage of using parent educators is the risk of burning out volunteers. In Washington, parents who agree to teach for a year, providing consistency and building relationships with the children in one classroom, get a rebate on Sunday school tuition for their own children. In Chicago, parents rotate, with each family signing up to teach two or three mornings each year, spreading the burden of work and introducing the students to more people and viewpoints.

Using a different approach, the IFC chapters in the New York area hire seminarians and local religious educators from outside the interfaith community to ensure expert knowledge. Historically, they have recruited teachers from Jewish Theological Seminary, a Conservative Jewish rabbinical school, and Union Theological Seminary, a progressive multidenominational training ground for Protestant ministers. These seminarians bring a more consistently high level of religious knowledge. They also have the possible advantage of not being parental figures—often they are young adults who are compelling mentors to adolescents.

Expertise, erudition, and collegiality were all in evidence when I sat in on a sixth-grade class working through a year-long Sacred Texts curriculum in the Westchester IFC chapter, co-taught by Jewish educator Andrew Rosenthal and veteran Catholic educator Denise Della Porta. At the start of each class, the teachers tape up index cards with the various books of the *Tanakh* (Jewish scriptures) written in both English and Hebrew script, alongside the books found only in Christian scriptures. The lively lesson also included breaking into small groups to interpret parables of Jesus and then debating interpretations with the full class.

HOW DO YOU TEACH ABOUT JESUS?

Whether parents or seminarians, interfaith teachers grapple with the same issues. Most notably, how do you talk about Jesus with children being raised with both Judaism and Christianity? In a Jewish context, the very mention of Jesus is often avoided as irrelevant, if not forbidden. Yet in an interfaith education program, children must learn the Jewish views of Jesus, along with the Christian views.

At IFFP, a year is devoted in the curriculum to the life and times of Jesus. The summary for parents explains:

The overarching question of the IFFP 5th-grade year is: Who was Jesus? And, if the students had met him in 1st-century Palestine, how would they have responded to him? The 5th graders learn about the life that Jesus, as a Jew, would have lived

2000 years ago. The class begins with an exploration of Hebrew history up until the birth of Jesus so that students will better understand the common historical roots of Judaism and Christianity. Then they take a look at Jesus in his contemporary setting to learn about the political and religious environment in which he lived. After that, the class reads stories about Hillel, another Jewish teacher from the same time period, to discuss the similarities between his teachings and the teachings of Jesus. By the end of the year, students are able to discuss the ways in which Jesus's teachings are both completely Jewish and a critique of the mainstream Judaism of his life and times.

Interfaith educators must tackle not only the life of Jesus but also his death. Reverend Jennings provided this guidance to parents and teachers at IFFP: "We don't say to the kids 'This is the answer.' We say, 'This is the resurrection story as the Bible tells it.' But mind you, it's different in every gospel. So we say, 'Some Christians believe this about it, some Christians believe that about it. Jews often believe this about it. I wonder what *you* believe?' We contextualize the question and give children permission to understand it in their own way. Because, honestly, that is what's true in the world. There are a lot of different understandings. And for these kids, this is normal."

In Chicago, sixth-grade students get an entire year of history in a class called One Root, Two Branches: How Christianity Grew From Judaism. The description reads,

As Christians, we want to teach our children lessons about the life of Jesus, his profound teachings, and the way he showed that God can become human in the world. Yet as Jews, how can we be true to our faith and teach our children about this man millions of others have accepted as the son of God and their Savior?

Moreover, how can we teach this material and not sound like the evangelical group Jews for Jesus? We answer these questions with a very Jewish approach, focused on the importance of learning history, a foundation of any good Jewish education. As many of our sister and brother Catholics have discovered, understanding the Jewishness of Jesus is key to a much deeper understanding of his wisdom and ministry—an understanding that we have experienced through our marriages with Jewish partners.

Teens and young adults who have gone through these programs tend to express consistently positive views of Jesus, though few claim him as the Messiah or as the only son of God. Responses to my survey question, "Who or what is Jesus for you?" included "a very wise man, or even a prophet, who sent a message of peace in a time of struggle. His message was, and is too often, ignored"; "a rabbi who openly expressed his very 'different' ideas"; and "a historical figure who was Jewish and preached charity and kindness. I think it is going against Jesus's own teachings to worship him." And an eighteen-year-old from Chicago wrote, "I don't necessarily know if he was the Messiah, but to me that doesn't matter. What matters is God and my relationship with God."

Again, in theological terms, interfaith education seems to be producing people who could be described variously as progressive Jews unafraid to admire Jesus, or progressive Christians or post-Christian universalists with exceptional appreciation of Judaism, or as people steeped in Christianity and Judaism who may or may not make a choice between them at some point.

WHAT ABOUT GOD?

Belief in God is the core belief shared by monotheistic religions, and the Abrahamic faiths of Judaism and Christianity share specific God concepts. I am puzzled when critics assert that interfaith children will end up godless. The shared belief in God provides essential common ground in interfaith education.

In Washington, though many parents come from secular backgrounds, IFFP provides opportunities to meditate, sing, and pray in the heart of the community, even for those who rarely attend synagogue or church. The community seeks to provide these opportunities independent of whether the parents or children believe in God. Children sing religious songs in the classrooms, meditate on the *Sh'ma* and the Lord's Prayer at Gatherings, and walk labyrinth pathways at retreat centers and go on solo wilderness experiences in the Coming of Age program. Secular parents may choose to skip the Gathering before Sunday school because they have no interest in shared spirituality. But to be comfortable with interfaith education for their children, they have to at least be comfortable with their children learning about the role of God in both religions and open to the possibility their child will choose to believe in God.

Many intermarried atheist parents are comfortable with letting their children come to their own decisions about God, just as they are comfortable letting their children come to their own decisions about religious affiliation. For these parents—and they represent a significant group—an interfaith community works fine. However, if they do not want their children exposed to the idea of God, they would probably find a better fit in a secular humanist community.

Parents are the most important religious teachers in the life of a child. Thus, it is presumably more likely that interfaith children who have secular parents, or who do not attend church or synagogue, will emerge as atheists themselves. These secular parents do not necessarily feel that producing religiously literate secular children is a negative outcome—in fact, it may be their goal. On the other hand, children who attend both church and synagogue with their parents in addition to being part of an interfaith community are presumably more likely to emerge with a traditional God-based faith. In the Chicago interfaith schools, the expectation is that families will attend both Mass and synagogue. Father John Cusick believes that interfaith education "really only works if you have a parent system, and therefore a family system, that is observant of their traditions. If it means nothing to you and there is no practice, this is going to be a vaccination that will not take. If it's not a lived faith, I think the possibilities are diminished."

In the survey, interfaith teens and young adults responded to the question, "Who or what is God for you?" with an array of answers, perhaps typical of any sample of people in this age range. In Chicago, a fourteen-year-old boy described God as "the supreme and ultimate being whom I have a close personal connection to, and seek insight from when I am going through hard times. He may not be the sole reason everything happens, but he does oversee all of humanity." A fifteen-year-old boy from Washington wrote, "God is the one in a million chance of actually having life in this galaxy—we are such a little speck in this idea of space—and we're actually alive."

A fourteen-year-old boy from Washington who defines his religious identity as "interfaith, agnostic" described the shifting landscape of his own theology: "On a particularly spiritual day, in which my mind is racing and I am maybe overanalyzing, I believe in the abstract concept that God is nature and/or love or everything beautiful in this world. I might think about it the next day and find that I completely 'tricked' myself into believing. Depends on the moment."

Many teens answered very simply that for them, there is no God. A seventeen-year-old from Washington wrote, "For me, the concept of god doesn't exist. I believe in the values preached by Jesus, the Bible and the Torah. I think the concept of god was created because most people need someone to tell them to follow those values."

Reverend Jennings, the parent of three teenage boys, says, "Youth, if they are in a supportive setting, are of course going to question everything. That's what they're supposed to do. What is important is that they have someone in their lives who is both completely accepting of their questioning and willing to turn it back on them. Someone who can say, 'I'm happy to hear what you don't believe, that's the deconstruction. Now I want to hear some construction. So tell me—what *do* you believe?'"

As yet, no one has made a longitudinal study of interfaith children into adulthood, tracking how their beliefs and practices change as they negotiate the inevitable shocks and traumas of life. But in New York, a twenty-seven-year-old woman raised in the earliest interfaith group testifies to her faith in a divinity: "God is the same in both faiths. God is everywhere . . . God probably does not directly affect what is happening in my life and the world, but I do (or have) spoken to some being (God, I guess) when very scared or worried."

HAS DUAL-FAITH EDUCATION SUCCEEDED?

One measure of the success of interfaith education is the overwhelmingly positive responses from the parents and children who have experienced it. When asked whether they would choose an interfaith education program again for their children, only two parents of 162 said they would not. And more than 90 percent of the grown children agreed that their parents had made a "good decision" when they decided to teach them both religions. When asked how they plan to raise their own children, the majority chose "interfaith group."

Another way to judge the success of interfaith education would be to try to determine how well these programs are meeting their stated goals. One common goal is to help children feel comfortable in synagogue and church. To the extent that they are learning fundamental prayers and songs and basic rituals, holidays, and theology, interfaith education can certainly help. However, children who have never set foot in a synagogue or church can still feel alienated. Here, again, parents are key as religious educators: in order for their children to feel comfortable in a place of worship, parents must take them there. In Chicago, the Interfaith Family School website states clearly that "The school is not intended to be a family's sole form of religious activity, but rather to supplement other choices each family makes." Many Chicago families attend Mass at Old Saint Pat's on Sunday mornings and the Family School there, and also attend Shabbat services at local synagogues. In Washington, the majority attend IFFP on a weekly basis and church or synagogue only on holidays with extended family.

Nevertheless, in the survey, 67 percent of the interfaith program graduates said they felt comfortable in a synagogue, and 64 percent said they felt comfortable in a church. About 15 percent said they did not feel comfortable in a synagogue, and about 10 percent said they did not feel comfortable in a church. (The remainder gave complex explanations of which synagogues or churches they did or did not feel comfortable in.) It is important to note that the parents of many of these children are themselves secularists who also do not feel comfortable in those environments and purposefully chose an interfaith community as an alternative.

The extent to which we feel accepted in a house of worship also has a direct effect on whether we feel comfortable there. One seventeen-year-old, when asked if she was comfortable in synagogues, said: "It depends upon how welcoming they are and whether I'm told by others that that sect recognizes me." When asked whether she felt comfortable in churches, a Washington teen replied, "It depends on the church. I feel fine in a Quaker church, but in the more conservative 'praise the Lord' ones I feel out of place."

Another common goal for parents joining these programs is religious literacy for their children. Granted, it can be challenging to teach the ways of two religions in the limited time most families are willing to devote to religious education. In Washington, the desire to give real depth of knowledge, coupled with membership demand for IFFP to be a full-service community, has led to expansion of the program to the point where it meets most weeks of the school year. It would be interesting to test the knowledge of students emerging from these programs. When asked about the greatest benefits of raising children with both religions, parents in the survey often praised the education programs. A Washington mother of three writes that her children are getting "[a] much deeper knowledge of Christianity than I ever had at their age, and a knowledge of Judaism that allows them to participate in holiday celebrations and prayers." Chicago parent Mary Beaudry writes, "I feel that we are all getting a great education about the common roots of the two religions." And Lisa Steven Brotmann, a mother of three teens in the New York area, writes, "We feel our three interfaith children are not only educated in both Christianity and Judaism but have great respect for both religions."

THE TEACHERS WEIGH IN

In the New York area, the Interfaith Community has gone to great lengths to ensure religious literacy in its students by hiring local Jewish and Christian seminarians. The perspective of these teachers with theology expertise is revealing. Rabbi Nehama Benmosche, who taught at IFC in New York, says, "Most of the time when we teach kids religion we're teaching them how to do religion or be religious, but we're not teaching them how to think about religion or the history of religion. We just don't do as much of that when we're in one religion." In contrast, she says, teaching both "requires a little bit more of a critical lens—how things came about and how they came together. It makes kids smarter about religion."

IFC teacher Anna DeWeese, a seminarian at Union Theological Seminary (UTS) and the daughter of a Methodist minister, was drawn right away to the idea of interfaith education: "These parents were trying to be ahead of their time and actually make the harder decision to try to find a way to represent both of the faith traditions and not capitulate to what the rest of society would want them to do, which would be just to choose one religion and move on."

Over her years of teaching, DeWeese's thinking about interfaith education has shifted. "When I started, I was probably a little more bright-eyed, thinking, 'Isn't this great, what a nice counter to the conservative institutional model [of choosing one religion].'" But now, DeWeese feels that the program may need to forge relationships with a synagogue and church. "I don't know if it's realistic to think that broader institutions would open themselves up to full membership for interfaith families," she says. "We know there's going to be a lot of pushback there: families have told us those stories." But DeWeese would still like to cultivate connections to specific houses of worship, "so that if you do make a decision to choose one religion, it becomes an outgrowth, instead of blindly going out and latching onto the community that seems to be the nicest to you the first couple of times you visit."

Another IFC teacher from UTS, Andrew Schwartz, a Lutheran, described his enthusiasm for the program: "I love the idea of allowing the kids to grow up in their own spirituality, to learn about both traditions and choose which option resonates with them, or the option of not choosing a tradition but creating their own and really working, struggling and grappling with what it means to be of a tradition, of a faith," he says. "I just love the honesty that IFC encourages, not just for the kids but for the parents, for the conversations it forces them to have."

Schwartz sees distinct advantages for the kids on this pathway: "There's a lot of pride that they have in being unique and being interfaith. From a very early age, they see that there's more than one way to see the world, and that is just so invaluable. In a social or cultural situation, it allows them to better see both sides of the story. The ability to discern and to really grapple with religion gives you tools that transcends just religious narratives."

Schwartz acknowledges that dual-faith education poses more of a problem for some of his Jewish co-teachers concerned about Jewish continuity. Yet he feels interfaith education is part of an inevitable cultural shift: "As much as tradition is lost in a fluid and dynamic world such as ours, I think such moves away from tradition are necessary and they allow a foundation for life and living that is completely necessary in our new and globalizing world." Schwartz sees interfaith education as meeting a real need for these families. "I'm fully confident that this movement will continue to survive and grow because people don't want to lose it," he says.

Ironically, of the teachers I interviewed, the one most skeptical about dual-faith education is an interfaith child himself. Like me, UTS student Andrew Rosenthal was raised as a Reform Jew by a Christian mother and Jewish father. Rosenthal describes himself as a "conservative person by nature, by temperament" and says, "I think it's much better for a child to be raised in one tradition." But he also allows, "I think it's good that they're getting a flavor of each, and that's better than nothing."

In contrast, IFC teacher Leslie Stern Abramowitz, who is also Jewish and an adult interfaith child, wishes that there had been an interfaith community for her family when she was growing up. She was raised with only secular holiday celebrations and chose to convert to Judaism in college. "Interfaith education really gives some sort of foundation for children and gives them a leg up that I didn't have," she says. "I felt that I really had to catch up. I wish there was something like that when I was growing up—making kids feel less alone or religions feel less taboo. I love the organization for doing that. I've come across people who say 'I don't get it.' These are people who've never had to make a choice. They feel it's watered down. I say 'Look, ideally yes, you'd have one religion and it wouldn't be confusing at all.' But you have to work in a way that works for people in a specific circumstance."

Jewish IFC teacher David (not his real name) continues to attempt to reconcile his positive experience teaching in an interfaith education program with the official disapproval of Jewish institutions. By the time this book comes out, he will be a young rabbi, wrestling with the fact that he has been ordained in a movement that prohibits interfaith marriage. "You can't control how people love and how people care," he says. "Am I going to say that God was not with a couple who are interfaith? God is all-connected."

Part of David's desire to embrace religious pluralism stems from an almost mystical experience of the *Aleinu* prayer, which states that one day "God will be one and God's name shall be one." David's interpretation: "It means that at the end of the day, whatever we decide to call God, or to call the greater force or greater meaning in the world, we have different names or different ways we understand it, but it's all a part of the same whole."

Driven by this passion for unity in diversity, David sought out his job as a teacher at IFC. "I wanted to be able to be exposed to the life of interfaith families, to understand where they were coming from, from the perspective of being both," he says, explaining, "While it is now acceptable for interfaith families to be part of the Jewish community, it is only if they decide to raise their kids Jewish." That exclusion troubled David. "It denies [children] a part of their religious heritage and tradition," he says.

David sees interfaith education as inspirational—as more than just "better than nothing." He says, "In my mind I see it as a task that has never existed before, to connect the religions together. If this were the only path to Judaism, it would be problematic. But it can be a positive thing, not just something we accept because it's here."

He describes the interfaith children he taught at IFC as unusually thoughtful about religion. "They exemplify certain characteristics of higher stages of faith, which it seems to me comes from the fact that they are exposed to multiple ways, early on," he says. "What I found is a certain nuanced sensitivity to conversations about God and life and meaning."

He contrasts these conversations with his experience in a single-faith setting. "A lot of Jewish-only settings focus on the social aspects of bringing Jews together, so that they will raise Jewish families and then the tradition will continue," he says. "And there's a long tradition as to why that makes sense, and a certain part of me believes in that goal. On the other hand, speaking as a Jewish leader and educator, it's troubling when our primary focus is on socialization, not on meaning making."

Rabbi Harold White expresses the same concern. He recalls walking into a third-grade classroom in a synagogue: "The teacher said to the students, 'You know why you're here? You're here so you won't marry a gentile.' And I said to myself, 'Oy vey.' That's the purpose of a religious education? If your only concern is the survival of peoplehood, without the values connected to it, we have a serious problem." Many Jewish communities are now working to infuse Jewish education with more spirituality. But interfaith couples continue to feel pressured by "outreach" programs with an overt agenda of "inmarriage," including the free Birthright Israel trips offered to Jewish teens and young adults.

Like Anna DeWeese, David would like to see the most progressive Christian and Jewish denominations work with interfaith communities, "so that an interfaith community is not stand-alone but is connected with a synagogue and a church, and can be a bridge between the two, to create more synergy for making this world a better place: to be able to use our differences and similarities for the benefits they bring." He envisions that this type of alliance would have to involve a Jewish denomination (not his) that accepts patrilineal Jewish children and a Christian denomination with a "more flexible understanding of Jesus."

At his Jewish seminary, David found quiet support for his involvement with an interfaith families community. "Most of the reaction has been overwhelmingly positive and curious, from colleagues and professors," he says. On the other hand, he points out, "Acknowledging the existence of it is problematic. You're giving an affirmation or approbation to the existence of that path. People want clarity, they do not want ambiguity. But life is ambiguous. If you put yourself in a position where you experience diversity, inevitably there's a part of you that will become diverse. And that's scary, especially in a Jewish context, and understandably so, since Judaism has had to deal with so much hatred and persecution over the course of our entire history. Talking about joining the non-Jewish world is very scary."

David calls working with interfaith families "this generation's challenge." He says, "I believe deeply that my rabbinate is tied to both my American-ness, which is that desire for diversity, and also my Jewishness, which is that connection to the people and the tradition—and wanting to keep them both alive. I don't really know yet where the boundaries are or if there are boundaries. Which is also scary."

As seminarians like David and the other IFC teachers go out into the world to become rabbis, ministers, full-time religious educators, or theologians, they take with them their experiences of working directly with dual-faith education. Presumably, this will help religious institutions to acknowledge interfaith family communities and begin to understand the benefits of dual-faith education for these children.

As parents, some of us arrive at interfaith communities lugging the baggage of our own stultifying Sunday school or Hebrew school experiences, or of our rejection by clergy and religious organizations. And yet we enroll our children in interfaith education programs because we still believe that religious knowledge has value. We are optimists, not cynics. We want our children to be inspired by the great intellectual traditions of questioning (whether Jesuit or Unitarian or Talmudic) and by the thirst for social justice of Dorothy Day and Paulo Freire, Paul Tillich and Martin Luther King Jr., Martin Buber and Abraham Joshua Heschel. We want our children to experience the comfort of ancient ritual and the expansion of the soul triggered by great liturgical music.

For some of us, secular religious literacy is enough. In England, government-funded schools require interfaith religious education for all students. In the United States, many school systems studiously avoid religious education, and parents (interfaith or single-faith) must seek it out. But beyond religious literacy, I believe that in learning all of the strands of their own family history, all of the traditions woven through the reality of their interfaith heritage, our children will discover and create new ways of being spiritual and religious in the twenty-first century.

 CHAPTER TEN

Interfaith Children Grow Up

What Do They Believe? Where Do They Go?

WHETHER WE ARE BORN into one religion or two (or more, or none), our spiritual identity evolves as long as we think and breathe. Faith may wax or wane, allegiance shift, inspiration arrive in the form of a brief mystical encounter or new love. Every one of us creates a complex map of personal religious and spiritual influences: grandma's Old World rosary, dad's worship of opera, a professor's eloquent presentation of Buddhism, an old boyfriend's passion for Israeli folk dancing, a small daughter's communing with deep forest spirits.

Because faith forms and reforms throughout life, it would be misleading to talk about how children raised with two religions "end up." But in this chapter, I provide a first opportunity for the graduates of the programs this book has described to share their own complex and mutable identities at one moment in time. This snapshot of teens and young adults who graduated from interfaith education programs is based on fifty responses to an original survey, in-depth follow-up interviews, and my experience raising two interfaith children with my husband over the past eighteen years. The survey respondents were self-selected, responding to listserv requests that went out to the interfaith communities, as well as teens still in classroom programs.

This group portrait is a work in progress. The first of the interfaith children who went through comprehensive (kindergarten through eighth grade) interfaith education are now in their early twenties. Approximately 57 percent of the respondents were women. Ages ranged from fourteen (just completing a program) to thirty-four (the oldest graduate of the earliest prototype program in the 1980s). They were raised in the communities in Washington, New York, Chicago, and California. Seventy percent had six or more years of interfaith education, and all had at least three years. About 40 percent have a Catholic and a Jewish parent; about 60 percent have a Protestant and a Jewish parent.

CHOOSING ONE

At this point, very few of the children surveyed have chosen to practice only one religion. One twenty-year-old daughter of a Presbyterian mother and Jewish father raised in New York has chosen to be Episcopalian. One seventeen-year-old son of a Jewish mother and Catholic father in Washington has chosen to be Quaker. The twenty-one-year-old daughter of a Jewish mother and Catholic father in Washington has chosen Judaism. And so has Chicago's Matthew Kolaczkowski.

Matthew Kolaczkowski: "Because I Was Able to Choose"

Matthew Kolaczkowski, twenty, is the son of a Jewish mother and a Catholic father who together helped to found Chicago's Interfaith Family School. Matthew and his two younger siblings grew up going to church or interfaith Sunday school every week and synagogue only on High Holy Days. "The synagogue didn't seem to be as accepting as the church was," he recalls.

Matthew deeply appreciated the interfaith education he received in the Family School. "It really showed me how important tolerance was and all the negative effects if that's ignored. We went over a lot of history, over and over again—the conflicts that could have been avoided."

Even when presented with the more traditional theology of the Catholic Church, Matthew did not find learning about both religions confusing. "It just makes you think, and that's exactly what you should be doing with your religious education," he expounds. "I think people should question everything. It's really answering those personal questions that makes it clear what's meant for you and what's not."

Matthew developed an appreciation for Jesus as a "very wise man who had excellent ideas that people to this day do not take to heart" and who "may have been a prophet." He believes that "What really lasts and what people should concern themselves with are his teachings."

At the same time, Matthew decided to deepen his knowledge of Judaism by becoming a bar mitzvah, and he was lucky to have Rabbi Allen Secher to support him in this. "At the time of my bar mitzvah, I worked really hard, studied to learn my portion, write my *dvar* [an analysis of the Torah portion]. It drew me really close," he recalls.

Matthew gives many reasons for his choice of a Jewish identity. "It was the teachings, the theology," he says. "I wasn't convinced that Jesus was the son of God. I really liked Jewish tradition, that it went back so far. I liked how Judaism focused a lot on questioning—the commentaries on the commentaries on the commentaries." But to be sure of his decision, Matthew continued attending Catholic confirmation classes even after his bar mitzvah. "I wanted to try it to make sure that my hunch was correct, that I was doing the right thing," he explains. By the time he was sixteen, he felt confident: "I feel even closer to the religion I ended up going with because I was able to choose it."

He also felt confident that his parents would understand his choice. "I didn't see it as choosing between parents, I saw it as a life-long decision I would have to live with, and I knew that my parents would support me either way," says Matthew. "It's a really important decision and it shouldn't be made on other people's agendas."

Now studying chemistry at the University of Illinois, Matthew intends to follow his father into the pharmaceutical industry. He has made a personal choice to be Jewish. But when he thinks about raising children, he still feels drawn, as do virtually all of the children raised with both, to the type of interfaith education he experienced. "I'm really happy with the education I received and I'd really like to pass that on if could," says Matthew. "It's almost a shame if I marry someone of the same religion."

"I WANT TO STAY BOTH"

An overwhelming majority of survey respondents continue to claim both religions as part of their identity. When asked, "How would you describe your religious identity at this point?," more than a dozen, more than a quarter of the sample, chose the label "interfaith." Eight others chose "Jewish and Catholic" or "Jewish and Christian." Seven chose "agnostic," and four chose "atheist." More than a quarter of the sample refused all of the offered labels and wrote their own. For instance, the fifteen-year-old son of a Conservative Jewish mother and Catholic father in Washington, described himself as "Zen, Catholic, and a little bit Jewish."

More than 80 percent of those identifying as interfaith responded that they do *not* expect to eventually choose a single religion. One fourteen-year-old who described himself as interfaith wrote that his identity "will probably always be changing, evolving, discovering, diving in, easing out, going up, going down, spinning around, running around, sitting down, and last but not least, floating." Some expressed concern that choosing would cause them to lose something positive. "If I choose one religion over the other, I fear I would become too single-minded," wrote a sixteen-year-old in San Francisco. And a seventeen-year-old from New York wrote, "I want to stay both, because it's original and it represents a part of who I am. There's no reason I need to choose either religion."

Many respondents pushed back against the whole idea of religious labeling. An eighteen-year-old from Chicago wrote, "I don't think the label is as important as what you actually believe, and what I believe probably has some aspects that are Christian, some that are Jewish and some that are neither or a blend of the two." A nineteen-year-old from Washington wrote, "I don't think it's really necessary to put a label on it. I believe in God (ish) and I believe in the goodness in people and the beauty of this world and I kind of don't care if that fits into any category."

Several respondents testified to dual-faith status as a spur, rather than an impediment, to developing spirituality. A twenty-three-year-old wrote, "I feel the coupling of both faiths has given me unique avenues to God. I think identifying with the benevolent, shared commonalities between them (rather than narrowing the path) can give a stronger connection to God."

One sixteen-year-old from Washington disputed the implication that her only options were Judaism or Christianity. She wrote, "I'd like to explore even more religions than just Jewish and Christian before I decide what I want to openly identify as." Another Washingtonian, seventeen, wrote, "I cannot be severed from either of these religions, nor be limited to Judaism and Christianity. Each lesson I learn, regardless of its origins, will find a niche in my natural landscape of beliefs to be considered."

David Brescia-Weiler: "People Have Complex Stories"

As a sophomore at Brown University, David Brescia-Weiler, twenty, feels comfortable in his interfaith skin. His mother, Jill Weiler, is a Reform Jew. His father, Steve Brescia, is Catholic. From the age of six, David attended IFFP. He went through the dual-faith education program, participated in a group Coming of Age ceremony in eighth grade, and joined the interfaith Teen Group.

David says he feels no pressure to choose one religion. "My parents have always been super-supportive of each other's faith, which has made it easier for me to accept both," explains David. "When we go to church at Christmas and Easter my mom always comes too. Religiously, if I said I'm agnostic or I wanted to convert to Islam, they'd be supportive no matter what I said. Because their religions are important to them, it's important to them that I understand their faiths. But I think they understand it as something I can find for myself."

David describes how others sometimes assign him a religious label based on their own beliefs, or project their own confusion onto him. "A lot of people say, 'Oh, you're a Jew,'" he explains. "And I would say 'I'm a Jew. But I'm also a Christian.' People ask me if I'm half. And I say 'No, because I don't think you can be half a religion.' I say I'm both. I don't think I can say I was ever confused about what I was, because I always just kind of understood that I was both."

At college, he has met other interfaith children but none with his dual-faith education. "Most of them have one religion that's dominant, or they did nothing," David notes. "I'm lucky in that I wasn't forced to choose, and I didn't do one just because one parent was more adamant. Through IFFP and through my parents, I learned to marry the two religions, so to speak, because they do share the basics: Love your neighbor, be generous. That's the way I made everything work out."

In terms of theology, David, like many of those with an interfaith education, sounds either like a Jewish kid who is educated about the historical Jesus, or a very liberal Christian. "I don't know if I see Jesus as the son of God," he explains. "I see him as a role model. I don't see him as a deity but as a person, a great person. Part of why he has been made into a godlike figure is that what he represents isn't really attainable by a normal human."

David has gravitated to Jewish friends in college. He joined a fraternity with a large Jewish membership, plays on an intramural basketball team called the Hebrew Heroes, and has a best friend who is the son of a rabbi. "I think he accepts that I'm also a Jew but that I choose to embody that in my own way," says David.

He has learned to advocate for himself and fill in gaps in his religious knowledge when needed. Last semester, he chose to take a tough upper-level seminar with the title "Radical Jewish Thinkers," taught by an Israeli professor. There were only two other students in the class. One had spent time in Israel, the other was the rabbi's son. "So I was a little bit the odd man out," admits David. "Sometimes the professor would throw out names in Hebrew and I wouldn't know if it was a person or a place or a magazine and I would be, like, 'Slow down and tell me what that is.'" But, he says, "I hung in there—I did all right."

David remains a strong advocate for interfaith education. "At this point, I am very content with what I believe," he says. "When I have kids, depending on my spouse's beliefs, we'll have to work something out, but I would ideally like to raise my children with both religions in their lives."

Michaela Gawley: "I Can See Myself Going in Any Direction"

In a way, Michaela Gawley, sixteen, is responsible for the flourishing IFC chapter on Long Island. "Michaela, when she was very little, was interested in questions of death and God," says her father, Steve, who was raised Catholic. "So that pushed us to do something sooner rather than later."

The Gawleys joined the IFC in Manhattan when Michaela was six years old. A few years later, Pam Gawley, who is Jewish, launched the Long Island chapter when they moved to the suburbs, and she continues to lead it a decade later. Since completing the IFC religious education program, Michaela continues to attend on Sundays, assisting in the classroom with younger children. "I like having a connection with the rabbi and the reverend: it's personal, and that makes it more enriching," she says.

Michaela accepts her role as an interfaith ambassador. In elementary school, she says, a friend told her, "You can't be interfaith. That's dumb. That's not real." So she took it upon herself to educate her friend. And by the end of eighth grade, when Michaela took part in the IFC commencement ceremony, her doubting friend was there to witness it.

At other times, she refuses to invest time in defending her interfaith identity. "If I know I'm never going to see these people again, and I know it's over these people's heads, I just say 'I'm Jewish' or 'I'm Christian.' I'm not going to sit there explaining it," she sighs. Michaela fiercely defends her right to a fluid religious identity. "It's like asking a bisexual person, 'Aren't you confused?'" she declares, indignant. And she also bristles when others try to label her based on Jewish laws of matrilineality. "You know what I say? My mom is Jewish, Judaism passes through her. My dad is Christian, Christianity passes through him. So you figure that one out."

Michaela feels confident that religion will always be a part of her life. "I can see myself going in any direction—being Episcopalian, being Jewish. I could see myself exploring other religions," she says. "I'm not comfortable with anything extreme. But in my own weird way, I get really touched when I'm in a religious setting. I believe in God: it's like a comfort."

LEANING JEWISH

Beyond the desire to retain a fluid identity and perhaps a heightened desire to study religion, is it possible to discern any trends in the choices these interfaith children are making? In the survey of parents with interfaith children of all ages, which had many more respondents, some 20 percent of parents reported that they had a child who had chosen a Jewish identity, versus only 5 percent with a child with a Christian identity. (The vast majority reported children having some form of interfaith identity.) The age at which the child chose a religion ranged from four through college age.

Many of the clergy members who have worked most closely with interfaith communities believe they are seeing more Judaism than Christianity manifested in the young adults who have passed through their programs. Reverend Julia Jarvis of IFFP says that about half of the program's graduates get involved with Hillel in college— far more than participate in Christian activities—and the survey seemed to confirm this. More than half the college students had attended Jewish High Holy Day services on campus, and less than half had attended any Christian services on campus—though this may reflect the fact that the Jewish High Holy Days fall during the school year, while Christmas and Easter usually fall on school vacations.

But Reverend Jarvis believes the stronger connection to Judaism is a real effect. "They do say they're both, but my sense is they have more leanings towards the Jewish traditions," she notes. "I think actually we've made Judaism very attractive, because we're not trying to force these kids to stay Jewish—because it's a choice."

Both Reverend Jarvis and Reverend Ellen Jennings agree that the simplicity of Jewish theology may be easier for interfaith children than the complexity of the Trinity, which many Jews see as counter to monotheism. Or, as my mother recently said to me, "The concept of the Trinity is a puzzle, even for us Christians."

Lily Felsenthal: Representing Judaism

Lily Felsenthal, nineteen, has been inspired by immersion in a Christian context to claim her Judaism. When she was growing up in Washington's IFFP, Lily, like many other kids, hated getting up on Sunday morning to go to Sunday school. Neither her Protestant mother nor her Jewish father came from strongly religious families. And Lily admits that she, like many teenagers, was skeptical about the concept of faith. "I discounted religion," she says. "You see TV evangelists, and it's easy to be cynical."

Then, she ended up at DePaul University in Chicago, the nation's largest Catholic university. For many students, living in close proximity to others of different faiths in the intimacy of a dormitory is a singular and formative experience. For interfaith children, college is just one in a series of lifelong interfaith experiences, but it can still have a strong impact.

Lily's freshman roommate was Catholic. "She felt called when she got here to build a relationship with God, to do Bible study," says Lily. "I had never had a friend [who] connected to a religion for themselves like that, through no obligation to their parents. It really opened my mind to people who have very strong faith, that they're more than the stereotype. People of faith are trying to make sense of the world." In her sophomore year, Lily chose to live with the same Catholic roommate, two other devout Christians, and an interfaith child raised without religion who ended up exploring her Jewish roots when she got to college, going on a Birthright trip to Israel on winter break and becoming a bat mitzvah.

Surrounded by strong religious currents, Lily found herself called to identify, at times, as Jewish. "I've had a lot of really good talks with my Jewish friends and I'm feeling more connected to that side of my heritage than I was," she explains. "There's another reason I sometimes say I'm Jewish. I'm trying to represent. Not a lot of people know a lot of Jewish people here—some of my friends here are from very small towns." On the other hand, Lily resists the idea that she should be Jewish for the sake of Jewish continuity. When a friend told her that "So many people suffered for you to be Jewish," her response was, "I don't like the idea that it should be a numerical thing. I would say that's not why people should choose a faith."

Instead, Lily has used the religious resources available at college to continue to explore her own spirituality. She took an Introduction to Religions course. She started going to Shabbat at Hillel with Jewish friends. But she also goes to the university chapel for Taize prayer, a form of musical worship founded by ecumenical Christian monks in France. At the moment, her identity remains fluid. "I don't think it's necessary for me to pick a label," she says. "I don't want to limit myself."

Lily rebuts the idea that interfaith family communities are evolving into some kind of third religion. "I don't think there's any danger of us putting other religions out of business," she says. "We're not trying to undermine other faiths at all. It's hard for me to accept that finding common ground between two faiths that have had a hard time getting along sometimes in history, that that could be a bad thing."

Lily realizes her beliefs sound "a little bit hippie" but she has put a lot of thought into the meaning of religion. "Religion was created to explain things we can't explain," she says. "So it's weird that people think they're so right about religion, when the whole basis of religion is that nobody really knows for sure. If you're kind and loving and you do your best to do good for the world, I support whatever tradition that helps you do that. Or if you don't have a religion, however you get there, I support that."

Casey and Jared McGrath: Two Siblings, Two Identities

As anyone with more than one child knows, you can raise two children with identical parenting, in identical schools, with identical family religious practices, and still they grow up to be individuals who make different choices, in religion as in all other domains of life. The McGrath siblings illustrate that point. Randi Field is Jewish, Matt McGrath is Catholic. They sent both their children to Catholic schools in the Washington, D.C., area and to the interfaith education program at IFFP. Both children are now in college, but Casey, twenty-one, usually identifies herself as Jewish, while Jared, twenty-four, identifies himself as both, after a period of leaning toward Catholicism.

Jared and Casey both appreciate their interfaith upbringing. "It's made me much more open-minded and accepting of other cultures and religions," says Casey. "It's given me the opportunity to think for myself and make decisions for myself." She is alienated by religious exclusivism and territorialism. "The religions have so much in common and are so intertwined. People spend time trying to find ways to make them different and saying 'This is mine,'" she says.

Jared believes his interfaith perspective primed him to engage with Catholic teachings on a deep level. "I had religion class at Catholic school—memorizing vocabulary about the Mass, transubstantiation, the Apostles' Creed. For the other kids, it was just like memorizing math," he says. "But for me, I had to really think for myself to explain it, to understand what I believed."

Jared recalls his Catholic-school classmates as being confounded when he described himself as not Catholic, not Jewish, but interfaith. "I remember for the first time feeling that it was empowering, that I was a unique individual, that it was something to be proud about," he recalls. "I would tell them, 'I think it's just as right and as wrong or fallible and infallible as what you guys are learning about. We're both learning about how to bring God into our lives, about faith, and I think we're doing it two different ways, and I think neither of them is perfect. I think they're parallel and coexisting.'"

As Jared describes it, his classmates tended to identify him as Jewish, either because they were aware of the idea of Jewish matrilineality, or simply because he was the most Jewish person in their midst. Jared recalls, "I'd say, 'My mom's Jewish, my dad's Catholic, I was raised with knowledge and appreciation of both.' And they'd say, 'So you're a Jew.'"

Despite, or perhaps because of, these attempts by others to assign him a Jewish religious identity, Jared found himself deeply attracted to Catholicism in middle school. "I became very interested in Catholic liturgy. I liked the structure of it," he recalls. Every Friday at school, he went to an hour-long Mass in the middle of the day. "After a while, I thought, 'I could lead this,'" says Jared. "For a little while, I thought about being Catholic. But I've always had a problem submitting completely to one idea—maybe that is because of the way I was raised, as an interfaith child."

In high school, Jared had a "powerful religious experience" contemplating God and life on a Christian retreat with classmates. He notes, "I don't think I would have had such a profound experience without my interfaith background. Some kids had really never thought about these deep questions—I had already been trying to explore my faith for many years."

Jared also found his high school coursework in Catholicism inspiring. He paraphrased the entire Gospel of Mark in his own words. He helped create a movie on the Christian references in C. S. Lewis's *Chronicles of Narnia*. And he deconstructed Mel Gibson's controversial film *The Passion of the Christ*. "You have to remember, Jesuits like to question," Jared says. "We were all fifteen and gung-ho about questioning everything we possibly could."

In college at the University of Maryland, Jared talked his way into an interfaith dialogue group that was supposed to have an even number of students from each of the represented religions. There were no slots designated for students identifying with more than one religion, but Jared convinced them that his interfaith perspective would be helpful and relevant.

In contrast, Jared's sister Casey responded to her minority status in the Catholic environment by more clearly identifying with Judaism. "Through high school I identified more and more with the Jewish faith," she says. For one, she rejected the theology of sin and confession. "I was a huge nerd in high school: I didn't drink or do drugs or even date," she notes. "Watching these crazy kids partying on the weekend and then going to confession and being told that they would go to heaven and I wouldn't. It just didn't make sense."

Part of her identification with a minority religion, she believes, comes from her struggle with dyslexia. "Having been an underdog myself for so long," she says, "I'm always rooting for the underdogs. I still really like a lot of aspects of Catholicism, but I'm more picky and choosy about what I like about Catholicism than I am with Judaism. And the Catholics feel it's all or nothing, with not a lot of room for questioning."

After high school, her identification with Judaism grew stronger. "At this point, I usually say I'm Jewish and identify a lot more with the Jewish belief system and culture. I was in Catholic school longer than Jared was—by the time I got out, I was fed up with it and wanted something else."

In her graduate nursing program at the University of Pennsylvania, Casey gravitated toward the "liberal, edgy, Jews from New York. I feel like I have more in common with them." Her preference for Judaism is both cultural and theological. "I think that Jesus was a great role model. He did amazing things. I think it's very possible that he could have had miraculous powers and healed people," she says. "But I feel like if Jesus was the Messiah, the world wouldn't be in the state it is today."

She sees the different religious identities she and her brother now have as confirmation that interfaith education works: "I think it's good that Jared and I have gone in different directions. It shows we've always felt free to believe what we want to believe."

LIVING WITH THE DISADVANTAGES

When asked about the disadvantages of interfaith upbringing, about one-third of the young adults who answered the question said they saw none. The most frequent disadvantages cited all had to do with having to explain interfaith identity and being accepted by others. A fourteen-year-old from Chicago points to "the constant nagging of 'You can't be both Jewish and Catholic.'" A seventeen-year-old from Washington describes the challenge as "being illegitimate in the eyes of many, being called out as such." A twenty-three-year-old from Washington says, "You may find yourself at odds with individuals who disagree with this mode of religious upbringing."

When asked specifically, "Do people ever challenge your right to your religious identity?" slightly more than half of respondents replied that they did. One Chicago fourteen-year-old writes, "ALL THE TIME!!!!" and a twenty-seven-year-old in New York writes, "They do, in a subtle way."

Often the challenge comes from extended family members who feel responsible for the religious guidance of interfaith grandchildren or nieces and nephews. "My grandmother is the only person that has really challenged my right to my religious identity. I calmly tell her that it's her opinion, and that she doesn't have to agree as long as I feel comfortable in my own religious identity," writes a seventeen-year-old in New York. A twenty-eight-year-old, also raised in New York, writes, "When I was a teenager, a

Christian uncle implored me to choose one or the other religion. He was afraid I would be lost without a church community to fall back on, or perhaps a set of prescribed beliefs. More recently, I have been lectured on raising my own potential children in one faith, by my mother-in-law."

In the survey, those who identify as interfaith were asked how they respond to people who question their identity. Clearly, some of the teens enjoy the sense of being different and the chance to spar verbally on this topic. "I say that I have had many years of education, and that it is my and only my decision to make," says a fourteen-year-old from Chicago. An eighteen-year-old from Washington responds with, "Who are you to tell me what to and what not to believe in?" A sixteen-year-old replies, "I say 'It's my religion not yours, so, goodbye!'"

As they age, some of those raised in two religions begin to see a benefit to having to prepare an articulate defense. "I have realized that a lot of people don't agree with my religious identity," says an eighteen-year-old from Chicago in her first year of college. "But, I feel because I have been forced to defend myself, it has made my religious identity stronger." Another eighteen-year-old from Chicago writes, "People judge you a lot and try to convince you that what you are doing is wrong. It requires you to have strong will-power at a young age, but I feel this creates a strong faith, which is an advantage."

As described throughout this book, interfaith teens and adults will encounter both Jews and Christians who want to label them based on the belief that Judaism can pass only through the mother, while interfaith family communities take an egalitarian approach, in which the Jewish partner's gender plays no role. When interfaith teens were asked, "Is it important to you whether it is the mother or the father that is the Jewish parent in an interfaith family?" more than 90 percent stated it was not.

Diego Vasquez: "Adamantly Both"

At age eleven, Diego Vasquez became the oldest child in the very first class of children in the IFFP religious education program. The son of a Latino Catholic father and a white Jewish mother, Adria Zeldin, Diego was also raised by a Jewish stepfather, Peter Gray, alongside a Jewish stepbrother, Jordan.

The religious cross-pollination in this blended family has led to many unexpected moments of harmony. When Diego's Catholic grandmother died, he chose to go to a Jewish service with a friend to grieve. And when his Jewish grandmother was in hospice care, Reverend Jarvis from IFFP provided pastoral comfort for her.

Diego, now twenty-six and a clarinetist at a New York conservatory, has a strongly secular identity. "My life just hasn't been focused around religion," he states. "But if they ask what I'm cooking, I'll say, 'Brisket! I'm Jewish!' In that moment I'm Jewish." His stepfather adds, "That's interesting, because that's sort of how Adria identifies—as a gastronomic Jew."

But Diego's primary identity is interfaith, even when this claim comes at a cost. This became apparent when his stepbrother Jordan asked Diego to join him on a Birthright trip, the program to send Jewish youth on a free trip to Israel. "My brother wanted to go, and we planned the trip together," recalls Diego. "So then I applied, and they ask you questions over the phone, and one of the first ones was, 'Are you Jewish?' And I said, 'I'm actually interfaith. I was raised Christian and Jewish. So for me to pick one over the other and say I'm just Jewish, it's kind of like asking me to pick if I'm white or Latino.'"

Adria knew that Diego could claim to be Jewish under hala-cha (traditional Jewish law) because he had a Jewish mother. But he wasn't willing to do that. Recalling her conversation with Diego, she says, "If you really wanted to go, all you had to do was say, 'Yes, I consider myself Jewish.' But you didn't compromise your principles."

Peter, who spent a formative period on a kibbutz himself, adds, "You'd think Diego would be the kind of person they would want on the trip. Because if they want to get people to associate more strongly with their Jewish identity, and here you have someone who is somewhat ambivalent or says he's interfaith . . ."

Diego interrupts, "It's not that I was ambivalent. I just was adamantly both." In the end, Jordan went on the trip without his brother. Diego muses, "I'd love to visit Israel, but on my own terms."

Anna Cohn: The Price of Exclusion

Diego was not the only one raised with both religions who described being excluded by a Jewish institution. A teenage girl in the New York area described how her mother was helping to plan an event for interfaith families at her synagogue: "The temple told us we couldn't go, because my parents are raising me both. My parents were upset, especially my Mom, who is Jewish. It was a little weird going to temple after that." It is interesting to note that this family, members of this Jewish congregation, continued to go to services even after being excluded. Will this incident impact the emerging sense of religious identity in this interfaith teen? Anna Cohn, a young woman raised in the Chicago interfaith groups, still feels deeply connected to Judaism, despite facing similar exclusions.

As a freshman at Denison University in Ohio, Anna, eighteen, wrote a paper for her sociology class on interfaith families. "I went to the library and there were maybe fifteen books on the subject, but only one of them seemed unbiased. It was really frustrating," she explains. "The books were all either, 'This is the Christian perspective, and this is why you shouldn't marry a Jew,' or 'This is the

Jewish perspective, and this is why you shouldn't marry a Christian.' The only neutral book was like, 'Here's both perspectives, and this is why neither of them likes to marry the other,' which was a step in the right direction. But none of the books really had a positive perspective."

So Anna drew on her own experience growing up in the Chicago interfaith families community. "My argument was that people say interfaith children will grow up confused but that's obviously not the case, because I'm living proof," she says. Anna's parents, Barbara and Steve Cohn, raised their only daughter in both religions with the support of the Jewish Catholic Couples Dialogue Group and the Interfaith Family School in Chicago. Steve, a Reform Jew, has taught Hebrew classes for Family School students who want to study for a bar or bat mitzvah. He also teaches a class on the Holocaust to the eighth grade each year, drawing on his mother's experiences in World War II.

When Barbara and Steve married, Barbara, who grew up Catholic, signed the required commitment to raise her children Catholic to the best of her ability, and the Catholic Church recognized their marriage. "Raising them both is to the best of our ability," she explains. "It's easier to do both because it's not excluding one of the spouses. But it's not always easy—I can fit into the Jewish traditions more than Steve can fit into my traditions. Sometimes it's easy to forget that."

The Cohns, like the other Chicago interfaith families, have been very lucky to have clergy who understand and support them. Rabbi Allen Secher and Father John Cusick were both there for Anna's First Communion and for her Bat Mitzvah. "Rabbi Secher and Father Cusick are both very important to me," says Anna. "Every step of the way, they both made sure that I was comfortable, that it was really something I wanted to do." However, Anna decided against Catholic Confirmation, which she understood as a more exclusive commitment to Catholicism.

Anna testifies to the fact that the Family School helped prepare interfaith children to make these religious decisions. "We had a set of triplets—one wanted to be only Christian, one wanted to be only Jewish, and one wanted to be both. Even growing up in the same family, it showed that it worked that each could make their own decision," she says.

And yet the Cohns faced exclusion as a family celebrating two religions. By the time of Anna's bat mitzvah, Rabbi Secher had retired to Montana and the family had joined a Reform synagogue. "They said that we could use the space for my bat mitzvah but because I was being raised both we couldn't use the rabbi or the *bimah* or the Torah," says Anna. "The woman had a long confrontation with my mother. She said my parents were confusing me—that I would grow up with no religion or faith."

Barbara still simmers over this rejection. "In the name of religion, for a child who wants to do this, you're going to turn a child away? They're going to turn her away because she's not 'pure'?" She adds, "We quickly quit that synagogue and joined another."

Later that same year, the Cohn family, including Steve's parents, took Anna to Israel. "We had a tour guide who was in the Israeli military, very knowledgeable but very set in his ways and his beliefs," Anna says. "He knew my mom was Christian from the beginning. But in the middle of the trip he found out that I was being raised both Jewish and Christian. He called me—and I can't even make this up—'Hitler's success.' My dad and grandparents got a little heated. I said to him, 'How can you say I'm not a Jew?' Honestly, because of my interfaith upbringing I feel like I know more about Judaism and Christianity than most Jews and Christians. I was forced to ask questions and find the differences and the similarities between the two. Whereas if you're just raised in one, you might just follow what your parents say."

While the analytical, compare-and-contrast approach to religious education may sound overly dry or intellectual, Anna, like many other interfaith children, has in fact derived a deep sense of spirituality from being raised with both. "For me, what matters is my relationship with God," she says. "So whether Jesus was the Messiah or not doesn't affect my relationship with God. The reason I practice both religions is that both have ceremonies and rituals and values that get me closer to God and allow me to have a stronger faith." And despite the exclusion from the synagogue and the confrontation in Israel, Anna maintains her right to claim Judaism. Her mother says, "I really think Anna has more of a Jewish soul."

As for how she will raise any future children, Anna reflects, "If it was up to me, and just me, I'd want to raise my children both Christian and Jewish. But I'm going to have a husband, and he's going to have his own point of view. If he's Muslim, then that's awesome, they'll get raised with three religions."

STRESS AND CONFUSION, OR THE LACK THEREOF

These interfaith children, even in an anonymous survey, almost never expressed confusion or stress over choosing religion. Only one youth described "a small fear that in choosing one or the other you are choosing one parent over the other—but I do know that my parents would accept and respect any decision I made." Interfaith communities work hard to alleviate the pressure to choose, by emphasizing to children that their parents have chosen an interfaith identity for them and by educating parents to gracefully accept any faith choice the child makes later in life.

When asked whether they found learning about two religions confusing, almost 90 percent said no. They gave a variety of explanations for their lack of confusion. One twenty-year-old from

Chicago wrote, "It does require some thought, but isn't that exactly what we should be doing? It is our responsibility to be informed about our decisions. How can we do so without being given all the facts?" And a sixteen-year-old from Washington writes, "How could it be confusing? It wasn't like there was a rabbi yelling at us Jewish beliefs in one ear and a pope yelling Christian beliefs in the other. They were presented as information that some people believe, which is not confusing." Some stressed that the similarities and connections alleviate any confusion. At thirty-four, one of the oldest graduates of the New York program writes that she was not confused because "they were taught to me as one emerging from the other chronologically, and the parallels in the religions were presented."

THE INTERFAITH ADVANTAGE

When asked whether being an interfaith child is an advantage or disadvantage over all, none of the survey respondents said it was a disadvantage. About 80 percent said it was an advantage, and 20 percent responded that it was neither. In describing the advantages, many teens and young adults cite some variation on "tolerance," "open-mindedness," or "broader worldview." A seventeen-year-old from Washington writes, "People use the term 'open-minded' so I like to think of interfaith as being 'open-souled.'" Others testified to the breadth of the religious education they received. A thirty-four-year-old from New York writes that she "got to learn twice as much about the world as other kids." And a fourteen-year-old notes, "Seeing the connections made me a better Christian and Jew." One of the respondents, twenty-seven, from New York, cites a whole list of pluses, including "I have the advantage (if it is one) of choosing to be one or the other in accordance with my future spouse" and "Because I was never forced one way or the other, I never learned to resent religious practice. I enjoy the duality of it."

Others describe using their stereoscopic vision, the ability to see from multiple perspectives, in domains of life beyond religion. A twenty-three-year-old observes, "If you grow up learning to bridge two religions that are not normally taught together, you will likely spend your adult life building new bridges as well." When asked specifically how interfaith education affects his outlook on the world, he adds, "Nothing is black and white. Every story has multiple sides, every issue multiple outlets. Dialogue is essential. It's the most powerful weapon against war. It must be fostered."

In answer to that same question about outlook on the world, a fourteen-year-old from Chicago responds, "I try to never accept someone's beliefs as my own unless I have reflected on it inwardly. I find my own interpretations and beliefs on all topics." And a twenty-year-old in Washington writes, "I find religious extremism of every kind to be out of line. It is people not being accepting of others that causes so much of the terror in the world."

Jonah, Ian, and Elana Gold: Three Bridge-Builders

Jimmy Gold and Promise Ahlstrom met in a sixth-grade ballroom dance class in New Haven, Connecticut. Promise, the daughter of a religious historian at Yale and granddaughter of a minister, grew up Episcopalian. On the other side of town, Jim Gold grew up as a cultural Jew in an entirely Jewish neighborhood. "My parents were both raised by vigorously antireligious socialist immigrants, so they had no religious education. They were High Holiday Jews," he recalls. In high school, Jim felt drawn to a local rabbi who had been involved in the civil rights movement. He began attending services with his Jewish friends from more observant homes, becoming the most practicing Jew in his family in three generations.

At the time of their marriage, Promise and Jim had not decided how to raise their children. "I remember saying to Jimmy's mother after our first child, Jonah, was born that if he didn't do something to start them being Jewish I was going to have them baptized. I think her mouth dropped open," recalls Promise. She never carried out the threat. Instead, the family joined IFFP in Washington. All three Gold children participated in IFFP's group interfaith Coming of Age program. All three also studied Hebrew and had bar or bat mitzvahs in which they chanted from the Torah. Jim feels they made the best of the situation but still worries about where his children will end up, religiously speaking. "I don't know that they'll feel at home in a church or a synagogue, and there aren't groups like IFFP everywhere," he says. Promise, on the other hand, feels confident that their children will settle into a religious identity—most likely a Jewish one. "I do think eventually Judaism will resonate more. I think it's hard to continue with this interfaith identity," she says. "My guess is they'll become the religion of whomever they will marry."

The three Gold siblings illustrate three different ways in which an interfaith education stimulates the formation of cultural bridge-building. The oldest, Jonah, twenty-six, studied Arabic at Tufts University, became a Middle East studies major, and spent a year as a student in Cairo. He now works in Morocco, promoting Muslim-Western dialogue.

Ian Gold, twenty-one, was still in high school when he joined a youth dialogue group called City at Peace, designed to forge connections between students of different races and socioeconomic backgrounds in D.C. "The ability to connect with people and share moments and help others is what defines my life. My spirituality is more rooted in people than in the heavens," he says. "There's something to coming together even if you have different beliefs, that creates a space for everyone to grow in."

Recently, on a trip to Berlin, he and his fellow students visited the Jewish Museum. Afterward, Ian returned on his own and spent three more hours there. When the group left Berlin, he stayed on and visited the Holocaust Memorial by himself. "I connect a lot more with my Jewish faith, which I think is true of my entire family," he says. "For my Dad, it was important to maintain my identity as a Jewish person because of our ancestors. I got a balance from IFFP, but in our house, Judaism was more important."

Contemplating the next generation, Ian must reconcile his desire to keep Judaism alive, with his appreciation for his own interfaith education. "I don't need to marry a Jewish person—I've had heated arguments with Jewish friends about that," he says. "So how to raise children is something I'd have to negotiate with my spouse. If there were something similar to an interfaith organization around where I was, I would go see if I like it."

Elana Gold, nineteen, a Latin American Studies major at Temple University, plans to be a human rights lawyer working on immigration. She directly connects her interfaith upbringing and her passion for justice. "I'm sure that the more accepting and open-minded I am, the better I will be at my job," she states. "I just think it's easier to be accepting when you come from two backgrounds."

As a regular at campus Hillel, she has had to hone her legal argumentation skills, explaining her identity to others. At a Shabbat dinner, she struck up a conversation with the rabbi, who told her she could not be Jewish and Christian. "I told him about IFFP and my Coming of Age, and how I read from the Torah yet also had Christian songs and had both a minister and a rabbi there, and how I really just identify as both Christian and Jewish," recalls Elana. "And the rabbi was like, 'Well, I guess you *can* be both.' I don't necessarily think I convinced him. I think he maybe just decided that it wasn't worth the fight."

In her first year at college, Elana also regularly attended Shabbat at the campus outpost of Chabad, the Orthodox sect with a mission to "win back" non-practicing Jews. While Elana and a Jewish friend were chatting with the rabbi there, the friend asked if she could bring a curious Christian friend to the next Shabbat. Elana recalls, "The rabbi said, 'Well, Chabad has very limited resources. We try to say just Jewish people can come.' This was after I'd been there many times; I'd established a relationship with him, made friends. So I told him, 'Well, you know, I'm not technically Jewish. My Dad is the Jewish one.' And he said, 'Well as I said before, we're really just trying to serve Jewish people.' So I never went back there."

WHETHER ON COLLEGE CAMPUSES OR in houses of worship, interfaith children are standing up for themselves, defending their right to formulate religious identities at their own pace and on their own terms, and speaking out on the benefits of interfaith education. For clergy, religious institutions, and extended family, the question going forward will be how to welcome this growing cohort of interfaith children and how to benefit from their unique perspectives and interfaith bridge-building skills.

CHAPTER ELEVEN

Muslims, Hindus, Buddhists

The Next Interfaith Wave

S O FAR, JEWISH AND Christian families have dominated the discussion on religious intermarriage in America. But we are not alone. There are now over two million Muslims, over a million Hindus, and over a million Buddhists in America, and they too are marrying across religious boundaries.

The kaleidoscope of American religious identity keeps turning, powered both by intermarriage and by adult Americans who continue to switch religious affiliations at an extraordinary rate. As we slide past and through each other in a seemingly infinite display of intricate patterns, we are creating interfaith families including Sikhs, Jains, Pagans, Wiccans, Baha'is, and Zoroastrians.

Each religious recombination creates unique challenges and unique synergies. Families celebrating Judaism and Islam find many shared rituals and beliefs in these sibling religions, yet feel burdened by the weight of Middle East conflict. Jews or Christians may practice Buddhism while retaining their original faiths, creating another model for religious dual identity. Celebrating a monotheistic faith such as Christianity, Islam, or Judaism alongside a mainly polytheistic faith such as Hinduism forces families to grapple with simultaneous "gods" and "God." And people from the dharmic faiths (Hinduism, Buddhism, Sikhism, Jainism) must face the real or perceived exclusionary nature of Abrahamic rituals.

With great excitement, I await the books that will be written by interfaith Buddhist, Muslim, Hindu, and Pagan parents and children to describe their experiences. My hope is that this book inspires next-wave interfaith couples of all combinations with two essential ideas. No family should feel forced to choose one religion. And children raised with two religions can grow up to be well-adjusted adults, spiritually deep and unafraid to affiliate with one or more religions.

MUSLIM INTERMARRIAGE

According to *Muslim Americans: Mostly Middle Class and Mainstream*, a 2007 study by the Pew Research Center, 62 percent of American Muslims said they personally believed that it was "okay" for Muslims and non-Muslims to intermarry.

Traditional Muslim clerics have held that Muslim men can marry "people of the book" (Christians and Jews) but that a Muslim woman can marry a non-Muslim man only if he converts to Islam. Dissenting Muslim voices argue that the Qur'an does not actually spell out these restrictions on women. Imam Khaleel Mohammad, a professor of religious studies at San Diego State University who officiates at interfaith weddings, states his much more progressive interpretation: ". . . an interfaith marriage can take place on condition that neither spouse will be forcibly converted to the other's religion."

And although the traditional Muslim view has been that the child will be the religion of the father, Imam Mohammad advocates for allowing children to be immersed in both religions. He writes, "As a Muslim scholar, I can tell you that the Qur'an advocates the use of the heart and mind in forming opinions. If both parents are faithful to their interpretations of the Creator's will, then the children will make informed decisions when they come of age." In both of the cases below, an intermarried Muslim father is raising children with both family religions.

In England, where the Muslim community is both larger than in the United States and constitutes a greater percentage of the population, a Muslim and Christian intermarriage support group has been meeting since the 1990s, and a group of Christian and Muslim clerics recently signed on to a document that discourages forced conversions and promotes the equal rights of men and women to intermarry. Muslim and Christian interfaith families groups also exist in France and Scotland. And in Chicago, Eileen O'Farrell Smith of the Interfaith Union has been facilitating a Muslim and Christian intermarriage support group, exploring the idea that her experiences in Jewish and Catholic interfaith communities will prove useful as a model.

Muslim and Christian: Reza and Jessica

Reza Aslan (a Muslim man) and Jessica Jackley (a Christian woman) have a high-profile intermarriage: they are each nationally prominent in their own fields. Reza, a religious studies scholar and author of five books, frequently comments on the Muslim world in the national media, including repeat appearances on Jon Stewart's *The Daily Show*. Jessica Jackley cofounded Kiva, a groundbreaking online network allowing individuals to make small loans to entrepreneurs in developing countries and the United States.

After mutual friends suggested they meet, Reza and Jessica were both so busy traveling that weeks went by before they managed to get together. That gave them time to "Google the hell out of each other," Reza says. By the time they met, "We both kind of had these intellectual crushes on each other."

While Reza is the Muslim in this intermarriage, his American experience primed him for religious pluralism and complexity. "My family was basically culturally Muslim, the way most Americans are culturally Christian," he says. "My grandmother was a very religious woman, so my mom had a deeper sense of her faith than my father did. My father was quite famous in Iran for his atheism."

After the fall of the Shah and the creation of the Islamic Republic of Iran in 1979, Reza's family fled to California, joining a flood of Iranians, most of whom "came away with a bad taste in their mouths" about religion, Reza notes. But he had a different reaction: "I think my childhood experiences of revolutionary Iran created an abiding interest in the power of religion and social change and what happens as a result of faith put into practice. It created a lasting impression," he says.

In high school, Reza was drawn to the fervor of Christian classmates and was "born again." From ages sixteen to twenty, he was an Evangelical Christian. "I went out there and saved souls, including my mother's soul," he says. She remains a Christian to this day. Then Reza went off to college at Santa Clara University, a Jesuit institution. "I decided to take my interest in religion into an academic realm, and it didn't take long to realize that everything I had been taught was wrong," he recalls. By the time he graduated, he was no longer an Evangelical but was still a Christian, on his way to Harvard Divinity School to study the New Testament. But before he left, his academic adviser at Santa Clara asked Reza some probing questions. As a practical matter, she suggested that the academic world needed more experts in Islam. But she also challenged him, saying, "I don't understand why you're so uninterested in your own culture and tradition, the faith of your forefathers."

By the time he arrived at Harvard in the fall, he was immersed in readings on Islam. "Everything I read, I just kept thinking to myself, 'This is what I believe. This is what I think. This is how I view it,'" he recalls. "Suddenly it became clear why my spiritual quest in Christianity was not satisfying me. The way that Islam talks about God and creation and the relationship between the creator and creation was stuff that I actually already believed, but that I didn't know had a name. In a truly Jungian sense, it was in me all along."

Inspired by Reza's discoveries, one of his sisters went to Iran to visit family and "came back wearing a veil," says Reza. His other sister remains an atheist, like her father. "So now in the family we have a Shia fundamentalist, a religion scholar, an Evangelical Christian, and two atheists. Two grumpy, grumpy atheists," laughs Reza.

Meanwhile, Jessica was growing up outside Pittsburgh, deeply involved in community service through her Evangelical church. "We went on service trips, and I found a lot of meaning and a huge part of my identity in that," she recalls. "We would go volunteer somewhere on Saturdays and paint schools or build playgrounds. I wanted to understand poverty and my role in it. My senior year, I went to Haiti with a dozen friends from church on a trip led by my dad, and that was pivotal for me. That broke me open and made me ask a lot of questions about my faith. You think you are going to give something, and you realize you receive and learn a lot more than you give. I had a bit of a breakdown. The next week was senior prom, and I was bawling in the middle of my prom with this big fluffy dress on knowing that there were children starving in Haiti and there was a supermarket in my suburb filled with food right down the street. I just didn't know how to make sense of it."

At Bucknell University, she studied philosophy, challenging her own fundamentalism with Nietzsche. "I think my professors were all shocked that I didn't graduate an atheist like many of them were. But I didn't, it strengthened my faith," she says.

Her passion for alleviating poverty led her to found Kiva with her first husband, a Christian. Though her strict identification with Evangelical Christianity fell away in the process of a divorce, she remains a Christian.

Jessica fell in love with Reza in part because of, not in spite of, his religious background. "I found the person who could understand and know me more than anyone, and that I wanted to know more than anyone. I felt like he had gone through the same things I had gone through. Maybe on the outside it would look like a different journey, but it wasn't. He knows the Bible better than I do. He's writing a book right now on Jesus. He understood my life better than most Christians. He brings such a richness to everything, but especially to this area of life."

For her Christian family, the idea that Jessica had chosen a Muslim as a partner did come as a shock. "As you can imagine, when Jessica first told her parents about me, her mom was very distressed," recalls Reza. "She said, 'I just don't know if I want my grandkids to grow up around all that violence.' She had never in her life met a Muslim. All she knew about Islam, and she admits this openly, was what Sean Hannity told her on Fox News. She has come from there and has done this incredible 180 where she adores me. We have the most wonderful relationship."

In fact, Jessica's brother, an Evangelical pastor, officiated at their wedding. As for many other interfaith couples, the process of thinking through the idea of marriage, independent of a religious script, was liberating for Jessica and Reza. "Our decision to get married was a process of reclaiming what marriage could be and redefining it for ourselves," says Jessica. Reza adds, "We wrote our own vows. We talked about the things that were important to us. There was a deep spiritualism to the ceremony but we did not ground the ceremony in any specific set of symbols or metaphors. It was neither Christian nor Muslim."

The couple now plans to raise their twin toddler sons with both family religions and with an awareness of all religions. "My dream is that we spend time, set aside as a family, and we all teach each other, and that we expose them to the world's religions in a pretty systematic way—not just to our own traditions but all sorts of faiths," says Jessica. "Holidays will be about family and our own traditions. But just as we redefined and reclaimed what marriage could be, I feel like we can redefine and reclaim holidays and how we talk about and think about God in our day-to-day."

Reza adds, "Jessica and I share the same beliefs; we share the same values. We also share the notion that our beliefs and values must be lived out in our lives, our choices, the activities that we engage in, in the world. The stories, the myths, and the rituals are different. But the values, the beliefs, the worldview are identical. For us, it's kind of a no-brainer. What we're going to teach our kids is the values, the beliefs, the activism, the worldview. And when it comes to the stories, we'll give them *all* of them. We'll give them Jessica's stories and my stories and Buddhist stories and Jain stories and Hindu stories and Jewish stories. And we'll make sure that they understand that what they're reading are *stories*. And that the ideals and aspirations behind the stories are exactly the same. It's what the stories mean that's important."

Second-Generation Interfaith: Adam and Maureen

Adam grew up Muslim, Maureen grew up Catholic (these are not their real names). They are raising their children with both religions. But looking to the past and the future, their family represents a trifecta of Abrahamic faiths, and perhaps the future of interfaith recombination. "In some sense I'm kind of the classic American melting pot," Adam explains. "My mother was born and raised Jewish. My father was Catholic, went to Catholic schools, and considered going into the priesthood." After seeking together for a common religion, they converted to Sufi Islam, a year before Adam was born.

In childhood, Adam learned to read Arabic script, memorized the Muslim prayers, and refrained from consuming pork or alcohol. But at the same time, the family kept ties to Judaism and Christianity. "We celebrated Christmas every year, because clearly the rest of the family on my father's side was Christian," says Adam. "We also had Passover seders at our house or at other people's houses." It helped that Adam's family lived in a multicultural neighborhood in a major urban center. "My parents tried to teach us about their previous faiths, but also about Buddhism, and all faiths. My godmother is Sikh. My brother's best friend was Baha'i. The overriding principle was focused more on spirituality and less on dogma," recalls Adam. For a while, he attended a Unitarian Sunday school, and for a few years, he attended classes at the Muslim community center.

In a high school science class, Adam met Maureen. She recalls, "I didn't know that he was Muslim. I think we actually started dating before religion came up. Obviously when you're seventeen you're not looking for a life partner. You think someone's cute, you're not thinking about what religion they are."

Adam explains, "Even at the time, which was before 9/11, people tended to have negative views of Islam. So along with all the other teenage insecurities, I had the religion one." When Adam finally confided that he was Muslim, Maureen was not deterred, despite her strong religious background. The product of a "big Irish Catholic family," Maureen says, "There were a lot of expectations that I would be Catholic forever and marry someone Catholic."

Nonetheless, the couple stayed together through college, then broke up for eight weeks. As Maureen describes it, "We had one brief crisis of faith where we weren't sure it was going to work out because of this sticking issue of how were we going to raise children." The decision to raise the children with both religions saved their relationship. Adam says: "It came down to raising them with exposure to both, giving them a good solid foundation. They can choose one of the two, or choose something else."

They married in the church where Maureen was baptized. "I elected not to have Communion at the wedding," says Maureen. "My mother was upset about it. But I didn't want to start the marriage doing something where Adam couldn't participate." At the wedding reception, they chose not to have alcohol, which struck Maureen's father at first as contrary to the spirit of being good hosts. In the end, he found a way to welcome guests by walking around offering a humidor of cigars instead.

The first three years of marriage sailed by smoothly; then a son arrived, and they faced the circumcision issue. Maureen gave birth with midwives, not in a hospital, so the circumcision could not be done at birth. "I didn't really want to circumcise my son," Maureen admits. She asked Adam to make the arrangements, but by the time they took him to a pediatric surgeon, they were told their son would have to abstain from nursing for twelve hours in preparation for general anesthesia for the procedure. Both Adam and Maureen rejected this option. Adam's Jewish-born mother came to the rescue, using her Jewish networks to find a mohel, a licensed Jewish ritual circumciser, who would perform a home circumcision for the child of a Muslim and a Catholic.

Next, it was Adam's turn to wrestle, this time with the issue of baptism. "Frankly, I didn't want it to happen," says Adam. "I don't believe in original sin, so I struggled with it." He was able to talk over the decision with his Catholic-born father. Eventually, he came to a universalist embrace of water in religious rituals, and this helped him to accept the idea. "Original sin aside, the act of cleansing is experienced in all faiths. As Muslims, we do it before prayers every day," he says. And so, their son was baptized in the Catholic Church.

But their second child never had a baptism. By the time their daughter arrived, Maureen's family, ardent supporters of Pope John Paul II, felt less connected to the Church. At the same time, the family had grown more comfortable with the idea of Adam as a Muslim.

The couple has followed through on their plan to expose the children, now ages seven and four, to both religions. "We have a very interfaith bedtime routine," says Maureen. Every night, Adam comes in to say Muslim prayers, and then Maureen says an Our Father and a Hail Mary. They host a Christmas celebration for extended family and also celebrate the major Muslim festivals, the *Eids*.

At the moment, the children attend only a Muslim Sunday school, learning Arabic script and *suras* (Qur'anic verses). "In order to have it be equal, you almost need to more formally educate them more about Islam. *My* prayers are in English, so they know them by heart," Maureen says.

At seven, their son now identifies himself as Muslim. Maureen says, "Early on, he said, 'I'm what Daddy is.' This is sort of what I knew would happen. You can't have a religion that gets practiced so routinely throughout the day and not have that feel closer to the children." Maureen points out, for instance, that the decision to avoid pork means they have told their son he cannot have the pepperoni pizza at school, a dietary prohibition that serves as a constant reminder of their Muslim practice.

And yet Adam and Maureen continue to read their children tales from all of the world's great religions, including Buddhism, as Adam's parents did. And they imagine there may come a time when they might even seek out a Unitarian Universalist religious education program for them. "Our focus has been less on textbook religion and more on the core beliefs and spirituality," says Adam.

Maureen has grown into her role as an interfaith bridge-builder, inspired by her relationship with Adam and in response to anti-Muslim discrimination. "I'm not converting," she says. "We're both comfortable with what we are. I'm not by any means a practicing Catholic. But what do you turn to in times of trouble? For me, it's always going to be the rosary, the prayers I learned when I was young. But at the same time, I am a bit of a goodwill ambassador now for Islam. Especially in the wake of 9/11, people who didn't feel comfortable asking Adam would ask me these delicate questions. When you find yourself having to constantly defend a religion because you're defending your husband and your family, you do find yourself starting to align yourself with those principles. You're trying so hard to make people understand that at the base it's really not that different."

Adam and Maureen see the benefits for their children of being an interfaith family. "When we talk to the kids about other faiths, the biggest thing is being respectful and accepting of everyone, because ultimately we're all trying to get up the same mountain, on whichever path works best for that person. Coming from an interfaith family shows them that there is not one way to do things."

Hindu and Catholic: Robbie and Keya

Keya Rajput and Robbie Milla met in law school in Chicago in 2005. Immediately, they were drawn together by all that they shared: strong faith, connections to family, deep cultural roots. And yet their faith is in different religions, their families from different cultures.

Keya grew up in an Indian American community in West Bloomfield, Michigan. Her family attended a Hindu temple nearby but also immersed Keya in religion at home. "My mom and my family taught me the importance of prayers at home, singing in the morning and on the way to school. I was told that if I was ever afraid or needed to talk to someone and my parents weren't there, I could always turn to God," she recalls. "I learned about the Hindu deities and the myths and the stories behind my religion and grew to appreciate that. So many of our family gatherings were centered around some kind of cultural, historical, or spiritual significance. It was really through family that I learned religion, more so than going to temple. And today I sort of have the same view. I don't go to temple daily, but I consider myself very spiritual and devout and I believe in the tenets of Hinduism."

Meanwhile, Robbie grew up Catholic on the Gulf coast of Florida. "My father is half Italian and half Spanish, my mother's from the Philippines, but our religion was unified. We knew we were Catholic—there was no doubt about that," he says. His mother attended Mass daily, his father weekly, and Robbie became an altar server.

While dating, Robbie and Keya each reveled in embracing the other's culture and family. "I went to family events, wore Indian garb," says Robbie. "Rather than shying away from it, I was full steam ahead, knowing this is a part of her life that is extremely important to her, so it's got to be important to me. It wasn't forced. It just came naturally. And in the same way, it was clear to me that when she was around my family, she was on board."

Keya's family welcomed Robbie with notable warmth. "We would go to temple, and her mother would make a point of sitting next to me and making things clear to me: 'This is what they're chanting. This is why they're saying it. This is the significance of these statues.' I wasn't left on my own feeling ostracized," says Robbie. "I was made to feel welcome. Even with prayer, they would say, 'Robbie, it's okay if you want to pray to your God.' It was a really welcoming environment that made me feel more in love with her because the family was so great."

Keya felt equally comfortable going to church with Robbie and his family. "My parents had always taught me that you can seek guidance wherever you are," she says. "I grew up in a predominantly Jewish community. I went to bar and bat mitzvahs by the dozens when I was in seventh grade. We felt very comfortable in any house of prayer. Hinduism is polytheistic but doesn't necessarily disagree with the concept that there is just one concept of God. My mom went to a Catholic school in India and knew those prayers. She always instilled in me the idea that I should feel comfortable praying wherever I am. When I'm in church with Robbie's family, praying and singing, I love the feeling that we are all a family attending church together."

But as the relationship became more serious, Keya became concerned about how they would teach any future child about the afterlife, given their theological differences. "I told him, 'We believe in reincarnation, and you believe in heaven and hell. I would not be able to handle it if my own daughter thought I wasn't going to go to a good place when I die.' He looked at me and said, 'If we both believe so strongly in God, we'll tell our child there's no God that would allow us to love each other and be together if we're not going to be together in the afterlife.'"

When they got married, they incorporated Catholic prayers and Filipino culture into a three-day traditional Indian wedding with a Hindu priest. Both mothers lit the Unity candle (a contemporary Christian wedding tradition) together. Some of Robbie's family wore traditional Filipino clothing. And they incorporated Filipino wedding traditions, including a veil spread over the bride and groom and a lasso roped around them in a figure eight, representing the binding of the two families. The couple was also bound, in Indian tradition, by garlands and the tying together of their clothing.

Robbie and Keya both knew that they would raise any future children with both religions. "Her faith is so strong, as is mine," says Robbie. "It was understood that when we have a child, she will know both." Keya elaborates, "We are taking each other as we are, and if we have a child together, that child is going to be both of us in every way."

That child has now become a reality. She's a year old and has been growing up with full Hindu and Catholic immersion. When Keya was seven months pregnant, a Hindu priest came to give traditional blessings over the unborn child. Keya explains, "All the portions of the belly—the uterus, the water—are protected and blessed by different divinities." Robbie adds, "I felt warm that these blessings were being showered on our child, who was being protected and looked after."

The baby's Catholic baptism was harder for Keya, at least at first. "I felt like I was going to be the outside member in a very important ritual and ceremony that my daughter was involved in," she says. "I did struggle with the idea a little bit, knowing that she was going to participate in a sacrament for a religion that is sometimes exclusionary, whereas Hinduism isn't often outwardly exclusionary in that way."

So Keya did her own research on the origins and meaning of baptism. "The more I read about it, the more I liked the idea behind baptism. I didn't think the symbolism of the baptism ceremony disagreed with any of the Hindu tenets." Keya may have been comforted by the fact that the family Catholic priest who performed the baptism happens to be Indian. She also credits Robbie's family with helping her through her moment of alienation. "Robbie's sisters said, 'She is never going to feel that because she's Catholic, she can't be Hindu too,'" Keya recalls. And Robbie's mother organized a feast of Indian food after the baptism.

When they think about their daughter's future religious identity, both Keya and Robbie have a hard time imagining their daughter with only one faith. Keya says, "Even if she leans one way more than the other, I hope that she still appreciates both of them and knows that they are very much a part of her." Robbie echoes this sentiment: "What would be upsetting, or sad, would be if one religion was shut out. I can live with her identifying with one more than the other but appreciating both of them."

THE APPEAL OF BUDDHISM

Both of my interfaith children feel drawn to Buddhism: at fifteen, my son describes his current religious identity on Facebook with an ice cream metaphor: "Jew Christian swirl interested in Buddhism." Whether through intermarriage or through the adoption of Zen meditation practices, Buddhism plays a growing role in twenty-first-century American interfaith families, just as Americans are becoming more conscious of Hinduism through the growing practice of yoga.

One of the friends who has brought Buddhism into my family is my daughter's godmother, Sharron Mendel Swain, who was raised by one Jewish and one Christian parent, found a spiritual home in Buddhism in her twenties, and now runs a UU religious education program. Her Buddhist practice is based on the teachings of peace activist and Vietnamese Buddhist monk Thich Nhat Hanh, who was nominated for the Nobel Peace Prize by Martin Luther King Jr.

Sharron explains the appeal of Buddhism for her as an interfaith child: "The beautiful thing about Buddhism is that it never, in my experience, asks someone to choose. It would be like asking a child 'Are you your father's child or your mother's child?' Of course, you are the child of both." This recognition of bothness stems from the central tenet of Buddhist practice called *interbeing*. She explains, "Interbeing is a deep recognition of how intricately interconnected our world is, from the subatomic level to the level of the cosmos. Looking deeply, it is possible to see that Christianity cannot exist without Judaism, and Judaism as it is today cannot exist independently of Christianity. For me, it is as if Christianity and Judaism are two rivers of my family's experience flowing into the ocean of my life and experience. Buddhism is the one place I have found that is big enough to embrace the whole ocean."

At the same time, many Buddhist practitioners from interfaith families do not abandon their birth religions. "An ironic thing about Buddhist practice is that it almost invariably leads the practitioner into a much closer examination of, and often deeper appreciation of, the religion with which they were raised," says Sharron. "This often helps people arrive at a much more mature appreciation of the treasures buried in their birth traditions."

For many Jews and Christians, simultaneous practice of Buddhism has become common and relatively accepted. The Jewish American love affair with Buddhism began in the nineteenth century, intensified in the 1960s, and continues unabated. Christian mystics, most notably Trappist monk and author Thomas Merton, have long been drawn to Buddhism. However, some Jews and Christians label Buddhism as a practice, rather than a religion, thus skirting the idea that they are dual-faith adherents.

From the Jewish standpoint, claiming both Judaism and Buddhism remains far less controversial than claiming Judaism and Christianity. "The Buddha is completely innocent when it comes to the question of Christ's death," says Sharron. "Jews have been burdened for centuries with false allegations around this event, and all manner of prejudice and discrimination that flows from that. Nonviolence and nonharm are central to Buddhism. People come into Buddhism with all kinds of wounds and baggage, but if they stick with it long enough, it helps transform all that. No matter how much anger or hatred is in us, we can shift the focus and nurture the altruism, the forgiveness, the kindness. This is a profoundly healing perspective."

Jewish, Christian, Buddhist: Ivan and Miral

For some interfaith families, layering Buddhism onto a Jewish and Christian relationship can actually help unite the couple, rather than create further complexity. For example, Ivan Kruh grew up Jewish, his wife, Miral, grew up as a Coptic Christian (an ancient Egyptian form of Christianity). Through his practice of Buddhism, Ivan has been able to deepen his appreciation of both of their religions. "Buddhism has helped my interfaith family immensely, although not necessarily intentionally. I found that I didn't need to be so tight about what was 'true' in Judaism and what wasn't—I could see the way Judaism holds multiple perspectives on many issues, some of which resonate and some of which don't, and I could see the things that didn't resonate as *koans*, or paradoxical and irrational questions for me to contemplate. Importantly, I was able to see freshly the psychological and spiritual depth of Judaism that had been missing from the Judaism I was raised with." This same perspective became essential to Ivan in accepting the Christianity of his wife. He explains, "Most fundamentally, Buddhism provided me the courage to walk into a religion that had been demonized in much I had been raised with, with an openness to see what this religion I ridiculed from a collective unconscious of fear had to teach me."

Ivan has encountered different forms of resistance to crossing the various religious boundaries. In his experience, Jews may welcome the exploration of Buddhism as a philosophy, "but exploring Christianity is still a serious no-no. In many Christian circles, Judaism is appreciated as the root of Christianity and is open to exploration, but Buddhism is 'godless' and is to be shunned. There are still so many walls people put up based on history and misunderstandings. Sometimes it makes me so sad to see. At least for our tri-religion family, each tradition and the interactions among the three have brought great joy and beauty into our lives."

Challenged by a local rabbi to explain how he would give a multireligious identity to any children they might have, Ivan wrote to his future children, saying, in part: "We will share with you the Jewish, Christian, and Buddhist ways, because they are ways that have nurtured and powerfully shaped us. These particular traditions are your birthright. Going deep into one or more of these traditions is very important to spiritual development, but so is the appreciation for the richness of the human experience that comes from the full family of spiritual traditions. Exploration across traditions can bring greater clarity and help prevent you from seeing the lens of any one tradition as exclusive Truth. God has always been patiently holding all of these unfolding traditions, and so can you."

CONCLUSION

Ambassadors for Peace

N O MATTER WHAT RELIGIOUS choices we make for them, or what choices they make for themselves, we must foster positive self-images for our interfaith children. We want them to feel inspired and motivated by their interfaith heritage, and if we bequeath to them a sense that the benefits of their birthright outweigh the challenges, I believe that prophecy can and will be fulfilled.

Interfaith families quite literally transgress (from the Latin for "step across") religious boundaries to pioneer a new life in the liminal space. We meet the other, embrace the other, fall in love with the other, have children with the other, and many of us refuse to get back inside neat religious identity boxes. As an interfaith child, I celebrate the discovery that the barrier is permeable, that cognitive dissonance can lead to creativity as well as chaos, that I can (as Walt Whitman declared) contain multitudes.

As those of us with multifaith backgrounds reach maturity, we are beginning to reach out to each other, to reflect on and confirm our own positive experiences, and to create our own zeitgeist. We thrive on seeing coevolution, sensing overlaps, making linkages. Jewish people sometimes joke that they can identify each other by "Jewdar," a sixth sense picking up on visual, cultural, verbal, and intellectual cues. I like to think I have the gift of "interfaithdar," meaning that I often correctly guess when someone has interfaith heritage, based on a certain open spirit and proclivity for crossing borders and making connections.

Recently, I read a press report about a tropical tree–canopy expert who was mapping out the religious significance of the trees planted around an Episcopal cathedral in Utah. Immediately, my "interfaithdar" went off. Sure enough, it turns out that ecologist Nalini Nadkarni was born to a Hindu father and a Jewish mother, attended Unitarian Sunday school, and married her husband in a "hybrid Hindu/Jewish/Presbyterian ceremony." In her book *Between Earth and Sky: Our Intimate Connections to Trees*, she links her thoughts on biology, poetry, and spirituality, vaulting gracefully across traditional academic boundaries. In her introduction, she uses the intermarriage metaphor explicitly to describe her work: "Although we are not of the same family, trees and humans are in a sense married into each other's families, with all the challenges, responsibilities, and benefits that come from being so linked."

I admit to feeling a sort of tribal (or perhaps anti-tribal) pride when I discover adult interfaith children who have transformed their experience with more than one religion into passionate good works fueled by empathy, or important thinking inspired by connections between disciplines, or compelling art created by dwelling in the borderlands. I see common positive traits, not genetic but created through interfaith experience or knowledge of interfaith heritage, in a long list of prominent heirs of intermarriage, including Barack Obama, Gabrielle Giffords, Fiorello LaGuardia, Paul Newman, Gloria Steinem, Saint Teresa of Avila, Raoul Wallenberg, Marcel Proust, Adrienne Rich, and Frida Kahlo.

As I write this conclusion, religious hatred continues to instill fear, incite violence, and prevent peace in the world. Christian supremacists open fire on Sikhs and burn American mosques to the ground. Muslim extremists drive moderate Sufi Muslims out of northern Mali. Jews, Muslims, and Christians still cannot seem to find a way to coexist peacefully in the Middle East. None of this violence has purely religious roots: the causes include ethnic and socioeconomic differences, political manipulation, territorial disputes. Yet demonizing other humans as religious "others" makes such violence psychologically possible.

As interfaith children, born with the potential to walk in more than one pair of religious shoes or to see through more than one religious lens, we have a unique role to play in reducing religious intolerance and promoting religious peace. By our very existence, strong interfaith families disarm those who believe there is only one true way to live a righteous life. By our very presence in the world, interfaith children make coexistence into a permanent reality. If the "other" is a wife or husband, if as interfaith children the "other" dwells within us, than there can truly be no "other."

After the trauma of 9/11, the long-standing formal interfaith dialogue between theologians opened up into a national movement of grassroots interfaith activists. What began with religious leaders meeting at conferences has expanded to include local congregations visiting each other, Jewish and Muslim teens going to summer camp together, and college students from many religious backgrounds joining with secular humanist students to do community service projects. On campuses, in part through Eboo Patel's dynamic and fast-growing Interfaith Youth Core, the word "interfaith" has even morphed from an adjective into a noun, as in, "Interfaith means so much to me" or "I want to get more involved in interfaith."

I hope the day comes soon when those who claim interfaith identity—and who have been practicing interfaith communication since birth—will be welcomed as leaders in interfaith dialogue. Religion scholar Karla Suomala notes that if those of us with complex religious identities are not invited to the interfaith dialogue table, "there won't be anyone left at the table." As intermarriage increases, we may feel frightened by what may be lost: the purity of each religious pathway, the unequivocal criteria of membership, the precision of boundaries. But at the same time, so much is gained: a growing population of couples, children, grandparents, uncles, aunts, cousins, coworkers, and friends who witness the fact that love can be more powerful than ancestral strife. When we embrace the other, when we bring into the world children who embody two or more religions and cultures, we create a protective network, invisible but as strong as silk, against intolerance.

Whether or not this was our original intention, when we live as interfaith families, we help to bring about peace in the world. If, as a Jew, I love my Christian husband, how can I demonize a Muslim or a Hindu? Interfaith children, from birth, can learn to cherish two religions just as they cherish two parents. If they are raised loving Quakerism and Hinduism, how can they disrespect Mormonism or Sikhism?

In the end, I did not feel I had a choice but to raise my children interfaith. As an interfaith child myself, I could not in good conscience make a choice for my own children that would require marginalizing their predominantly Christian family tree. But neither could I turn my back on my beloved Judaism.

But I did not anticipate how choosing both would create *joy*, and not simply compromise, in our lives. My husband and I have reveled in the pleasure of our intellectual interfaith collaboration and lovingly shared our traditions with each other and with our children. We have been able to sit together as a family in a church pew, in a synagogue, and in our interfaith families community, feeling intensely fulfilled in each environment.

My children are now on the brink of adulthood. As I finish writing this book, my daughter is heading off to college, ready to continue her religious explorations and make her own decisions about affiliation and identity. I hope that she goes to Shabbat services with the Hillel group at her college and bakes with the campus nonprofit "Challah for Hunger." I hope she explores chapels and cathedrals and seeks out gospel choirs. I hope that she studies the religions of the world, bringing her own radically inclusive viewpoint to the classroom. I hope that she finds a pathway that brings her strength and fulfillment. And I hope the skills she has honed as an interfaith communicator will be appreciated by interfaith activists.

We have given both of our children love for two cultures and literacy in two religions. We have given them the gifts of seeing connections and contrasts, of going beyond embrace of the other to actually embody the other. We have given them the gift of joyful interfaithness. They have learned to take spiritual delight in nature and music, and to feel an organic connection to both family religions. Now may their interfaith childhoods inspire them to strive for greater peace in the world.

ACKNOWLEDGMENTS

AFTER WORKING ON THIS book, on some level, for my entire lifetime, I have many thanks to give. First, thank you to Reverend Julia Jarvis and Rabbi Harold White for their extraordinary collaboration. To Mary Heléne Pottker Rosenbaum and Stanley Ned Rosenbaum (may his memory be for a blessing) for paving the way. To Sheila Gordon, Mary Joel Holin, Stacey Katz, Irene Landsman, Laura Sternberg, and everyone else who has worked to create interfaith-family communities. To the village that helped to raise my children, including Johanna Janssens and Jeff Bartholet; Marika Partridge and Larry Ravitz; Emily Piccirillo and Gordon Clark; Katherine Russell and George Askew; Diane Singerman and Paul Wapner; and Denise Jones, Rhonda Kranz, and Sharron Mendel Swain. For the love and support of Martha Katz, David Katz, and James Katz. For the joy of theological discussion: Reverend Fred Alling, the late Wilson Alling, Judy Bolton-Fasman, Reverend Ellen Jennings, Rabbi Tamara Miller, and Ian Spatz. To my steadfast writing group, Calliope: Colleen Cordes, Christine Intagliata, Robyn Jackson, Mandy Katz, Diane MacEachern, Susan Orlins, and Karen Paul-Stern. To visionary agents, May Wuthrich and Rob Weisbach. And to editors Amy Caldwell and Will Myers, and the whole team at Beacon, who took a leap of faith(s) to bring the world this book.

Above all, to my parents, William Emanuel Katz and Martha Legg Katz, for loving each other and for extraordinary support of all their children; to my husband, Paul Miller, for the gift of time to pursue this dream throughout our decades together; and to my Aimee and Ben, for their patience as my obsession with this book took up much of their childhood. They embody everything I hoped that interfaith children could grow up to be.

SELECTED AND
ANNOTATED RESOURCES

INTERFAITH MARRIAGE AND INTERFAITH CHILDREN

Blecher, Arthur. *The New American Judaism: The Way Forward on Challenging Issues from Intermarriage to Jewish Identity.* New York: Palgrave Macmillan, 2007. Makes the case that intermarriage may be good for Judaism.

Christian Muslim Forum. *When Two Faiths Meet: Marriage, Family and Pastoral Care; Ethical Principles.* 2012. http://www.christianmuslimforum.org/images/When%20Two%20Faiths%20Meet%20guidelines.pdf. A guide for clergy and families on Christian/Muslim marriage in the United Kingdom.

Cohen, Steven, et al. *The Jewish Community Study of New York: 2011.* http://www.ujafedny.org/jewish-community-study-of-new-york-2011/, UJA-Federation of New York, 2012. Shows the increase in people identifying as "partially Jewish" in New York.

Cox, Harvey. *Common Prayers: Faith, Family, and a Christian's Journey Through the Jewish Year.* New York: Houghton Mifflin Harcourt, 2001. How Judaism can be meaningful for an intermarried Christian parent raising a Jewish child.

Fishman, Sylvia Barack. *Double or Nothing? Jewish Families and Mixed Marriage.* Lebanon, NH: Brandeis University Press, 2004. In-depth interviews and research, funded by Jewish institutions concerned about intermarriage.

Forum for Interfaith Marriages with Equality. http://www.interfaithshaadi.org/. Issues raised when those from dharmic religions (Buddhism/Hinduism/Jainism) marry those from Abrahamic religions (Judaism/Christianity/Islam).

Gibel Azoulay, Katya. *Black, Jewish and Interracial.* Durham, NC: Duke University Press, 1997. A scholarly work on the children of African American and Jewish families.

Gillick, Jeremy. "The Coming of the Intermarried Rabbi," *New Voices,* April 23, 2009. http://newvoices.org/2009/04/23/0007–3/. Important investigative journalism on rabbinical students in interfaith relationships.

Goodman-Malamuth, Leslie, and Robin Margolis. *Between Two Worlds: Choices for Grown Children of Jewish-Christian Parents.* New York: Pocket Books, 1992. The first book by and about adult interfaith children, written just as interfaith communities were starting up.

Greek Orthodox Archdiocese of America, Office of Interfaith Marriage. http://www.goarch.org/archdiocese/departments/marriage/interfaith. Greek Orthodox policies and advice on intermarriage.

Gruzen, Lee. *Raising Your Jewish/Christian Child* (rev. 2nd edition). New York: Newmarket, 2001. The book that first proposed raising children with both religions.

"Half-Jewish? The Heirs of Intermarriage." http://iishj.org/colloquium-12.html. 2012 colloquium sponsored by the International Institute for Secular Humanistic Judaism.

Hawxhurst, Joan. *The Interfaith Family Guidebook: Practical Advice for Jewish and Christian Partners.* Kalamazoo, MI: Dovetail Publishing, 1998. Advice from an author open to raising children with both religions.

Interfaithfamily.com. http://www.interfaithfamily.com/. Lively and comprehensive website primarily for interfaith couples raising Jewish children.

Islamic Interfaith Marriage Blessing. https://www.irshadmanji.com/Interfaith-Couples. Muslim author Irshad Manji defends the idea that both Muslim men and women can intermarry.

Klein, Daniel, and Freke Vuijst. *The Half-Jewish Book: A Celebration.* New York: Villard, 2000. A defense of "half-Jewish" as an identity: comedy, pop culture, some serious essays.

Kosmin, Barry A., Egon Mayer, and Ariela Keysar. *American Religious Identification Survey 2001* and *2008.* http://commons.trincoll.edu/aris/. Surveys on American religious identification.

Mayer, Egon. *Love and Tradition: Marriage Between Jews and Christians.* New York: Plenum, 1985. A classic early book on intermarriage by a noted researcher.

Miller, Susan Katz. *On Being Both.* https://onbeingboth.com/. Blog with essays on raising children in an interfaith family, interfaith identity, and interfaith community celebrations.

O'Hearn, Claudine Chiawei, ed. *Half and Half: Writers on Growing Up Biracial and Bicultural.* New York: Pantheon, 1998. Essays on complex identity.

"Patrilineal and Matrilineal Descent." Central Conference of American Rabbis, October 1983. http://data.ccarnet.org/cgi-bin/respdisp .pl?file=38&year=carr. Explains the Reform rabbinic reasoning behind accepting "patrilineal Jews."

Pew Forum on Religion and Public Life. *Many Americans Mix Multiple Faiths.* 2009. http://www.pewforum.org/Other-Beliefs-and-Practices/ Many-Americans-Mix-Multiple-Faiths.aspx. Survey finding a high rate of Americans attending more than one place of worship.

Pew Forum on Religion and Public Life. *Muslim Americans: Middle Class and Mostly Mainstream.* 2007. http://pewresearch.org/pubs/483/ muslim-americans. Survey finding that the majority of Muslim Americans think interfaith marriage is "okay."

Pew Forum on Religion and Public Life. *U.S. Religious Landscape Survey.* 2009. http://religions.pewforum.org/reports. Survey documenting the high rate of Americans changing or dropping religious affiliation, and intermarriage between people of different religious identities.

Riley, Naomi Schaefer. *'Til Faith Do Us Part.* New York: Oxford University Press, 2013. Focuses on challenges and divorce, with funding from conservative foundations.

Rosenbaum, Mary Heléne, and Stanley Ned Rosenbaum. *Celebrating Our Differences: Living Two Faiths in One Marriage.* Shippensburg, PA: Ragged Edge Press, 1994. The first book on raising children with Judaism and Christianity; published in the era before interfaith communities.

Rosenstone, Robert A. "My Wife, the Muslim." *Antioch Review*, March 22, 2005. A Jewish man marries a Muslim woman in a ceremony officiated by a Buddhist.

Schaper, Donna. *Raising Interfaith Children: Spiritual Orphans or Spiritual Heirs?* New York: Crossroad Publishing, 1999. A Christian minister married to a Jewish man raises children with both religions.

Seamon, Erika B. *Interfaith Marriage in America: The Transformation of Religion and Christianity.* New York: Palgrave MacMillan, 2012. Study of the impact of interfaith marriage.

Smith, Eileen O'Farrell. *Making Our Way to Shore: An Interfaith Guide to Baby-Naming and Baptism.* College Station, TX: Virtualbookworm. com, 2004. Guide to Jewish and Catholic baby-welcoming ceremonies.

Sheskin, Ira. "Comparisons of Jewish Communities: Intermarriage." Berman Institute-North American Jewish Data Bank, 2012. http:// www.jewishdatabank.org/study.asp?sid=90188&tp=5. Percentages of children being raised "partially Jewish" (i.e., with both religions).

Snyder, Laurel, ed. *Half/Life: Jew-ish Tales from Interfaith Homes.* Brooklyn, NY: Soft Skull Press, 2006. Essays by adult interfaith children who grew up before interfaith family communities.

Swirl. http://www.swirlinc.org/. National organization supporting people with mixed-race identities

Union for Reform Judaism. "Revisiting the 1995 Resolution on Religious School Enrollment." 2005. http://urj.org//cong/outreach/resources// ?syspage=document&item_id=13652. Reaffirming the policy that children should not be educated in two religions.

Walker, Rebecca. *Black, White and Jewish: Autobiography of a Shifting Self.* New York: Riverhead Trade, 2002. Memoir by author Alice Walker's daughter, an interfaith child.

INTERFAITH RELATIONS AND INTERFAITH HISTORY

Armstrong, Karen. *A History of God: The 4,000-Year Quest of Judaism, Christianity and Islam.* New York: Ballantine, 1994.

Boorstein, Sylvia. *That's Funny, You Don't Look Buddhist: On Being a Faithful Jew and a Passionate Buddhist.* San Francisco: HarperOne, 1998.

Boyarin, Daniel. *The Jewish Gospels: The Story of the Jewish Christ.* New York: The New Press, 2012.

Brettler, Marc Zvi, and Amy-Jill Levine. *The Jewish Annotated New Testament.* New York: Oxford University Press, 2011.

Bruteau, Beatrice, ed. *Jesus Through Jewish Eyes: Rabbis and Scholars Engage an Ancient Brother in a New Conversation.* New York: Orbis, 2001.

Cornille, Catherine, ed. *Many Mansions? Multiple Religious Belonging and Christian Identity.* Eugene, OR: Wipf and Stock, 2010.

Eck, Diana. *A New Religious America: How a "Christian Country" Has Become the World's Most Religiously Diverse Nation.* San Francisco: HarperSanFrancisco, 2002.

Klausner, Joseph. *Jesus of Nazareth: His Life, Times and Teaching.* New York: Bloch Publishing, 1997.

Knitter, Paul F. *Without Buddha I Could Not Be a Christian.* Oxford, UK: Oneworld, 2009.

Levenson, Jon Douglas, and Kevin J. Madigan. *Resurrection: The Power of God for Christians and Jews.* New Haven, CT: Yale University Press, 2009.

Miller, Susan Katz. "Why Include Interfaith Children in Interfaith Dialogue?" *Huffington Post,* July 8, 2011. http://www.huffingtonpost .com/susan-katz-miller/why-include-interfaith-ch_b_893526.html.

Patel, Eboo. *Acts of Faith: The Story of an American Muslim, in the Struggle for the Soul of a Generation.* Boston: Beacon Press, 2010.

Putnam, Robert D., and David E. Campbell. *American Grace: How Religion Divides and Unites Us.* New York: Simon & Schuster, 2012.

Smith, Huston. *The World's Religions.* San Francisco: HarperOne, 2009.

Spong, John Shelby. *Jesus for the Non-Religious.* San Francisco: Harper-One, 2008.

Stedman, Chris. *Faithiest.* Boston: Beacon Press, 2012.

Suomala, Karla, "Complex Religious Identity in the Context of Interfaith Dialogue." *Crosscurrents* 62, no. 3 (September 2012): 360–70.

INTERFAITH FAMILY COMMUNITIES AND SUPPORT

Doppel:halb ("Double:half"). http://www.doppelhalb.de/english.html. German group for people with part-Jewish ancestry.

The Family School. http://the-family-school.org/. Education for Jewish and Catholic interfaith children in downtown Chicago.

Groupe des Foyers Islamo Chretiens. http://gfic.net/Pub4/Accueil.asp. Muslim/Christian families in France.

The Half-Jewish Network. http://half-jewish.net/. Advocacy group for heirs of intermarriage.

Interfaith Community. http://interfaithcommunity.org/. Jewish and Christian interfaith family groups and education programs in New York, Connecticut, New Jersey, and Boston.

Interfaith Families Project of Greater Washington, D.C. http://iffp.net/. Jewish and Christian interfaith community and education program in the Washington, D.C., area.

InterFaith Families Project of Philadelphia. http://www.iffp-philly.org/. A community for Jewish and Christian interfaith families in the Philadelphia area.

The Inter-faith Marriage Network. http://www.interfaithmarriage.org.uk/. Resources for interfaith couples in the United Kingdom.

The Interfaith Union. http://www.theinterfaithunion.org/. Provides Jewish/Catholic baby-welcomings, interfaith education, and a Muslim/Christian support group in suburban Chicago.

The Jewish Catholic Couples Dialogue Group. http://www.jcdg.org/. Supports interfaith couples, meets in downtown Chicago.

Muslim Christian Couples Scotland. https://www.facebook.com/groups/128788780603985/?ref=ts&fref=ts. Support network in Scotland.

Muslim/Christian Marriage Support Group. http://www.mcmarriage.org.uk/. Support network in London.

Unitarian Universalists for Jewish Awareness. http://uuja.org/. Supports UUs from Jewish backgrounds and all UUs interested in Judaism.

INDEX